Studies in Discourse Representation Theory and the Theory of Generalized Quantifiers

Groningen-Amsterdam Studies in Semantics (GRASS)

This series of books on the semantics of natural language contains collections of original research on selected topics as well as monographs in this area. Contributions from linguists, philosophers, logicians, computer-scientists and cognitive psychologists are brought together to promote interdisciplinary and international research.

Editors
Alice ter Meulen
Martin Stokhof

Editorial Board
Renate Bartsch
  University of Amsterdam
Johan van Benthem
  University of Amsterdam
Henk Verkuyl
  University of Utrecht

All communications to the editors can be sent to:
Department of Philosophy   *or*   Department of Linguistics, GN 40
University of Amsterdam   University of Washington
Grimburgwal 10   Seattle, Washington 98195
1012 GA Amsterdam   U.S.A
The Netherlands

Jeroen Groenendijk,
Dick de Jongh,
Martin Stokhof (eds.)

Studies in Discourse Representation Theory and the Theory of Generalized Quantifiers

1987
FORIS PUBLICATIONS
Dordrecht - Holland/Providence - U.S.A.

Published by:
Foris Publications Holland
P.O. Box 509
3300 AM Dordrecht, The Netherlands

Sole distributor for the U.S.A. and Canada:
Foris Publications USA , Inc.
P.O. Box 5904
Providence RI 02903
USA

CIP-DATA

Studies

Studies in Discourse, Representation Theory and the Theory of Generalized Quantifiers /
Jeroen Groenendijk, Dick de Jongh, Martin Stokhof (eds.). – Dordrecht [etc.]: Foris. –
(Groningen-Amsterdam Studies in Semantics ; 8)
ISBN 90-6765-266-0 bound
ISBN 90-6765-267-9 paper
SISO 805.5   UDC 801.5
Subject heading: semantics (linguistics).

ISBN 90 6765 266 0 (Bound)
ISBN 90 6765 267 9 (Paper)

Printed in the Netherlands by ICG Printing, Dordrecht.

Table of Contents

Preface

This volume contains a selection of the papers that were presented at the Fifth Amsterdam Colloquium, which took place in August 1984. The papers collected in this book are contributions to the theory of generalized quantifiers, or to discourse representation theory (or to both).

The paper by van Benthem explores the idea of giving a procedural, rather than a declarative meaning to quantifier expressions, by treating them as 'semantic automata'. The Chomsky-hierarchy, familiar from mathematical linguistics and automata theory, turns out to make sense in this semantic field as well, providing us with a means to develop a fine-grained notion of 'complexity' for denotations. Taking a procedural view also allows us to give a new twist to matters of definability, shedding new light on the constraints used in characterizing logical determiners in earlier work. Keenan's contribution deals with the issue of the relative freedom that natural languages allow themselves in expressing possible denotations by means of lexical expressions. He claims that this freedom is a function of the size of the set of all possible denotations: small categories have more freedom than large ones. Though his analysis deals with several kinds of categories, the main inspiration for this investigation clearly derives from results in the theory of generalized quantifiers, to which it is another contribution as well. Löbner's paper is concerned with extending the theory of quantification in another direction. Quantification, he claims, is not a phenomenon that is restricted to noun phrases, but its application extends to several kinds of adverbs, modal verbs, verbs taking various types of complements, certain types of adjectives, and so on. In every such case, the notions and principles of the theory of generalized quantifiers (such as duality and monotonicity) can be applied fruitfully. Analyzing the meanings of non-nominal quantifiers such as *already/still, enough/too, big/small*, Löbner develops the conception of 'phase quantification', which he offers as a candidate for the general format of natural language quantification. In Verkuyl's paper we find an application of the theory of generalized quantifiers to yet another descriptive set of problems: the determination of the aspectual properties of sentences. Considering the basic aspectual opposition to be that between 'durative' and 'non-durative' aspect, Verkuyl develops a combinatorial mechanism that allows one to derive the marked one of these two: non-durativity.

With Partee's paper we are at the borderline between the two main topics of this volume. Her objective is to show that the theory of NP-interpretation from generalized quantifier theory, and referential analyses of NP's such as definite descriptions, or the referential semantic analysis of indefinites that we know from discourse representation theory, can be reconciled if we allow ourselves more flexibility in relating syntax and semantics. General type-shifting principles, applicable in other domains of analysis as well, will allow us to go from one interpretation to another, thus giving us the best of both worlds, at least in semantics. A related paper is the one by Turner. Whereas Partee argues for a flexible relation between the categories of syntax and the types of semantics, Turner claims that natural language, in view of its possibilities of direct and indirect selfreference for example, needs a type-free theory. In his paper Turner not only wants to substantiate this claim, which he does by discussing various problems in the semantics of nominalizations, he also sets out to develop the foundations of a type-free theory which can be applied in natural language semantics. The paper by Klein is primarily devoted to a descriptive issue, the analysis of verb phrase ellipsis in discourse representation theory, but behind it lies a theoretical question: can the theory be made to conform to the 'rule-to-rule' format of compositionality, familiar from standard Montague grammar? While not tackling this question in its full generality, Klein argues for extending the formalism of discourse representation theory to incorporate a device similar to lambda-abstraction. This both facilitates the treatment of VP-representation, and also has the side-effect of allowing Kamp's treatment of *every* and *a* to be assimilated to the pattern of generalized quantifiers. Zeevat's paper investigates to what extent discourse representation theory can be interpreted as a formalization of a phenomenological theory of thoughts. In terms of this interpretation the theory is then applied by Zeevat to the semantics of belief-sentences, addressing many of the well-known problems in this area.

From this brief indication of the contents of the various contributions, it may be clear that they share a common theoretical and philosophical interest in the foundations and applications of semantics, yet that they also display a variety of approaches and frameworks. 'Logical' semantics in the broad sense of that word is no longer tied to a particular framework or set of principles, as it was at the stage of its inception. Rather it is a many-coloured thing. We hope that the papers in this volume may help to convince the reader that this is a virtue, rather than a vice.

A companion to this volume, containing various papers read at the colloquium which deal with the foundations of pragmatics and lexical semantics, appears as GRASS 7.

The Amsterdam Colloquium was organized by the Department of Philosophy of the University of Amsterdam, with financial support of the Department of Mathematics of the same university and of the Royal Dutch Academy of Sciences, which is gratefully acknowledged.

Finally, the editors would like to thank the authors for their cooperation and patience in bringing this volume into being.

The Editors

Chapter 1

Semantic Automata

Johan van Benthem

1. INTRODUCTION

An attractive, but never very central idea in modern semantics has been to regard linguistic expressions as denoting certain "procedures" performed within models for the language. For instance, truth tables for propositional connectives may be viewed as computational instructions for finding truth values. Another example is the proposal in Suppes (1982) to correlate certain adjectives with procedures for locating an individual in some underlying comparative order. And finally, the frequent proposals in a more computer-oriented setting for translating from natural language into programming languages are congenial too. The purpose of this paper is to apply this perspective to yet another linguistic category of expression, viz., determiners, or more in particular, quantifier expressions ('all', 'some', 'ten', 'most', etc.).

In order to correlate quantifiers with procedures, the so-called "generalized quantifier" perspective will be used. Here, a quantifier denotes a functor $Q_E XY$, assigning, to each universe E, a binary relation among its subsets. (Compare van Benthem, 1984c, for an exposition, as well as a development of some logical theory to be used in the present paper.) Viewed procedurally, the quantifier has to decide which truth value to give, when presented with an enumeration of the individuals in E marked for their (non-)membership of X and Y. Equivalently, the quantifier has to recognize a "language" of admissible sequences in a 4-symbol alphabet (as there are four distinct types of X, Y-behaviour). But then, we have arrived at a very familiar perspective: that of ordinary mathematical linguistics and automata theory.

This observation turns out to be more than a mere formal perspectival trick. We shall find surprising connections. In particular, the Chomsky Hierarchy turns out to make eminent semantic sense, both in its coarse and its fine structure. For instance, the border-line "regular"/"context-free" corresponds (in a sense) to that between first-order and higher-order definability. But also, within these broad classes, machine fine structure is correlated with a significant semantic hierarchy. Various examples and theorems will illustrate these points. Thus, what is often regarded as the main formal stronghold of pure syntax, can also be enlisted in the service of semantics.

Another motive for this study comes from within the theory of generalized quantifiers itself. For instance, in van Benthem (1984c), the idea was mentioned to view quantifiers as procedures, in order to obtain a better insight into their hierarchy of complexity. Nevertheless, there, another road was pursued, with classifications depending on certain "homogeneity" or "uniformity" constraints on truth value patterns for quantifiers. The present perspective provides the latter with a perhaps more solid and convincing background.

Evidently, quantifiers form one very special type of linguistic expression. But, as in the above-mentioned generalized quantifier theory, extensions of notions and results are often possible to other types of expression − sometimes even to all categories. (See also van Benthem, 1984a, on this issue of generality.) Usually, such extensions require sensitivity to further model-theoretic structure than mere feature lists (as in the above). Some examples will be mentioned in section 6. (For more detailed proposals and results, see van Benthem 1986). This further step is reminiscent of the move in contemporary mathematical linguistics towards "tree automata" recognizing more structured syntactic objects than flat linear sequences.

There are some interesting general aspects to procedural semantics. Notably, the denotations studied here are "intensional", in the sense that one and the same input/output behaviour for a quantifier may be produced by widely different automata. (This particular issue will be taken up in Sec. 4 below.) But also, this functional − in the pre-Cantorian sense − view of denotations still has obvious links with the extensional approach embodied in common type-theoretic denotations. Such general issues will be discussed in Section 6 as well.

Finally, the procedural perspective may also be viewed as a way of extending contemporary concerns in "computational linguistics" to the area of semantics as well. Complexity and computability, with their background questions of recognition and learning, seem just as relevant to semantic understanding as they are to syntactic parsing.

All considered, the claim of this paper is not that the procedural view is a unique favoured one in semantics, either philosophically or empirically. But, the concrete results of our study, to be presented below, do indicate that this perspective is an enlightening one. And where there is light, there must be truth.

2. QUANTIFIERS

In this preliminary section, some basic notions concerning quantifiers will be reviewed. (See van Benthem, 1983a, for a more detailed linguistic exposition.) As stated above, quantifier words or phrases, with Montague categorial type $(e,t),((e,t),t)$, denote relations between predicates (extensionally: sets of individuals) on each universe of discourse: $Q_E XY$.

Not every mathematically possible denotation of this type is actually realized in natural language, and hence there has been a search for reasonable global *constraints*. For instance, quantifiers should be "context-neutral", being insensitive to extensions of the universe:

EXT if $X, Y \subseteq E \subseteq E'$, then $Q_E XY$ iff $Q_E XY$.

Moreover, quantifiers should be "topic-neutral", disregarding individual peculiarities of objects, beyond their mere quantities:

QUANT if $X, Y \subseteq E$, and π is some permutation of E, then
$Q_E XY$ iff $Q_E \pi[X]\pi[Y]$.

Finally, quantifiers are "left-leaning" (or 'conservative', as the literature has it), their first argument setting the stage:

CONS $Q_E XY$ iff $Q_E X(Y \cap X)$.

For a discussion of the linguistic motivation behind these various conditions, see also Keenan and Stavi (1981).

The cumulative effect of the above conditions may be pictured in the traditional Venn Diagrams. The original picture is as follows

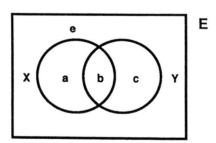

Then, QUANT makes for dependence on the mere numbers a, b, c, e. EXT removes the box E, and hence the dependence upon e. Finally, CONS removes the dependence on Y-X; i.e., on c. Thus, in the end, the behaviour of Q is completely specified by the set of all couples of cardinalities (a, b) which it accepts.

But then, a simple geometrical representation becomes possible, by displaying all relevant couples in the so-called "Tree of Numbers":

$$
\begin{array}{lll}
|X| = 0 & & 0,0 \\
|X| = 1 & & 1,0 \quad 0,0 \quad 0,1 \\
|X| = 2 & 2,0 \quad 1,1 \quad 0,2
\end{array}
$$

More prosaically, this tree may be viewed as the north-eastern quadrant of the Cartesian product of the integers with the integers.

A quantifier Q is now determined by a plus (minus) – marking of those positions in the tree which it accepts (rejects). This representation, equivalent to imposing the above three constraints, has already proved very useful – and we shall find some further ways of exploiting it here.

Various more special conditions on quantifiers that have been studied in the literature are now mirrored by simple geometrical constraints on Q-patterns in the tree. For instance, there are the well-known properties of Monotonicity:

$$Q_E XY, \ Y \subseteq Y' \text{ only if } Q_E XY',$$

and its cousin Persistence:

$$Q_E XY, \ X \subseteq X' \text{ only if } Q_E X'Y.$$

In the tree, the first amounts to the following:

'any node to the right of a node in Q is itself in Q',

while the second becomes

'any node in Q has its entire generated downward subtree in Q'.

The latter observations have been used to give explicit definitions for all "doubly monotone" quantifiers.

For the special purposes of this paper, a geometric look is needed at *first-order definability* of quantifiers – meaning that there exists some sentence in the monadic first-order language with identity and unary predicates "X", "Y" such that for all universes E with $X,\ Y \subseteq E$, $Q_E XY$ iff $< E,X,Y > \vDash \phi$.

By the Fraïssé characterization of the latter notion, in terms of "semantic insensitivity" beyond a certain threshold size of the universe (measured by the quantifier depth of the sentence), the first-order definable quantifiers are precisely those displaying the following tree pattern:

- up to some finite level $2N$, arbitrary $(+/-)$-behaviour,
- at level $2N$: truth values in the interval $[2N, 0 \ldots N, N)$ propagate downward in a south-westerly direction, those within $(N, N \ldots 0, 2N]$ propagate toward the south-east, while the pivot position $N,\ N$ determines the truth value of its entire generated downward triangle.

For an illustration, the reader may draw the patterns for the first-order quantifiers in the traditional Square of Opposition: 'all', 'some', 'no', 'not all'. By way of contrast, notice how the eternally zigzagging pattern for the higher-order quantifier "most" violates the above description.

The above tree picture certainly suggests (even though it does not actually presuppose) a restriction to finite cardinalities $a,\ b$; i.e., to *finite universes E*. This restriction will indeed be assumed here (except for one passage in Sec. 4): in a computational perspective, it makes good sense. For a critical discussion of the motivation of this constraint in linguistic semantics, see the contributions by van Deemter and Thijsse in van Benthem and ter Meulen (1985).

3. QUANTIFIERS AND AUTOMATA

The action of a quantifier Q may be viewed as follows. For any pair of arguments $X,\ Y$, it is fed a list of members of X, which can be tested one by one for membership of Y. At each stage, Q is to be ready to state whether it accepts or rejects the sequence just read. In its simplest mathematical formulation, then, Q is just presented with finite sequences of zeroes and ones (standing for cases in X-Y and $X \cap Y$, respectively), of which it has to recognize those for which the couple "number of zeroes, number of ones" belongs to Q in the earlier sense. In other words, Q corresponds to a language on the alphabet $\{0,1\}$. Moreover, its language is a rather special one, in that different enumerations of the argument set would not have affected acceptance: quantifier languages are *permutation-closed*. (Eventually, of course, the potential dependence on order of presentation may be put to good use in describing certain more contextual, or pragmatic phenomena. For instance, the quantifier "every other" may be presentation-dependent in this sense. (Cf. also Löbner, this volume.))

Actually, we could also have given the following discussion in terms of a four-element alphabet, enumerating universes E with the four labels

$$X - Y, \ X \cap Y, \ Y - X \text{ and } E - (X \cup Y).$$

But, in the present context, the two additional symbols would remain "inert", only encumbering notation. Moreover, there are certain mathematical differences between languages with a two-element alphabet and more complex ones, that will be exploited to good effect in Section 5. For the relevant mathematical theory, here and elsewhere, the reader is referred to Ginsburg (1966), Hopcroft and Ullman (1979).

Now, one of the main themes in mathematical linguistics is the duality between the notion of a language and its description by means of accepting (or generating) automata. And indeed, the familiar quantifiers turn out to be computable by means of well-known automata.

3.1. Example: The quantifier "all" is recognized by the following finite state machine:

Here, the initial state A is accepting (B is not). Alternatively, it suffices to present the "all" language in Kleene regular set notation: 1^*. Similar two-state finite state machines will compute the remaining quantifiers in the Square of Opposition.

Other quantifiers may lead beyond regular languages and finite state machines.

3.2. Example: The quantifier "most" is not recognized by any finite state machine. This fact follows from the Pumping Lemma. Its language is context-free, however − and so it can be recognized by a push-down automaton. The idea of the latter is simply to store values read, crossing out complementary pairs 0,1 or 1,0 of top stack symbol and symbol read, as they occur. When the string has been read, the stack should contain symbols 1 only. (Actually, this description does not quite fit the usual format of a push-down automaton. But, such further subtleties will be postponed until Sec. 5 below.)

Thus, higher-order quantifiers may induce context-free languages. Interestingly, it is not all that easy to advance beyond this stage, finding non-contrived natural language quantifiers whose associated procedure would be essentially of the complexity of some Turing machine. One (not uncontroversial) example is "(relatively) many", in the numerical sense of "the proportion of Y's in X exceeds that of the Y's in the whole universe E". This case will be considered in more detail in Section 5. But on the whole, we find natural language quantifiers, even the higher-order ones, within the context-free realm. Thus, they are essentially "additive" in a logical sense to be explained later on. There is some foundational significance to this observation, as *additive arithmetic* is still an axiomatizable (indeed, decidable) fragment of mathematics. The "Gödel Border" of non-axiomatizability only arises in the next step, when adding *multiplication* to the theory. (Compare Mendelson, 1964, on this point.) Thus, natural language seems to show a wise restraint in these matters.

Apart from purely technical insights, mathematical linguistics also provides one with interesting more general points of view in this area. For instance, the well-known concerns about learnability of grammars can now be related to similar questions about learnability of meanings. The latter is surely an issue which semanticists have worried about, often without having very definite ideas about how to make their concerns mathematically articulate. The present study provides one way of doing so.

4. FIRST-ORDER QUANTIFIERS AND FINITE STATE MACHINES

Definability

The first examples in the preceding section motivate an obvious conjecture; which turns out to be justified.

4.1. Theorem: All first-order definable quantifiers are computable by means of finite state machines.

Proof: Recall the tree pattern for first-order quantifiers described in Section 2. It consists of some arbitrary finite top triangle, followed by a "decisive row" at level $2N$. Now, the theorem is proved if the associated language can be shown to be regular.

The first top triangle declares some fixed finite set of sequences to be in Q, and all the corresponding singleton sets are of course regular. Moreover, any finite union of regular languages remains regular. Then, the decisive row adds a finite number of accepted patterns, of (at most) the following three types
- exactly i occurrences of 1, at least j occurrences of 0,
- at least i occurrences of 1, at least j occurrences of 0,
- at least i occurrences of 1, exactly j occurrences of 0.

It remains to be checked that the latter types of language are indeed regular.

An example will make this clear. "Exactly two 1's, at least five 0's" may be described as follows in Kleene notation. Take all (finitely many) possible distributions of five 0's over three slots formed by two 1 boundaries, and then "fill up" with suitable iterations 0* wherever possible. QED

Through this connection, existing results about finite state machines become available for first-order quantifiers, given by their definitions. For instance, it follows that, for any two such quantifiers, the question is decidable if they are equivalent.

Given the simple nature of finite state automata, a converse of Theorem 4.1 seems likely. But, there are counter-examples.

4.2. Example: The following automaton recognizes the (non-first-order) quantifier "an even number of":

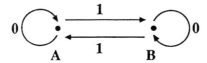

Here, the initial state of *A* is accepting (*B* is not).

Thus, an additional restriction is needed to filter out the procedures corresponding to logically elementary quantifiers among all finite state machines. And in fact, the earlier examples suggest the following distinction. The machine graph for "an even number of" has a non-trivial loop between two states − something which did not occur with "all," "some," etc. Let us call a finite state machine *acyclic* if it contains no loops connecting two or more states. This notion is quite common and useful: basically, such graphs allow 'inductive' enumeration (cf. van Benthem, 1983b).

Moreover, a condition is needed reflecting the earlier-mentioned permutation closure of our associated quantifier languages. A machine graph will be called *permutation-invariant* if the possibility of traveling from state *A* to state *B* by means of some 1,0-sequence implies that any permutation of that sequence will also force the passage from *A* to *B*. Note that the given automata for "all" and "an even number of" both had this property. Evidently, such automata recognize only permutation-closed languages. The converse is true as well: see the Addenda to this paper.

Evidently, permutation closure is a strong restriction on our classes of languages. It should be kept in mind, however, that we can always decide to drop it when studying more involved linguistic constructions. On the other hand, the restriction is a mathematically interesting one. Contrary to initial beliefs, our experience is that it does not collapse the general theory of automata and languages, leading rather to new versions of old questions. Some examples will appear in what follows.

As an illustration, it may be observed that permutation-invariant and acyclic finite state machines are "convergent": all non-stationary paths end eventually in one single absorbing state. This observation will be significant (although it is not actually used) in the proof of the following result.

4.3. Theorem: The first-order quantifiers are precisely those which can be recognized by permutation-invariant acyclic finite state machines.

Proof: First, a closer look is required now into the automata associated with first-order quantifiers. Interestingly, the earlier Tree of Numbers now proves to be computationally significant too.

Let Q be a first-order quantifier described in this tree, with the earlier-mentioned Fraïssé pattern. Now, interpret this structure *itself* as a graph for a machine M_Q with infinitely many states corresponding to the tree nodes. Its starting state is $(0, 0)$. The transition arrows for reading a zero go from states (a, b) to $(a + 1, b)$, those for reading a one from (a, b) to $(a, b + 1)$. Finally, the accepting states will be those in Q.

Claim: M_Q accepts a finite sequence s if and only if the couple $0(s)$, $1(s)$ = number of zeroes in s, number of ones in s, belongs to Q.

Proof: By induction on the length of sequences s, it may be shown that reading s will take M_Q from its starting state to the state $0(s)$, $1(s)$. The claim then follows. QED

Now, with a first-order pattern for Q, this infinite accepting device M_Q may be reduced to an equivalent *finite* state machine. Recall the earlier "decisive row", at level $2N$. Above it, the state graph remains as before; on it, one concludes with the following picture:

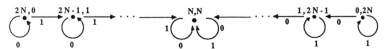

It is easy to check that this modified machine still accepts the same language.

Finally, inspection shows that machine graphs of the latter kind are both acyclic and permutation-invariant. This concludes the first half of the argument.

The converse direction of the theorem follows from the above-mentioned inductive character of acyclic finite state machines. In such automata, for any accepting state, there is only a *finite* number of types of path leading to it (from the starting state), driven by successive transitions of the four types 0, 1, 0* or 1*. Thus, such states accept sequences of essentially the following types

- exactly i times: 1, exactly j times: 0
- exactly i times: 1, at least j times: 0

- at least i times: 1, at least j times: 1
- at least i times: 1, exactly j times: 0.

Now, all these types by themselves are first-order definable – and hence so is their disjunction (which is the 'yield' of the accepting state considered). Finally, the whole machine itself again accepts the disjunction of everything admitted in its individual accepting states. QED

Some further illustrations of these methods may be obtained by comparing "tree-based" automata for first-order quantifiers with those found in an ad-hoc fashion. For instance, the tree approach for "all" would give a 3-state automaton, which may be simplified to the earlier 2-state one. Conversely, given automata for first-order quantifiers may be "normalized" into a tree-like form.

It may be noted here that the above theorem can be extended to the more general class of merely Quantitative quantifiers (not necessarily obeying CONS). The same notion of first-order definability may be employed then, but there is a four-letter alphabet, as in the earliest Venn Diagram of Section 2.

Finally, the question remains to describe the class of *all* quantifiers computed by finite state automata. Our conjecture is that these are all definable in a first-order language with a suitable addition of "periodicity quantifiers," such as "a k-multiple number of."

Fine-structure

In addition to the above global definability questions, matters of finer detail are relevant too in the study of actual quantifiers. For instance, one particularly important case is that where the states correspond directly to the semantic *truth values*. In the present setting, this leaves only finite state machines having two states, one accepting, the other rejecting.

4.4. Theorem: The permutation-closed languages or quantifiers recognized by finite two-state automata are the following:
- 'all', 'some', 'no', 'not all'
- 'an even number of', 'an odd number of', 'all but an even number of', 'all but an odd number of', together with the extreme cases
- 'empty sequence only', 'non-empty sequences only', 'sequences of odd length', 'sequences of even length'.

Proof: By brute force; enumerating all possible automata. *QED*

This enumeration result is reminiscent of similar ones in van Benthem (1984c), employing "Homogeneity" or "Uniformity" constraints on quantifier patterns in the Tree of Numbers. For instance, the so-called "Strong Homogeneity" condition stated that a truth-value change under the influence of a transition (a, b) to $(a + 1, b)$, or to $(a, b + 1)$, will be the same throughout the tree. But, this amounts to sanctioning operating with one "true" and one "false" state, with fixed responses for their departing zero and one transition arrows.

Additional states may be needed for quantifiers of higher complexity.

4.5. Example: "(Precisely) one" can be recognized by an automaton with three states; but no less.

Of course, all quantifiers mentioned can also be correlated with machines having large numbers of additional states. Thus, there is an issue of "minimal representation," as in the well-known Nerode Theorem, representing input/output functions in terms of state transition machines. In fact, the Nerode representation method could be applied to first-order quantifier languages as well.

4.6. Example: Consider the class ONE of sequences with exactly one occurrence of 1. The crucial Nerode equivalence relation is the following:

$s1$ E $s2$ if, for all sequences s, $s1$-followed-by-s is in ONE
iff $s2$-followed-by-s is in ONE.

Its equivalence classes are the following three: sequences with exactly *no, one* or *two* occurrences of 1. These then will be the states in the minimal representation, with the transition function defined by the stipulation

equivalence class of s, read symbol x =>
equivalence class of s-followed-by-x.

The outcome is the automaton of the previous example.

Infinite models

When *infinite* models are considered, matters become less perspicuous. Of course, the earlier machines can operate on infinite sequences just as well as on finite ones − but, the problem is to find a well-motivated convention for acceptance, given a non-ending sequence of states traversed.

One possibility is to admit only those infinite sequences which cause the machine to remain in some accepting state after a finite number of steps. By inspection of the earlier Fraïssé recognizers, it may be seen that all first-order definable quantifiers are recognized in this way. But also, certain genuinely "infinitary" cases are admitted:

4.7. Example: The following two-state machine recognizes the quantifier "almost all," in the sense of "with at most finitely many exceptions":

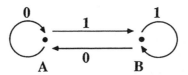

Here, *B* is an accepting state. Notice that this machine is not permutation-invariant – although its set of infinite accepted sequences is permutation-closed.

Another essentially infinite quantifier of this kind is "virtually no", in the sense of "only finitely many". Indeed, it would be of interest to chart the effects of all our earlier two-state machines here.

What distinguishes the first-order quantifiers from the infinitary cases is that their rejection is also finitary: non-acceptable sequences lead the machine to some stable non-accepting state after a finite number of steps. Again, this may be seen from the earlier Fraïssé recognizers.

4.8. Conjecture: On the sets of countably infinite sequences, the first-order quantifiers are exactly those with a finitary acceptance and rejection behaviour.

Further relaxations of the acceptance convention are possible, such as allowing recurring *cycles* of accepting states – or even recognizing by certain infinite patterns. Clearly, the "yield" of our machine classes will be rather sensitive to such stipulations. A deeper investigation of this phenomenon must be left to another occasion.

5. HIGHER-ORDER QUANTIFIERS AND PUSH-DOWN AUTOMATA

Examples

With higher-order quantifiers, finite state machines usually become insufficient as computing devices – and the next level in the machine hierarchy is needed, that of push-down automata, handling a stack in addition to changing state when reading new input. The usual definition of these machines is rather restricted: the transition function takes only the top stack symbol into account, recognition is by empty stack only. However, by a suitable re-encoding of instructions, it may be assumed that the machine can keep track of a *fixed finite* top part of the stack, with a final read-off convention performing a finite state machine check on the stack contents. One way of simulating these effects in the orthodox format is by having new states q, $\langle q, s1 \rangle$, ..., $\langle q, s1, \ldots sk \rangle$ encoding tuples of old states q with up to k top stack positions. Then, suitable "ϵ-moves" (Cf. Hopcroft and Ullman 1979) are to allow a trade-off between encoded sequence and top stack symbols displayed. Finally, another set of ϵ-moves will allow us to carry out the finite state machine instructions without consuming any more input.

For instance, the earlier-mentioned quantifier "most" would have an awkward corresponding automaton in the original sense, whereas it has an easy intuitive one in this more liberal version (compare Sec. 3). Significantly, though, writing a context-free grammar for the "most"-language is not an entirely trivial exercise.

Before passing on to further examples, some general remarks should be made on push-down automata. First, the present discussion is couched in terms of *non-deterministic* machines of this kind. Deterministic push-down automata recognize a smaller class of languages, less natural mathematically than the context-free realm. Incidentally, the examples from the literature establishing this non-inclusion all seem to lack permutation closure. But, it seems probable that certain quantifiers in our sense (more specifically, various disjunctive ones) would require essentially non-deterministic push-down automata too. Even so, most basic examples of quantifiers considered here can be calculated by deterministic machines – and hence an obvious narrower enquiry remains.

Also, recognition of sequences will be made by inspection of stack content. One could also pursue the analogy with the finite state machine case here, recognizing by designated states: an equivalent procedure, in general. Either way, the earlier-mentioned parallel between machine states and semantic truth values becomes less direct.

Besides "most," other prominent higher-order quantifiers occurring in natural language are "almost all", "many", "few", "hardly any", etc. Evidently, the meaning of these expressions is underdetermined – as is the case, indeed, with "most" itself. To get an impression of their complexity in the present terms, then, reasonable formal explications are to be considered. The following seem fair approximations of their spirit:

'many': 'at least one-thirds'
'almost all': 'at least nine-tenths'.

Thus, on this reading, the above quantifiers all express "proportionality".

Now, the complexity of the latter phenomenon is essentially context-free. A simple illustration is the following.

5.1. Example: A push-down automaton recognizing "at least two-third" will operate as follows. It keeps track of two top stack positions, checking with the next symbol read. In case it encounters a symbol 1, with 1, 0 occuring on top (in any order), it erases the latter two, and continues. Likewise, with a symbol 0 read and two symbols 1 on top. In all other cases, the symbol read is simply stored on top of the stack. At the end of the process, the machine checks if the stack contains only symbols 1: only then does it recognize the sequence just read.

The above automaton recognizes the right strings, by a simple combinatorial argument. A similar procedure, somewhat more involved, will recognize "almost all". The case of "many" will be treated somewhat differently here, to illustrate an important non-deterministic procedure too.

5.2. Example: "At least one-third" may be recognized as follows. The machine now keeps track of three top stack positions, having the following (non-deterministic) instructions. Symbols read may be pushed onto the stack. But moreover, the following moves are allowed (without consuming input): combinations of two 0/one 1, one 0/one 1, or one 1 only, may be erased from the top of the stack. This time, the final recognition is simply by empty stack.

The arithmetical idea behind this procedure is that all couples (a, b) with $a \leq 2b$ are generated, starting from $(0, 0)$, by means of the following operations: add $(2, 1)$/ add $(1, 1)$/ add $(0, 1)$. Obviously, if a string is accepted by the above machine, it has such an arithmetical form. Conversely, if a string has contents a, b of the form $x(2, 1) + y(1, 1) + z(0, 1)$, then a judicious process of reading and erasing will produce an empty stack in the end. (A more general procedure in this spirit will be given in the proof of Theorem 5.5 below.)

Many other examples in the same spirit can be analyzed in these terms. We shall now investigate the situation from a higher logical point of view.

Arithmetical definability

When viewed arithmetically, the above quantifiers all express extremely simple conditions on the two variables a (number of zeroes) and b (number of ones). For instance, 'all': $a = 0$, 'some': $b \neq 0$, 'one': $a = 1$, 'most': $a < b$, 'many': $a \leq b + b$.

Thus, simple first-order quantifiers employ just a, b, fixed natural numbers and identity, others add "smaller than", and eventually, addition is needed. These were atomic cases; but, e.g., the earlier example "an even number of" would also require the quantified formula "for some x, $a = x + x$".

In fact, once arbitrary first-order conditions on a, b involving $+$ are considered, the notion $<$ becomes definable, and hence so are all specific natural numbers n. Thus, we are dealing with first order formulas $\phi(=, +, a, b)$, interpreted as standard arithmetical statements. Now, we shall derive a general characterization of the present area of complexity.

5.3. Digression: One natural preliminary notion to consider is first-order arithmetical definability in $=$, 0 and S('successor') only. It is easy to see that all first-order definable quantifiers (in the earlier X, Y, $=$ sense) are definable here already. (For instance, 'at least two' is defined by: $b \neq 0$ and $b \neq S\ 0$.) The converse fails, however. Thus, the arithmetical formula $a = b$ defines the quantifier "exactly half", which is not even recognizable by a finite state machine. But also, not every finite state recognizable quantifier is definable here: a counter-example is "an even number of." In this light, the better behaviour of "additive first-order definability", to be studied below, is all the more surprising.

Some preliminary notions and results are needed for the above purpose.

First, there is the fundamental *Parikh Theorem*, stating that each context-free language L, in alphabet $a1$, $\ldots$, ak (say), induces a *semi-linear* set of k-tuples of natural numbers

> { (number of symbols $a1$ in s, $\ldots$, number of symbols ak in s) |
> all sequences s in L }.

Here, a "semi-linear" set of k-tuples is a finite union of *linear* sets, consisting of all k-tuples produced by a schema of the following form:

$$(m1, \ldots, mk) + x1(m11, \ldots, m1k) + \ldots + xn(mn1, \ldots, mnk)$$
$$(x1, \ldots, xn \text{ non-negative integers}).$$

All semi-linear sets correspond to first-order additively definable k-ary relations on the natural numbers — as the given arithmetical schema can be written out in first-order terms. For instance, $(1, 2) + x(0, 1) + y(2, 2)$ would become:

$$\exists xy(a = 1 + y + y \quad \& \quad b = 2 + x + y + y).$$

Now, a first conclusion may be drawn.

5.4. Theorem: Every quantifier computable by a push-down automaton is first-order additively definable.

Proof: The set of "Parikh couples" for the (context-free) language of the quantifier is semi-linear, and hence definable in the required sense. Moreover, because of the permutation closure of this language, the latter definition fits it exactly. QED

In general, however, Parikh's Theorem cannot be converted, not even for permutation-closed languages. A standard counter-example on a 3-symbol alphabet is the following non-context-free set: "all sequences with equal numbers of occurrences of the three symbols". The corresponding arithmetical predicate is semi-linear; but the language is not context-free: when intersected with the regular $(abc)^*$, it produces the well-known counterexample $a^n b^n c^n$.

Fortunately, the present binary alphabet admits of a more interesting conclusion, matching the above theorem. That such restrictions may produce strong effects is not unknown: recall the theorem that, on a one-symbol alphabet, every context-free language is already regular.

First, observe that all our previous examples were semi-linear. This was indicated already for the case of "at least one-third," being $(0, 0) + x(0, 1) + y(1, 1) + z(2, 1)$. But also, e.g., "at least two-third" has such a form: $(0, 0) + x(0, 1) + y(1, 2)$.

To proceed more generally, a result is now needed from Ginsburg and Spanier (1966), who proved that the semi-linear predicates actually coincide with the first-order additively definable ones. Their idea was to use *Presburger's* early description of the latter predicates (cf. Mendelson, 1964, pp. 116−117). Through the method of quantifier elimination, these turn out to be equivalent to all Boolean combinations of "atomic" formulas

$$t1 = t2, \; t1 < t2 \text{ and } t1 = t2 \pmod{k} \text{ (i.e., } \exists x(t1 = t2 + x \; \vee \; t2 = t1 + x)).$$

Here, $t1$, $t2$ are terms employing individual variables, 0, S and $+$. Now, all Presburger predicates can be shown to be semi-linear. (This result is not trivial. For instance, it is not obvious that the intersection of two semi-linear sets is again semi-linear.)

Thus, first-order additively definable predicates correspond to semi-linear sets − and it remains to find suitable automata for the latter, generalizing the earlier examples. In view of earlier observations, the restriction to a two-symbol alphabet must play some essential role here.

5.5. Theorem: Every first-order additively definable quantifier is computable by a push-down automaton.

Proof: Every quantifier of this first-order form corresponds to a semi-linear set of *couples*, by the Ginsberg and Spanier result. And the latter's corresponding set of 0, 1-sequences may be recognized by a push-down automaton. An elegant construction of this kind was found by Stan Peters and Bill Marsh. Here, we adapt their idea to the kind of automaton used in our original examples.

First, attention may be restricted to *linear* predicates, as finite unions of context-free languages are themselves context-free. Thus, suppose that our predicate has the form

$(m1, m2) + x1(m11, m12) + \ldots + xn(mn1, mn2)$.

Let N be the maximum of all natural numbers mi, mij involved. Our automaton will have $2(N.N)$ states, being all couples of the forms (i, j), $(i, j)^*$ $(1 \leq i, j \leq N)$. What these encode will become clear presently. The instructions are the following:

Reading: reading a symbol 0 in state (i, j) $(i < N)$,
$\qquad$ either go to $(i + 1, j)$, or remain in (i, j), adding a 0 to the stack;
$\qquad$ reading 0 in state (N, j),
$\qquad$ remain in (N, j) and add 0 to the stack.
$\qquad$ Likewise, for reading a symbol 1.
Similar moves are allowed for the *-states: here, and wherever appropriate.
Exchanging: the following ϵ-moves are possible,
$\qquad$ from $(i + 1, j)$ to (i, j), pushing a 0 onto the stack;
$\qquad$ likewise, with $(i, j + 1)$ and a symbol 1.
$\qquad$ Conversely, if $i < N$, a 0 may be popped from the stack,
$\qquad$ going from state (i, j) to $(i + 1, j)$;
$\qquad$ likewise, for $j < N$ and popping a symbol 1.
Lowering: when $i \geq mk1, j \geq mk2$, it is possible to jump
$\qquad$ from state (i, j) to $(i - mk1, j - mk2)$.
Crossing: when $i \geq m1, j \geq m2$, it is possible to jump
$\qquad$ from state (i, j) to $(i - m1, j - m2)^*$.

Finally, the initial state is $(0, 0)$ − and recognition is by empty stack and designated state $(0, 0)^*$.

The point of these stipulations lies in the following observation.

Claim: At each stage in the computation, with state (i, j), there exist numbers $x1, \ldots, xn$ such that
• $i +$ the number of symbols 0 in the stack equals the number of symbols 0 read $- x1.m11 - \ldots - xn.mn1$
• $j +$ the number of symbols 1 in the stack equals the number of symbols 1 read $- x1.m12 - \ldots - xn.mn2$.

For *-states, a similar assertion holds, but with two more subtractions − viz., for $m1, m2$, respectively.

The proof of the claim is by induction on the number of admissible moves in a computation. Clearly, each of them preserves this invariant statement.

Moreover, once in the final state, with the sum on the left-hand side equal to zero, the sequence processed must have had the above arithmetical character. Thus, only correct sequences are recognized.

Conversely, a judicious sequence of admissible moves will recognize any string with the correct amounts. To see this, the following assertion may be proved, by induction on the sum $x1 + \ldots + xn$.

Claim: If the stack has either all zeroes or all ones, the state is $(0, 0)$, and the occurrence totals of symbols 0, 1 in stack plus sequence still to be read are of the form $(m1, m2) + x1(m11, m12) + xn(mn1, mn2)$, then the machine will proceed to recognition. Likewise, in state $(0, 0)*$ without the initial factor $(m1, m2)$.

Proof: For $x1 + \ldots + xn = 0$, the only non-trivial task is to recognize a string of $m1$ zeroes and $m2$ ones. By obvious steps, state $(m1, m2)$ can be reached here, popping and reading − and then, one crossing produces the desired final state. For $x1 + \ldots + xn > 0$, the machine is to continue reading until the first couple of occurrence numbers $(mi1, mi2)$ is exceeded (or perhaps $(m1, m2)$ itself) − as is bound to happen. Say, we started reading symbols 1, stacking all of these, while using symbols 0 to raise the state. Then, transferring enough symbols 1 from stack to state, we arrive at the state $(mi1, mi2)$ − from where we may drop to $(0, 0)$, leaving a "homogeneous" stack. See the Addenda for some further explanation. QED

From the claim, it follows at once that all correct strings will indeed be recognized. QED

Notice that our proof implies the weaker result of Ginsburg and Spanier that semi-linear sets of 2-tuples correspond to context-free "bounded" languages in the universe $1*0*$. For, the intersection of a context-free set with a regular one is again context-free.

Our original argument for Theorem 5.5 proceeded by enumeration, providing suitable push-down automata for each of the above Presburger types − trying to circumvent the fact that context-free languages in general are not closed under intersection.

Still, the latter approach also provides some interesting concrete examples. Arithmetical predicates in a, b may be represented as point sets in the north-eastern quadrant $a \geq 0$, $b \geq 0$ (or equivalently, in the Tree of Numbers of Sec. 2) − and, by this geometrical representation, conjunctions of Presburger formulas are often seen to reduce to manageable patterns.

Thus, we have obtained an elegant characterization of all quantifiers computed by push-down automata.

Natural language quantifiers; computational concerns

With the above technical apparatus, several questions arise concerning quantifiers actually occurring in natural language.

As there is such a host of push-down automata, and so few linguistically realized quantifiers exploiting them, *additional* constraints seem of interest. For instance, earlier on, a possible restriction was mentioned to *deterministic* automata. One possibility here is to use deterministic push-down automata scanning some fixed finite top portion of the stack, provided with an additional facility for a final finite state machine check of stack contents. This type of automaton seems appropriate for all of the earlier-mentioned concrete examples. (Thus, e.g., 'at least one-third' may also be recognized deterministically, at least in this wider sense.)

In this light also, another topic to be investigated is the possible connection between important "semantic" conditions on denotations featuring in the orthodox approach, and natural restrictions on machine instructions. In other words, what are the *computational effects* of traditional notions in studies of generalized quantifiers?

One early example of this connection is found in van Benthem (1984a), where an equivalence is proven between quantifiers that are of *minimal count complexity* and those that are *continuous*. The latter condition requires a more traditional type of denotational behaviour; amongst others that

if $Y1 \subseteq Y \subseteq Y2$ and $QXY1$, $QXY2$, then QXY;
and likewise for not-Q.

Its precise total effect has a convenient formulation in the Tree of Numbers:

"in each of the three main directions of variation in the Tree,
viz., increasing a (traveling along a /-diagonal),
    increasing b (traveling along a \-diagonal),
    playing off a and b (traveling along a horizontal line),
the quantifier experiences at most one truth-value change".

Notice that all our previous examples of basic quantifiers satisfy this strong condition. Still, it may be seen that *uncountably* many cases share this property. In particular, any pattern of similar rows " $- - \ldots + +$ " (or " $+ + \ldots - -$ ") will qualify, whose true/false boundary shifts at most one position at a time, going down the Tree. Thus, it is of some interest to combine the latter condition with our present computability restriction, that to semi-linear, or even just linear sets. (Again, our previous basic, examples were all linear.)

As more often in these matters, one additional restriction will be useful to make the possibilities surveyable; viz., *Variety*. That is, at each non-trivial row, the quantifier should be "alive":

VAR   For all non-empty X, there exist $Y, Y' \subseteq E$
      such that $Q_E XY$, and not $Q_E XY'$.

In the Tree, this means that every row below the top level has both $+$ and $-$ positions for Q.

Now, our two computability conditions produce strong restrictions. Only a countable number of very regular patterns remains, viz., those dividing the Tree into a true and a false part with a "periodic" boundary. Alternatively, these sets may be described arithmetically, using special constraints on their linear representations. Various attractive mathematical diversions are possible here.

But, there is a reason for yet another restriction. The above semantic conditions of Continuity and Variety are symmetric: holding for Q if and only if they hold for its negation. Thus, it seems of interest to require the same concerning linearity: strengthening it to *bi-linearity*. Then, the following classification results of our "strongly computable" quantifiers.

5.6. Theorem (VAR): The bilinear continuous quantifiers are precisely those of the following forms ($n = 0, 1, \ldots$):

"at least $1/n + 1$", "at most $n/n + 1$",
"less than $1/n + 1$", "more than $n/n + 1$".

Comment: For $n = 0$, this gives the four quantifiers in the Square of Opposition. For $n = 1$, one gets 'most', 'not most', 'least' and 'not least'. Thus, a hierarchy arises, as in van Benthem (1984a), which also supplied the inspiration for the following type of argument. This time, however, the motivation of the conditions employed is computational.

Proof: It suffices to consider one case only, the others being analogous. Suppose that $(0, 0) \in Q$, with $(1, 0) \notin Q$, $(0, 1) \in Q$. Because Q is linear, this must mean that $(0, 0)$ is its basic case, while it allows steps of $+ x(0, 1)$. Moreover, non-Q has basic case $(1, 0)$. Also, because of Continuity in /-diagonals, $(2, 0) \notin Q$, and so forth: that is, non-Q allows steps $+ x(1, 0)$. Now Q, being linear, has only finitely many possibilities for occupying positions on the diagonal adjoining the non-Q left-hand edge; say, at most down to $(n, 1)$. By Continuity, it will then also occupy $(0, 1) \ldots, (n, 1)$ − but nothing beyond that. Thus, non-Q can make the jump $(n + 1, 1)$. By bilinearity then, as well as the already described properties of Q and non-Q, their boundary is fixed, to form the pattern of 'at least $1/n + 1$' ($n = 0$, 1, $\ldots$). QED

It may be checked that all quantifiers mentioned in this theorem are deterministic in the wider sense introduced earlier (D. de Jongh).

Also, as in Section 4, questions of *fine-structure* arise here. For instance, one natural class of push-down automata to consider are those with two states, whose stack alphabet is restricted to 0, 1. Even there, a hierarchy of further possibilities exists, depending on which actions are permitted in rewriting the stack, and which final reading-off convention is chosen. The 'most' machine exemplified about the simplest case here, with additions or removals of at most one stack symbol at a time, and a final convention which essentially just inspects the top stack symbol. Of the latter variety, there seem to be only a few representatives, notably the first two layers in the hierarchy of Theorem 5.6 above. The relevant calculations have been omitted here.

Are there any natural language quantifiers beyond the context-free realm? Of course, it is easy to make up such examples, such as 'a square number of'. A more serious non-contrived candidate is the earlier-mentioned '(relatively) many', stating (in terms of the numbers displayed in Sec. 2) that

$$b/a + b > b + c/a + b + c + e;$$

or equivalently, that

$$a.c < b.e.$$

5.7. Example: "(Relatively) many" is not computable by means of a push-down automaton. The reason is that the above predicate is not semi-linear, as it essentially involves multiplication. Thus, the assertion follows by Parikh's Theorem.

Still, the above example is not a pure quantifier in the narrower sense; and we know of no natural non-additive examples in the latter area. Thus, as was observed in Section 3, a deep result from logic becomes relevant: the quantifier system of natural language stops just short of the arithmetical border line where incompleteness and undecidability set in. Thus, while relatively strong, it still enjoys the theoretical properties of additive arithmetic. In particular, many questions about behaviour or comparison of even higher-order quantifiers must be decidable.

Actually, some caution is in order here. The above arguments only provide an effective road for obtaining push-down automata for arithmetically given quantifiers. The converse requires some supplementary reasoning. First, given a push-down automaton computing a quantifier, an equivalent context-free grammar is to be found. The standard proof of this correspondence in the literature is effective. Then, the proof of Parikh's Theorem provides an effective method for assigning a semi-linear set to a grammar. And finally, transcription of the latter into the format of additive arithmetic is effective too. Thus, for instance, equivalence of quantifiers as procedures (in the present sense) is indeed decidable. This is somewhat surprising, as equivalence of push-down automata in general is known to be undecidable. Evidently, our restriction to permutation-closed languages plays a major role in this respect.

6. EXTENDING THE FRAMEWORK

Many details of the preceding sections are tied up with special features of determiners, or even quantifiers in particular. Nevertheless, other types of linguistic expression also suggest procedural interpretations.

For instance, when evaluating *conditions*, viewed as generalized quantifiers between sets of antecedent and consequent occasions (cf. van Benthem 1984b), 'similarity graphs' of possible worlds are to be searched, where relative position is as important as numbers. Likewise, Suppes 1982 proposes procedural denotations for *adjectives*, locating individuals in certain comparative orders. These and similar cases can be subsumed under the notion of a *graph automaton* traversing acyclic graphs of nodes, possibly carrying features. Precise definitions, as well as a first study of the theory of the latter (extending the results of this paper) are found in van Benthem 1986a,b.

Taking procedures for actual denotations of certain linguistic expressions turns out to be a fruitful perspective, suggesting various new semantic questions. Indeed, Suppes has suggested that the idea extends to all of natural language − citing even a "procedural" view of proper names, as "criteria of identity". When the enterprise is proposed in this generality, some caution is due.

First, the proper name case may point at a possible confusion. Of course, even on the orthodox view, in every interpretation of language, there is some functional connection between linguistic items and their denotations − and this function may come with a procedure. Thus, "Julia" denotes the girl Julia; but, a procedure may be needed to recognize her if you saw her. Put differently, a procedural view might be appropriate to Fregean *senses*, while leaving traditional denotations undisturbed.

But, the procedural view proper is not external in this sense. It is supposed to apply "inside models", so to speak. Even so, a facile overapplicability threatens. For, in a type-theoretic framework, virtually every denotation is a function − and as such, may be thought of as a procedure. Thus, the procedural perspective only acquires some bite by descending from this general level.

But then, it might seem as if semantic population problems only get worse. One function, in the set-theoretic input/output sense, will correspond to many intensionally different procedures for computing it. On the other hand, though, this intensional move also suggests a more "categorial" perspective upon type-theoretic models, with each functional domain containing enough, but not necessarily all set-theoretically possible arrows. Actually, for other reasons too, semanticists might take advantage of the known correspondences between models for a typed lambda calculus (their usual haunt) and Cartesian closed categories.

Even so, the categorial perspective does not suggest concrete restrictions of the set of all possible procedures. To obtain the latter, we might try to articulate general conditions of computability for semantic meanings. For instance, should attention be restricted to *recursive* functions? This particular proposal has its obvious defects: on finite domains, it holds trivially, on infinite ones, it breaks down too soon. (Notice, e.g., that 'some', as non-empty intersection, is not a recursive predicate, even on recursive sets.) But then, it has been claimed that the notion of a *continuous* function is the proper one here (in the sense of Scott's domain semantics) — when used in conjunction with suitable model structures. But again, such global notions seem rather far removed from the actual examples which gave the idea of procedural semantics its initial flavour.

Therefore, pursuing further case studies, like the ones in this paper, may be a more sensible way of finding substantial forms of procedural semantics. Regardless of the eventual outcome, however, it should be stressed that this enterprise is not incompatible with the usual denotational views. There is always a distinction available between "truth conditions" and "verification conditions" (suitably understood). The latter view may complement the former, by introducing contemporary concerns of computability (and perhaps learnability) into semantics. If this paper has provided a foothold for such a development, it will have amply fulfilled its purpose.

Acknowledgement

I would like to thank Pat Suppes for an inspiring conversation, and especially Stan Peters, without whose continuing advice and encouragement this paper could not have been written. The center for the Study of Language and Information, provided the setting of all this. (An earlier version appeared as CSLI-report 85-27, July 1985.)

REFERENCES

Ginsburg, S.: (1966), *The Mathematical Theory of Context-Free Languages.* New York: McGraw-Hill.

Ginsburg, S., & Spanier, E.: (1966), Semi-Groups, Presburger Formulas and Languages. *Pacific Journal of Mathematics* 16, 285–296.

Hopcroft, J., & Ullman, J.: (1979), *Introduction to Automata Theory, Languages and Computation.* Reading, Mass.: Addison-Wesley.

Keenan, E., & Stavi, Y.: (1981), A Semantic Characterization of Natural Language Determiners, Linguistics and Philosophy. To appear.

Mendelson, E.: (1964), *Introduction to Mathematical Logic.* Princeton: Van Nostrand.

Suppes, P.: (1982), Variable-Free Semantics with Remarks on Procedural Extensions, In T. Simon and R. Scholes (Eds.), *Language, Mind and Brain.* Hillsdale, N.J.: Lawrence Erlbaum. 21–31.

Ter Meulen, A., & Van Benthem, J. (Eds.): (1985), *Generalized Quantifiers: Theory and Applications*. GRASS Series 4. Foris, Dordrecht and Cinnaminson.

Van Benthem, J., (1983a), Determiners and Logic. *Linguistics and Philosophy* 6, 447–478.

Van Benthem, J.: (1983b), Five Easy Pieces. In A. Ter Meulen (Ed.), *Studies in Model-theoretic Semantics*. GRASS Series 1:1–17. Foris, Dordrecht and Cinnaminson.

Van Benthem, J.: (1984a), A Linguistic Turn: New Directions in Logic. To appear in R. Marcus et al. (Eds.): (1986), *Proceedings 7th International Congress of Logic, Methodology and Philosophy of Science. Salzburg 1983.* Studies in Logic 114: 205–240. Amsterdam: North-Holland.

Van Benthem, J.: (1984b), Foundations of Conditional Logic. *Journal of Philosophical Logic* 13:3, 303–349.

Van Benthem, J.: (1984c), Questions about Quantifiers. *Journal of Symbolic Logic* 49:2, 443–466.

Van Benthem, J.: (1986a), *Essays in Logical Semantics*, Reidel, Dordrecht (Studies in Linguistics and Philosophy, vol. 29).

Van Benthem, J.: (1986b), Towards a Computational Semantics, to appear in R. Cooper, E. Engdahl and P. Gärdenfors (eds.), *Proceedings Lund Workshop on Generalized Quantifiers*, Reidel, Dordrecht (Studies in Linguistics and Philosophy).

ADDENDA

Since this paper was written (June '84), some further developments have occurred. As for the general procedural approach, a congenial perspective is found in S. Löbner, "Quantification as a major module of natural language semantics" [this volume]. Löbner adduces a wide range of linguistic material showing that evaluating quantifiers and related constructions involves surveying the domain in some order. Some further technical results and observations are grouped below, under the three main headings of this paper.

FINITE STATE AUTOMATA

The first-order quantifiers were shown to be those having a finite state automaton that is *permutation-invariant* and *acyclic*. Permutation-invariant automata recognize permutation-closed languages, as was noted above. The converse also holds: the Nerode-representation will automatically provide a permutation-closed regular language with a permutation-invariant recognizing machine. As for the notion "acyclic", it may be shown that languages having an acyclic finite state recognizer are precisely the *testable* regular languages playing a central role in W. McNaughton & S. Papert, *Counter-free Automata*, MIT Press, 1971, Cambridge (Mass.).

PUSH-DOWN AUTOMATA

Here are some comments on the proof of push-down computability for semi-linear languages with a two-symbol alphabet.

(1) How to read and act in order to recognize a sequence with numbers 0, 1 given by $(m1, m2) + x1(m11, m12) + \ldots + xn(mn1, mn2)$?

Suppose that we have a homogeneous stack of symbols 1, are in state $(0, 0)$, and the correct invariant holds (i.e., the totals of occurrences for 0, 1 in ⟨ state & stack & sequence to be read ⟩ still satisfy our linear schema). We want to read ahead to pick up enough 0's and 1's to reach the first $mi1$, $mi2$ (or perhaps $m1$, $m2$ itself) in occurrence totals for ⟨ state & stack ⟩. (Then, we 'drop state', or 'cross over', and repeat the process.) Now, in order to get this

*mi*1, *mi*2, we may have to pick up *too many* 0 or 1 (though not *both*). E.g., suppose it's too many 0 ('too many 1' just remain on the stack). Then, we first transfer all symbols 1 from stack to state (this must be possible: if there were too many 1's already there, then there would have been no need to pick up more than the required number of 0's) − putting all symbols 1 read into the state, and *enough* symbols 0 (stacking the others).
(2) Why does this work for two-symbol alphabets only?

With, say, three symbols, we cannot maintain a "homogeneous" stack − which is vital to the argument. E.g., suppose that we have stored "regularly" as follows: 0 ... 0 1 ... 1. Now, the first triple comes along, say (4, 2, 1). One problem: stacking additional symbols 0 read will disturb homogeneity. More seriously, suppose that we have encountered our first symbol 2 after having read enough 0 and 1. It may be *impossible* to get to the required state by popping, as too many intervening symbols 1 could block us from the initial symbols 0. And, other ways of stacking have similar problems.

GRAPH AUTOMATA

The action of our graph automaton, on *acyclic rooted finite* graphs, moving upward from daughters to mothers, can be described as follows:
• a finite state machine is given;
• first, the features at the currently inspected node are considered, to decide in which state to start up the machine,
• which then searches through all final symbols on the daughters, left as end-products of the machine's earlier action there,
• and ends in a final state, which leaves a mark on our node.
Theoretical questions about this kind of machine include the following:
• which properties of graphs with features are computed in this way?
In general, the class of graphs accepted by a machine M will be definable by a *monadic existential second-order* condition π_M. But in many cases, we can do better than this. π_M is often given *recursively* in terms of simple conditions on predecessors of the top node of the graph − and we can try to 'unwind' this to some *equally simple explicit* definition. Notably, there is the following question.
• given a recursive description of the machine M in terms of a *first-order* condition on the end-states on the daughters, can π_M be converted into an explicit first-order definition of the class of trees recognized? In general, the answer is negative: *Beth's Theorem* fails on this non-elementary class of graphs.
But, a great improvement occurs when the machine is allowed to inspect *all* predecessors, instead of only daughters. In that case, a formal analogy can be exploited with the semantics for *modal provability logic* of arithmetic (see C. Smoryński, 'Modal Logic and Self-Reference', in D. Gabbay and F. Guenthner (Eds.): (1984), *Handbook of Philosophical Logic*, vol. 2, Reidel, Dordrecht and Boston, 441−495). In particular, the algorithm used in the proof of the De Jongh-Sambin Fixed-Point Theorem may be used to calculate explicit π_M for simple machines M.

Actually, there is an interesting feed-back to the above area. From our point of view, two generalizations of the above theorem are minimally necessary. There can be more than one accepting state, and hence we need "multiple fixed points". Moreover, our machines will employ arbitrary first-order quantifiers on predecessors (not just ∃, ∀) and so we need arbitrary "first-order" fixed points. As it turns out, both generalizations are valid (Boolos; De Jongh, respectively). With higher automata, this result may fail, however: no "explicitization" result holds for, e.g., the quantifier *in most successors* (De Jongh). So again, the automata hierarchy turns out to be significant.

There remains a converse type of question, of which the following is a prominent example.
• Given some first-order condition on graphs with features, can one find a finite state graph automaton computing it?
For further information on this, and the preceding topics, see van Benthem 1986b.

Chapter 2

Lexical Freedom and Large Categories*

Edward L. Keenan

SUMMARY

Grammatical categories of English expressions are shown to differ with regard to the freedom we have in semantically interpreting their lexical (= syntactically simplest) expressions. Section 1 reviews the categories of expression we consider. Section 2 empirically supports that certain of these categories are *lexically free*, a notion we formally define, in the sense that anything which is denotable by a complex expression in the category is available as a denotation for lexical expressions in the category. Other categories are shown to be not lexically free. Thus for those categories the interpretation of lexical expressions is inherently constrained compared to the interpretation of the full class of expressions in the category.

In section 3 we establish the principle generalization of this paper: *small categories are lexically free, large ones are not*, where the size of a category is formally defined in terms of the full range of extensional distinctions expressible by expressions in the category. In terms of this generalization we suggest an explanation for the distribution of lexical freedom established in section 2.

We conclude with a generalization of the notion *lexical freedom* and present some partial results, leaving certain problems open.

1. CATEGORIES CONSIDERED

Below we present, with suitable mnemonics, the categories of expression we consider. We shall assume that these categories of expression form part of a formal languae L, the precise nature of which is unimportant here. The language given in K&F (Keenan & Faltz, 1985) will do, as will the languages given in Montague (1970 and 1973) with trivial modifications.

   CN or (*zero place*) *common noun phrase: man, tall man, man who Sue loves*

---

* At several points in this paper I have benefitted from discussion and comment from Johan van Benthem, Peter van Emde Boas, Dick de Jongh, and Larry Moss. In addition I wish to thank the Max-Planck Institute für Psycholinguistik, Nijmegen for having supported the research herein.

NP or *full noun phrase: John, every man, John and no other student, more students than teachers*

CN_1 or *one place (transitive) common noun phrase: friend (of), brother (of)*. They combine with NP's to form CN's: *friend of the President, brother of some senator.*

AP or *zero place adjective phrase: female, tall, who Sue loves*

AP_1 or *one place (transitive) adjective phrase: fond (of), jealous (of)*. They combine with NP's to form AP's: *fond of both John and Mary*, as in *Every student fond of both John and Mary came to their aid.*

Det_k or k-*place determiners:* they combine with k CN's to form an NP. Some Det_1's (or just Dets for short) are: *every, no student's,* (as in *no student's cat*), *more male than female* (as in *more male than female students [passed the exam]*).

Some Det_2*'s are: more ... than ..., exactly as many ... as ...,* as in *more students than teachers [attended the meeting].*

P_k or k-*place predicates*; We identify P_0 with S (Sentence).

Some P_1's are: *walk, walk but not talk, walk slowly in the garden.* Some P_2's are: *hug, kiss, hug and kiss.* Some P_3's are: *show, give, show and give.* We do not consider L to have P_k's for $k \geq 4$.

PM or *predicate modifier: here, slowly, in the garden.* PM's combine with P_k's to form P_k's, $k \geq 1$. Some also combine with CN_k's to form CN_k's.

Prep or *transitive PM's: in, at, on.* They form PM's from NP's.

Remarks on the syntax

(i) We shall not treat PM's and Prepositions directly, though we shall treat CN_k's and P_k's formed from them. We shall not treat Det_k's for $k > 2$. The extensive list of Det_1's we consider is given in K&S (Keenan & Stavi, 1981 and to appear). The class of Det_2's considered is given in K&M (Keenan & Moss, 1984). In addition, certain subcategories of the categories noted above will be treated.

(ii) For C any of the categories considered, we write C_{lex} for the set of syntactically simplest expressions of category C. Elements of C_{lex} will be referred to as *lexical expressions of category* C. They normally coincide with the one word expressions in C, though in a few cases such as P_0 and Det_2 it may be that the syntactically simplest expressions are more than one word long (e.g. *John walks,* and *more ... than ... respectively*).

2. LEXICAL FREEDOM

We shall first illustrate the concept of lexical freedom by arguing that the category P_1 is lexically free and that the category NP is not lexically free. Then we give the category independent definition of lexical freedom.

Extensionally we think of (first order) P_1's as being true or false of individuals. E.g. in a world ("model") of six individuals I_1, I_2, ..., I_6 it might be the case that the P_1 *walk slowly in the garden* is interpreted in such a way as to be true of, say, I_1, I_2, and I_3 and I_5 (and fails of all the other individuals[1]). And in such a case it is logically possible that the lexical P_1 *whistle* is also true of just I_1, I_2, I_3 and I_5. That is, there is nothing about the meaning of *walk slowly in the garden* which prevents it from being the case that the individuals who are walking slowly in the garden are just those who are whistling. This and similar examples show that complex P_1's formed from PM's (Predicate Modifiers) such as *slowly* and *in the garden* do not associate truth values with individuals in ways which are inherently unavailable for lexical P_1's such as *whistle*.

Moreover, what holds for P_1's formed with PM's holds for all ways of forming syntactically complex P_1's. That is, the various ways of building syntactically complex P_1's do not lead to P_1's which are true of individuals in ways which are in principle unavailable to lexical P_1's. And this is what we mean when we say that P_1 is *lexically free*. Any way of assigning truth values to individuals which are available for complex P_1's is also available for lexical P_1's.

To see that P_1 is in fact lexically free let us consider briefly the various ways in which complex P_1's may be formed. Modification with PM's has already been considered. Another way of forming complex P_1's is by taking boolean combinations in *and, or* and *not* (as well as *but, neither ... nor,* and a few others). Again, there is nothing about the meaning of, say, *walk but not talk* which prevents it from being the case that the individuals who are walking but not talking are just those who are smiling. So whenever *walk but not talk* is true of certain individuals it is logically possible that *smile* is also true of just those individuals. Third, consider P_1's formed from P_2's plus NP arguments, as *hug* and *kiss some student*. Obviously it is logically possible that the individuals who are both hugging and kissing some student are just those who are standing, so the lexical P_1 *stand* can in principle be interpreted in such a way as to be true of whatever individuals *hug* and *kiss some student* is true of. Fourth, consider P_1's formed by operations such as Passive, Reflexive, and Unspecified Object Deletion, as in *John was kissed, Mary admires herself*, and *Fred is reading*. Obviously, no matter which individuals were kissed, it is possible that just those individuals were *sleeping*, so the passive P_1 *was kissed* does not in principle hold of individuals which a lexical P_1 such as *sleep* could not hold of. Analogous claims hold for the P_1's *admire oneself* and *read*. As a last example consider P_1's form-ed from P_2's which take infinitival arguments, as in *want/begin/try* to *read this book*. Again it obviously could be the case that whatever individuals want to read this book are just the individuals who are humming, so such P_1's do not associate truth values with individuals in ways which are unavailable to lexical P_1's such as *hum*.

We conclude then that the category P_1 in English is lexically free. Moreover the informal arguments which support this claim are based on judgments which seem sufficiently banal as to make us wonder just how a category could really fail to be lexically free. There are however several such cases, among them the category NP considered below.

The category NP is not lexically free. Many complex NP's, such as *every student, more students than teachers*, etc. are built up from CN's (*student, teacher*), so just how such NP's are semantically interpreted will depend in part on how the CN's they are formed from are interpreted. We may (stan-dardly enough) think of CN's as denoting *properties* of individuals, and we regard two CN's as extensionally distinct if, in some model, the individuals which have the property denoted by one are not exactly the same as those with the property denoted by the other. For example, *doctor* and *fat lawyer* are extensionally distinct since we can easily imagine a state of affairs in which the doctors and the fat lawyers are not exactly the same individuals. Up to isomorphism then, we may think of a CN as (extensionally) denoting a set of individuals.

Given this understanding of CN's, we may (up to isomorphism) think of full NP's as denoting sets of properties, i.e. sets of possible CN denotations. On this view, a sentence such as *Every doctor is a vegetarian* is true if the property denoted by *vegetarian* is an element of the set denoted by *every doctor*, and false otherwise.

Now, to show that NP is not lexically free, we will show that there are property sets denotable by complex NP's which are in principle undenotable by lexical NP's. The lexical NP's are largely just the proper nouns (*John, Mary*) and the singular personal pronouns (*he, she*). We might also include the demonstratives (*this, that*) as well as possessive deictics such as *mine, yours*. Let us further include (though most linguists would treat them as syn-tactically complex) the plural pronouns, such as *we, they, these, ours*.

Note that all these NP's denote property sets which are *increasing*, which we define as follows: A set K of properties is *increasing* iff for all properties p, q, if p ∈ K and every individual with p is also one with q, then q ∈ K. An NP is *increasing* if it always denotes an increasing set.

To check whether an NP is increasing (cf. Barwise & Cooper, 1981) check that it satisfies the entailment paradigm given below when substituted for X:

(1)   Every doctor is a vegetarian
        X is a doctor
        Therefore, X is a vegetarian

The lexical NP's noted above are all obviously increasing, and it is tempting to conclude that all lexical NP's are increasing. There is however another class of NP's which at least are phonological words and might be considered by some to be syntactically simple. These are items often referred to in traditional grammars as "indefinite" pronouns, e.g. *all, none, someone, everyone, noone*. If we count these NP's as lexical, we must note that *none* and *noone* are not increasing. They are however *decreasing*, where a set K of properties is *decreasing* iff for all properties p, q, if q $\in$ K and every p is a q then p $\in$ K. To check that X is a decreasing NP verify that the following argument is valid:

(2)   Every doctor is a vegetarian
        X is a vegetarian
        Therefore, X is a doctor

A NP is called *monotonic* just in case it is either increasing or decreasing. Clearly the candidates for lexical NP's considered above are all monotonic, and as these exhaust our candidates we conclude that all syntactically simple NP's in English denote monotonic sets of properties. (In fact, not all monotonic sets can be denoted by these NP's, but the condition as it stands is sufficient for our purposes.)

Now to show that NP is not lexically free it is sufficient to find complex NP's which can denote non-monotonic sets. And in fact all major ways of forming syntactically complex NP's yield ones which may denote non-monotonic sets. Some examples formed from Det's plus CN's are: *exactly one boy, between five and ten boys, more male than female students, all but one student, every student's but not every teacher's bicycle*. Examples formed from Det$_2$ and two CN's are: *more students than teachers, fewer students than teachers*, and *exactly as many students as teachers*. Finally, examples formed by boolean combinations of NP's include: *John but not Mary, every boy but not every girl, either fewer than five students or else more than a hundred students*. (We invite the reader to test e.g. *exactly one boy* in the paradigms given in (1) and (2) to satisfy himself that this NP is neither increasing nor decreasing.)

Since lexical NP's in principle cannot denote non-monotonic sets we conclude that NP is not lexically free.

We may note however that if NP$_{prop}$, the set of proper nouns (*John, Mary*), can be distinguished on syntactic grounds as a (sub)-category, then it is lexically free. Indeed, some would doubtless say that there are no syntactically complex proper nouns, in which case it is trivial that anything which can be denoted by a complex proper noun can be denoted by a simple one. There are however certain syntactically complex expressions which we might consider to be proper nouns. For example, certain AP + proper noun combinations, as *Little John, Mighty Mo*. Similarly Proper Noun + family name expressions such as *John Smith, Ebeneezer Cooke*. Also Proper Noun plus epithet constructions, as *Eric the Red, Charles the Bald*. But in all cases these complex expressions denote individuals and so do not denote anything which is undenotable by simple proper nouns. So NP$_{prop}$, if a syntactically definable subcategory, is lexically free.

2.1 A general characterization of lexical freedom

The arguments above that P$_1$ is lexically free and that NP is not are ones based more or less directly on our judgments of entailment and logical equivalence among English sentences. In assessing the lexical freedom of other categories the arguments will have this same informal character, as they do not depend crucially on adopting one or another semantic formalism. It is nonetheless important to see that our considerations can be made formally precise. We sketch in this section one way of doing that. The reader who is satisfied with the informal treatment of lexical freedom already given may skip this section without loss of continuity.

The notion of lexical freedom basically compares the range of extensional distinctions which can be expressed by the lexical items in a category with the range expressible by the entire set of expressions in the category. Now informally we have regarded two expressions of a given category C as extensionally distinct if we can ultimately distinguish their meanings in terms of the properties possessed by individuals, and more generally the relations which individuals bear to one another. More formally, we shall measure the range of extensional distinctions expressible by a category C by the sets in which expressions of category C denote in an extensional model of our language L. Exactly what sets these are depends on which individuals there are. Given a set I of individuals, we shall write Den$_I$ C for the set in which expressions of category C denote. For example, given I, and chosing C to be P$_1$, we may think of Den$_I$ C as the set of functions from I into the set $\{T, F\}$ of truth values. So a P$_1$ then will denote some function which assigns T (= **true**) to some of the individuals in I and F (= **false**) to the others. Similarly, chosing C to be P$_2$ we may take Den$_I$ C to be the set of functions from pairs of individuals in I into $\{T, F\}$. So two P$_2$'s are extensionally distinct just in case for some universe I of individuals, they assign different truth values to at least one pair of elements of I. In general in what follows we shall introduce the denotation sets Den$_I$ C on a category by category basis.

Here it is only important to note that the $Den_I C$ are defined strictly in terms of the set I of individuals and the fixed set $\{T, F\}$ of truth values. Since I can be any (non-empty) set, we cannot give the range of extensional distinctions expressible by, say, P_1 in absolute terms. It depends on what I is chosen, and can only be expressed as a function of I. We can of course give this function precisely. If I is chosen with n (possibly infinite) members, there will be 2^n functions from I into $\{T, F\}$. In section 3 we shall define the relative "sizes" of categories in terms of how fast their denotation sets grow as a function of the number of individuals in the universe.

Given a universe I of individuals there are typically many ways of assigning elements of $Den_I C$ to expressions of category C. A specification of one of these ways basically defines a model for our language. Formally, a *model for* L is a pair (I, m), where I is a non-empty set of individuals[2] and m is a denotation function, called an *interpretation of L relative to I*, which assigns to each expression d of category C some element of $Den_I C$. The acceptable interpreting functions m are required to satisfy two types of condition. The first is Compositionality. Namely, the value of m at a syntactically complex expression d is determined by the value of m at the syntactic parts of d. So an interpreting function has no freedom in assigning denotations to syntactically complex expressions. The second type of condition limits the freedom in assigning denotations to lexical (= syntactically simple) expressions. In the first place, some expressions such as *every, be*, and *true* are "logical constants" in the sense that given two models (I, m) and (I, m') with the same universe, we require that m and m' assign the same values to these expressions. E.g. given I, there is only one function from $I \times I$ into $\{T, F\}$ which is an acceptable denotation for *be*. Moreover, even for lexical items which are not logical constants we find that an interpreting function may not assign values with complete freedom: some expressions are constrained in their interpretation relative to the interpretation of others. For example, if m(*kill*) is true of a pair of individuals (I_1, I_2) the m(*die*) must assign T to I_2.

Nonetheless, when all these conditions on acceptable interpreting functions are given, it is still the case that many lexical items exhibit considerable freedom in which elements of their denotation sets they may be interpreted as (= denote). And in fact for any non-empty universe I, there is always more than one interpretation of L relative to I. That is, there are at least two models (I, m) and (I, m') with the same universe I but with different interpreting functions m and m'.

With these preliminaries, we may formally define lexical freedom as follows (where 'C' in the definition ranges over the categories of expression considered):

Def 1: a.   For all universes I and all $K \subseteq C$,

$Den_I K = \{ m(d): d \in K \ \& \ m$ is an interpretation of L
relative to I$\}$

b.   C is *lexically free* iff for all universes I, $Den_I C_{lex} = Den_I C$

Recall here that C_{lex} is the set of syntactically simplest expressions of category C. So trivially $C_{lex} \subseteq C$, whence $Den_I C_{lex} \subseteq Den_I C$, all I. So to show that a category C is not lexically free it is sufficient and necessary to show that for some universe I of individuals, $Den_I C$ properly includes $Den_I C_{lex}$. That is, for some universe I, there is something which can be denoted by some expression in C but which cannot be denoted by any lexical expression of C. Conversely, to show that C is lexically free we must show that for all universes I, anything that can be denoted by an expression of C can be denoted by a lexical expression of C.

Notice also a notational subtlety which actually raises an interesting theoretical question (though not one we pursue here). Namely, given a category C and a universe of individuals I, we write $Den_I C$ for some set in which the expressions of category denote. $Den_I C$ is defined strictly in terms of I and $\{ T, F \}$. $Den_I C$ however, defined in Def 1 above, in addition refers to all ways m of interpreting expressions of category C. Trivially $Den_I C$ is a subset of $Den_I C$. We might like to require as an adequacy condition on approaches to model theoretic semantics for natural language that the reverse containment also hold. Why should we put elements in $Den_I C$ which can never be the denotation of an expression of category C under any interpretation of L? Nonetheless, several approaches, e.g. Montague (1973), do not satisfy the reverse inclusion. Further, while the definition of model in Montague (1973) could be appropriately modified, it is not obvious that there is a natural way to design the definition of the $Den_I C$, all I and all C, so that inclusion does obtain. It might happen for example that the natural and normally very simple definitions guarantee the inclusion when I is finite but leave some elements of $Den_I C$ inherently undenotable when I is infinite. See K&M for some relevant discussion.

2.2 The distribution of lexically free categories

CLAIM 1: The categories in A. below are lexically free, those in B. are not

A.   CN, CN_1, P_0, P_1, P_2, P_3, NP_{prop}, AP_{abs}, AP_1
B.   NP, AP, Det_1, Det_2

We consider first Claim (1.A.). P_1 and NP_{prop} (if it is a category) have already been argued to be lexically free. The arguments that P_2 and P_3 are L-free follow the same monotonous pattern as for P_1, noting that in general the ways of forming complex P_2's and P_3's are somewhat less productive than the ways of forming complex P_1's. We should however make explicit two restrictions we have been assuming on the class of P_n's we consider. First, we only consider "first order" predicates — ones which predicate of individuals rather than sets of individuals or more complicated objects. Thus we do not consider P_1's such as *love each other, be the two students I know best*, etc. which are most naturally thought of as predicating of sets of individuals. Nor do we consider P_2's such as *outnumber* which relates sets of individuals, not mere individuals. Further, this first order restriction applies where appropriate to other categories. For example, among AP's we do not consider ones such as *neighboring* and *parallel* as in *neighboring villages, parallel lines*, nor do we consider these CN's, as they do not denote properties of individuals but rather properties of sets of individuals.

Second, we limit ourselves to expressions which can be treated extensionally. E.g. we do not consider P_2's such as *seek* and *need*, nor do we consider AP's such as *skillful, fake*, and *apparent*. (Note that *skillful* and many other though not all, scalar AP's are not extensional in the sense that if the extensions of say *doctor and lawyer* are the same, i.e. the doctors and the lawyers are the same individuals, it does not follow that the extensions of *skillful doctor* and *skillful lawyer* are the same, i.e. the skillful doctors and the skillful lawyers may still be different individuals. We refer the reader to K&F (Keenan & Faltz, 1985) for a more thorough characterization of non-extensional subcategories of the categories we consider here.

Turning to the other categories mentioned in Claim (1.A), we have that P_0 is trivially L-free since clearly the simplest expressions of that category may be either true or false, so all elements of $Den_I P_0$ are denotable by elements of $(P_0)_{lex}$.

The claim that CN is L-free is slightly more interesting. We have earlier referred to CN denotations as *properties* (of individuals). Extensionally a property may be thought of as a set of individuals (i.e. those which have the property) and we may take, to use the formalism of the previous section, $Den_I CN$ to be the power set of I, the set of individuals of the model. Now to show CN to be L-free we must show that any way of forming syntactically complex CN's does not result in CN's which may denote properties inherently undenotable by lexical CN's. The most productive way of forming complex CN's is by modification with AP's, relative clauses, and PM's. But clearly, given any universe I of individuals, those who have the property expressed by *tall and handsome doctor* could be just those with the *bachelor* property, so CN's formed by AP modification do not take us outside the set of properties denotable by lexical CN's. Analogous claims hold for CN's such as *doctor who Susan kissed* and *child on the floor*, so CN's formed by relative clause and PM modification do not lead to anything extensionally new. Similarly, CN's formed from CN_1's plus NP arguments, as *friend of every senator*, are also not extensionally new. Clearly the individuals who are friends of every senator could be just the doctors. Finally, CN's formed by boolean combinations (not as productive as with many other categories) are not extensionally new. It is logically possible that the individuals with the property expressed by *non-doctor and non-lawyer* are just those with the vegetarian property. As this appears to exhaust the ways of forming complex CN's we conclude that the category CN is lexically free.

Consider now the less well studied case of CN_1's such as *friend (of)*. Extensionally we may think of them as denoting functions from individuals to properties (CN denotations). E.g. semantically *friend (of)* associates with each individuals J a property, friend of J. K&F investigate two ways of forming complex CN_1's: boolean combinations and modification. It is at least reasonable to consider that *friend and colleague (of)* is a complex CN_1 formed by conjoining *friend (of)* with *colleague (of)*. But it is clearly possible that for each individual J, the friends and colleagues of J are just the brothers of J, so *friend and colleague (of)* does not denote a function in principle undenotable by lexical CN_1's such as *brother (of)*.

Concerning modified CN_1's, K&F suggest that the classical ambiguity in *old friend of the President* may be represented by the scope of the modifier *old*. On the analysis on which *old* combines with the CN *friend of the President* it yields the property an individual has iff he is a friend of the President and he is old. In the case of interest, it combines with the CN_1 *friend (of)* to yield the CN_1 *old friend (of)*, which semantically maps each individual J to the property an individual has iff he has been a friend of J for a long time. But again there is no reason why, for each J, the old friends of J in this sense could not be the brothers of J, so *old friend (of)* does not denote any function which is undenotable by lexical CN_1's such as *brother (of)*. And as we can think of no further ways of forming complex CN_1's we conclude that CN_1 is a lexically free category.

The remaining categories listed in Claim (1.A) are adjectival and will be considered under the more difficult but more interesting Claim (1.B), to which we now turn.

NP has already been shown not to be lexically free. Consider Det (= Det_1). We may represent dets extensionally as functions from properties to sets of properties. E.g. *every* will denote that function which associates with each property p the set of those properties q common to all individuals with p. Now, to show Det to be not L-free we must find some property of lexical det denotations not shared by det denotations in general. (3) below, adapted from K&S, is intended as an essentially exhaustive list of lexical dets:

(3)   every, each, all, both, neither, most, half (the), the$_{sg}$, the$_{pl}$, a, some, zero, one, . . . , twenty, no, several, a few, a score of, a dozen, finitely many, infinitely many, many, few, this, these, them, my, his

We have been generous (here and elsewhere) in counting certain expressions in (3) as syntactically simple so as to not make our claim that Det is not L-free depend on an unjustified choice of what we regard as syntactically simple. For similar reasons we have included several dets which cannot (see K&S) be treated extensionally, such as *many, few,* and the demonstratives (*this, my*). We may however think of *occurrences* of these expressions as being interpreted the same as various properly extensional dets. For example, *many* on any given occurrence will denote something like *more than n,* where n is some number determined by context. Similarly, in a given context, an occurrence of *this* identifies an individual J and associates a property p with J if J has p (otherwise it associates the empty set Ø of properties with p).

Now it is easy to see that most of the dets in (3) always denote increasing functions, where a function f from properties to property sets is increasing if its value at any property is an increasing set. However, *no, neither, few* (extensionalized as above) and (*just*) *finitely many* denote decreasing and not increasing functions.

It would appear then that like NP, lexical dets denote monotonic functions. We believe this to be correct, as do Barwise & Cooper (1981). However some (e.g. Thijsse, 1983) consider that bare numerals such as *two* are to be interpreted in the sense of *exactly two* and not in these of *at least two,* in which case they denote functions which are not monotonic. We prefer the "at least" sense: it is unnatural to think that a question such as *Are there two free seats in the front row?* would be truly answered *No* in a situation in which there were three free seats there.

However, even accepting that bare numerals have an "exactly n" reading, it is not difficult to show that Det is still not L-free. A general observation which establishes this is that the non-increasing dets in (3) are all "logical". That is, they are always interpreted by functions which are *automorphism* (*permutation*) *invariant* (AI). Informally, to say that a function f from properties to sets of properties is AI is to say that in deciding whether to put a property q in the set it associates with a property p, f ignores which particular individuals with p have q. f may however be sensitive to how many p's have q and more generally to what proportion of the individuals with p have q. To appreciate the difference between AI and non-AI dets consider the interpretative differences between (4a, b, c) below:

(4)   a.   Some doctor is a vegetarian
          b.   Every doctor is a vegetarian
          c.   John's doctor is a vegetarian

Clearly the truth of (4a) and (4b) is determined once we have specified which individuals are doctors and which are vegetarians. But that information is insufficient to determine the truth of (4c). For that we must in addition specify which individual John is and which individuals he "has". Thus the function which interprets *John's* makes a real world commitment as to which individuals have which properties and which ones are related to which others. So *John's*, in distinction to *some* and *every*, is not AI. (A properly general, i.e. category independent definition of AI is given in the Appendix. See also Westerstahl (1984) for a slightly different treatment, one not incompatible with ours).

We may then consider that lexical dets are either increasing or AI. And to show that Det is not L-free it is sufficient to find complex dets which are neither. There are many such. One class is given by possessive dets such as *only John's, neither John's nor Mary's, no student's, exactly two students'.* Another class is given by comparative AP dets such as *more male than female, fewer male than female*, etc. Exception dets are another group: *every . . . but John* (as in *Every student but John left early*), *no . . . but John, every . . . but John's*, etc.

We conclude then that Det_1 is not lexically free. Analogous arguments show that Det_2 is not L-free. The simplest det_2's are ones like *more . . . than . . .* and satisfy the very weak condition of being either AI or increasing. But complex det_2's such as *more of John's . . . than of Mary's . . .* (as in *More of John's dogs than of Mary's cats*) and *more male . . . than female . . .* (as in *More male dogs than female cats*) are neither AI nor even monotonic.

We consider finally the more complicated case of AP's. Extensionally AP's may be represented by functions from (extensional) properties to (extensional) properties. K&F observe that extensional AP's always denote *restricting* functions, i.e. functions f such that all f(p)'s are p's. E.g. all female artists are artists, all tall doctors are doctors, etc. Within this class there are two semantically distinct sorts of lexical AP's: *absolute* ones and *relative* ones. We consider first the absolute AP's (AP_{abs}). They are illustrated by lexical AP's such as *male* and *female* as well as by more complex AP's of the relative clause sort (*who Sue kissed*). To say that *female* is absolute is to say e.g. that the female artists are just the artists who are female *individuals. Relative* AP's such as *tall* do not license this inference: A tall artist need not be a tall individual (i.e. "absolutely" tall), he need only be tall relative to artists. Note that two absolute AP's are extensionally distinct just in case their values at the property of being an individual are different. It is in fact easily seen (K&F) that the set of absolute functions is isomorphic to the set of properties (the function h sending each absolute function f to the value of f at the individual property being the isomorphism).

Given this correspondence between absolute AP's and properties it is perhaps unsurprising that syntactically they behave more like CN's than do properly relative AP's. E.g. they combine more freely with dets to form NP's, as in *The university hires more males than females* but *The university *hires more talls than shorts.* There may then be syntactic grounds for distinguishing absolute AP's from others, in which case we may observe that the category AP_{abs} is lexically free. As the point has some independent interest in what follows let us establish that fact.

There are several ways of forming complex absolute AP's. For example, relative clauses (formed on extensional positions) are absolute. E.g. a student who Sue kissed is a student and an individual who Sue kissed. Similarly (though often awkward to form) boolean combinations of absolute AP's are absolute. E.g. a *non-male* student is a student who is a non-male individual. Third, comparatives of relative AP's with NP arguments are absolute: A student *taller than Bill*[3] is a student who is an individual taller than Bill. Equally, as Manfred Bierwisch (pc) pointed out to me, relative AP's combined with measure phrases such as *five feet tall* are absolute. A student five feet tall is a student who is an individual five feet tall, not just five feet tall relative to students but perhaps some other height relative to, say, vegetarians. Finally, and important in what follows, AP's formed from AP_1's plus NP's appear to be absolute. E.g. a student *fond of Mary* is a student who is an individual fond of Mary. A student *angry at every teacher* is a student who is an individual angry at every teacher. And since these complex AP's are absolute they do not denote functions inherently undenotable by lexical absolute AP's. I.e. it could be that for each p, the p's who Sue kissed are just the male p's.

We conclude then that if AP_{abs} is a grammatically definable subcategory it is lexically free. But the full category AP itself is not lexically free. To see this, consider that lexical relative AP's are not interpreted as arbitrary restricting functions. They must meet a variety of very strong conditions (see e.g. Kamp, 1975, and Bartsch, 1975 for much discussion). One such condition is exemplified in (5) below.

(5)   *Continuity Condition:* if John and Bill are both doctors and also both lawyers and John is a tall doctor but Bill is not, then it is not the case that Bill is a tall lawyer and John not.

The antecedent of (5) guarantees that John is taller than Bill. If it were so that Bill was a tall lawyer and John not, that would imply in addition that Bill was taller than John, an obvious impossibility.

It appears then that lexical AP's must denote restricting functions which are either absolute or continuous as above. (In fact many additional conditions must be satisfied by the lexical relative AP's, but Continuity is sufficient for our purposes here).

Now it is not difficult (but it is slightly tedious) to show that boolean combinations of relative AP's need not satisfy Continuity. Consider e.g. *neither tall nor short.* Let p be a property possessed by just the individuals I_5, I_4, and I_3 where I_k is k feet tall. It is clearly possible that I_5 would be the only tall p, I_3 the only short one, and I_4 a neither tall nor short p. Now let q be the property possessed by just I_7, I_6, and the individuals with p, where I_7 is 7 feet tall, etc. It is surely plausible that the tall q's are just I_7 and I_6, the short q's are just I_4 and I_3, and the neither tall nor short q's are just I_5. But in such a case (more individuals can be added improving plausibility) Continuity fails. To see this, write f for the function denoted by *neither tall nor short*. Then we have that both I_5 and I_4 are p's and also q's. And I_4 is an f(p) and I_5 is not. But I_5 is an f(q) and I_4 is not, so *neither tall nor short* fails Continuity.

We infer then that AP is not lexically free. But note, as Dick de Jongh points out, that our argument relies crucially on the empirical claim that English possesses no lexical AP *blik* with the meaning of *neither tall nor short*. Might we not try such AP's as *average*, or *middling?* But clearly *an average man* is not synonymous with *a neither tall nor short man*. What is needed here is a complex AP such as *of average height*. It appears then to be a non-trivial fact concerning the expressive nature of English that it does not lexically codify the middle range of scales determined by relative AP's such as *tall* and *short*. So we are claiming that *blik* above with the meaning given is not a possible extension of English.

Finally, let us note, perhaps surprisingly, that AP_1 does appear to be lexically free. Extensionally such expressions (*fond (of)*, etc.) denote functions from individuals to AP denotations − in fact to absolute AP denotations. And there appear to be several ways of forming complex AP_1's. Some combine with intensifiers like *very*, as in *very fond (of)*. But obviously it could be that for each individual J, the property of being very fond of J was possessed by just those individuals who were proud of J, so *very fond (of)* does not extensionally denote a function in principle undenotable by a lexical AP_1 such as *proud (of)*. Similarly boolean combinations do not lead to extensionally new functions. It could be that, for each individual J, the individuals who are *fond but not envious of* J are just those who are *proud of* J. And finally, complex comparative forms such as *much taller than*, *twice as tall as* are not extensionally new. It could be that for each individual J, those who are twice as tall as J are just those who are fond of J.

We conclude then that AP_1 is lexically free and thus that Claim 1 is established.

3. EXPLAINING LEXICAL FREEDOM

We should like to know whether the fact that certain categories are L-free and others are not is merely an accidental fact about English or whether there is some principled basis for expecting just the distribution of L-freedom given in Claim 1. More specifically, does the property of being L-free correlate with any other semantic property of the categories which might be used to predict, or at least lead us to expect, that the L-free categories are just those indicated?

We shall show here that L-freedom correlates with the "size" of a category, and moreover, that this property may plausibly be used as a basis for explaining the distribution of L-freedom across categories.

Regarding "size", observe that in a model with n individuals, there are 2^n extensionally distinct CN denotations, one for each set of individuals. Similarly there are just 2^n extensionally distinct P_1 denotations and 2^n AP_{abs} denotations. Further, the set of extensional P_2 denotations (as well as the CN_1 and AP_1 denotations) corresponds to the sets of ordered pairs of individuals, whence there are 2^{n^2} such. Similarly there are 2^{n^3} extensional P_3 denotations. These facts and others are summarized in the table below, where we write n for the cardinality of the set 1 of individuals of the model and, as before, $Den_I C$ is the set of possible denotations of expressions of category C in a model with universe I.

(6)

				Lexically Free Categories C				
	P_0	NP_{prop}	P_1	CN	AP_{abs}	CN_1	AP_1	P_3
$\lvert Den_I C \rvert$	2	n	2^n	2^n	2^n	2^{n^2}	2^{n^2}	2^{n^3}

By contrast consider the comparable figures for categories which are not L-free:

(7)

	Lexically Restricted Categories C			
	NP	AP	Det_1	Det_k
$\lvert Den_I C \rvert$	2^{2^n}	$2n.2^{n-1}$	2^{3n}	$2(2^{k+1}-1)^n$

Justifying the figures in (7) is rather more difficult than for those in (6) and raises one question of some theoretical interest.

Consider the figure given under the heading NP. In a model with n individuals (n may be infinite) there are 2^n properties (sets of individuals) and thus 2^{2^n} sets of properties. But are all of these properties sets possible full NP denotations? That is, given any property set, can one guarantee that there is an English NP which may be interpreted as that set? The answer to this question (and the comparable ones for the other categories above) is far from obvious, and requires a serious study of the actual expressive power of English. Several such questions are investigated in K&M and several partial results are obtained, but equally several questions remain open. In the case at hand, NP, we may infer that the answer is yes when n is finite. If n is infinite it is unknown whether an arbitrary infinite property set is denotable by an English NP under some acceptable interpretation.

The positive answer for the finite case follows directly from a theorem in K&S which gives a positive answer for Det_1. Note first that Det_1's denote functions from properties to sets of properties. The total number of such functions is thus 2^{2^n} raised to the power 2^n, which computes out to 2^{4^n}. However K&S argue on empirical grounds that not all of these functions are needed as denotations for English Det_1's. Rather we only need functions f which satisfy the Conservativity condition given below:

(8)   f is *conservative* iff for all properties p, q,
       $p \in f(q)$ iff $(p \wedge q) \in f(q)$

In effect the condition says e.g. that *every doctor is a vegetarian* iff *every doctor is both a doctor and a vegetarian*, and moreover, the equivalence remains true no matter what English Det_1 is substituted for *every*. We may compute then (K&S, Thijsse 1983) that only 2^{3^n} functions satisfy the Conservativity condition. But is this condition sufficient? That is, is every conservative function a possible Det_1 denotation, or may we impose still further conditions? K&S show that for n finite no further conditions may be imposed. That is, given any conservative function f over a finite universe, K&S provide a way of constructing an English Det_1 which may be interpreted as f. This then justifies the figure given under Det_1 in (7), a point of some importance in what follows.

It is now easy to see that the figure in (7) for NP is accurate. For the nonce, write 1 for that property which all individuals have. So 1 is arguably the denotation of the CN *individual* (or at least the complex CN *object which is either animate or inanimate*). It is then easy to prove that for any set Q of properties, the function f_Q which sends 1 to Q and all other properties to Ø, the empty set, is conservative. It follows then that *d individuals* will denote Q, where d is the English Det_1 interpreted as f_Q whose existence is guaranteed by the theorem in K&S.

The figure given for AP in (7) is empirically more problematic. That figure is the number of restricting functions from properties to properties, where, recall, such a function f is restricting iff for each property p, the individuals with f(p) are a subset of those with p. But as we have seen, lexical AP's are not freely interpreted in the set of restricting functions. Some, such as *male* and *female*, may only be interpreted by absolute functions. Others, the relative AP's like *tall*, must meet the Continuity condition (5), and in fact must meet somewhat stronger conditions. The issue then is whether we have sufficiently rich ways of forming complex AP's so as to allow us to denote any restricting function (at least over a finite universe). Under one plausible set of assumptions concerning these stronger conditions, which space prevents us from presenting here, we may prove that any restricting function may be built up as a finite boolean combination of ones meeting the stronger conditions. To this extent then the figure given in (7) under AP is reasonable. But more work is needed to determine whether we might not be able to impose even stronger conditions yet on the interpretations of lexical AP's.

Finally, the general figure given for Det_k's in (7) is simply the number of k-place conservative functions given in K&M. We have no proof comparable to that in K&S for Det_1's that, even over a finite universe, any k-place conservative function can actually be expressed in English. However, for purposes of what follows, it is sufficient that the figure given for Det_k be at least as large as that given for Det_1, and a quick perusal of K&M shows that to be the case.

Consider now the significance of the figures in (6) compared with those in (7). It is obvious that the denotation sets for L-restricted categories grow much faster as a function of the size, n, of the universe than is the case for L-free categories. For example, choosing n infinite, the denotation set for any L-restricted category has size 2^{2^n}, which is strictly larger than that for any L-free category, whose size is always $\leq 2^n$. In fact, for all but the smallest universes ($n \leq 9$) the denotation set for any L-restricted category is strictly larger than that for any L-free category.

Let us define then a category C to be *small* if its denotation set always has size $\leq 2^{f(n)}$, where f(n) is a polynomial function in n. And call C *large* if its size is always $2^{g(n)}$, where g(n) is itself a non-trivial exponential function in n. We then have the following generalization:

GEN 1: Small categories are lexically free, large ones are not[4]

Note that GEN-1 is simply an empirical generalization about English. It has perhaps the status of a "law" in (roughly) the sense of Werner's Law or Grimm's Law — namely, an empirical regularity in the observed data.

It does however suggest an explanation for the distribution of lexical freedom among our categories: Let us think of the relative sizes of the denotation sets as a *measure* of the relative complexity in learning the meaning of, and interpreting on an occasion of use, an arbitrary expression in the category. Such a measure has some intuitive appeal. Correct application of an arbitrary expression from a small category requires being able to discriminate among many fewer states of affairs than for an arbitrary expression from a large category. E.g. assuming for the moment perfect knowledge of the world, imagine that we are faced with the use of a new vocabulary item, say, *blik* used as a P_1, as in *John bliks*. To know whether the statement is true or not we need merely be able to discriminate among 2^n possible states of affairs, where n is the number of individuals in our relevant universe of discourse. But if our interlocuter asserted *Blik students are vegetarians* we should have to be able to discriminate among 2^{3^n} possible states of affairs (were the category Det_1 is not lexically restricted).

Further, the learning and use problem can be expected to be greater for lexical items in a category then for syntactically complex ones, since the interpretation of complex expressions is (modulo idioms, etc.) determined as a function of the interpretations of their syntactic parts. But for lexical items there precisely are no syntactic parts, so the meanings of these elements must be learned directly. Thus the problem of determining the meaning distinctions among lexical expressions in a large category is reasonably considered more difficult than that for small categories. It is then cognitively advantageous in learning and using the meanings of expressions in large categories if the learners and users can assume that the lexical expressions in those categories do not denote freely in the set in which expressions in that category in general denote, but rather they may only denote in a very limited subset of that set.

While these considerations are admittedly speculative, they receive further support from the fact that in general it appears that the set of possible denotations we need for the set of lexical expressions of a large category is itself small.

Consider first Det_{lex}, the set of lexical one place dets. Several of these dets are deictic (*this, these, my, your*). That is, we understand that their reference is given by the context in which they are used. Reasonably then the use problem here is minimal. Equally "pronominal" dets such as *his, their* have their reference provided by the linguistic or non-linguistic context of use. Calling all of these elements deictic, we see that the learning and use problem for lexical dets largely reduces to that for the non-deictic items. Now most of those items are in fact logical constants. They are "logical" in the sense that they denote AI functions, and they are constant in that mostly there is only one function from properties to property sets which they denote (in each case). The learning and use problem then virtually reduces to that of learning the meanings of a handful of items – say 35 to be safe, and is not of the order expressed by 2^{3^n}, the size of Den_1Det. However, certain lexical dets such as *several* and *a few* appear not to be constant, though they still denote AI functions. But even if they denoted freely in the AI set (which they don't – e.g. *several* is increasing), we may compute (K&S, Thijsse, 1983), that there are only $2^{(n+1)(n+2)/2}$ such functions. Thus we may infer that the denotation set for Det_{lex} is by our definition small.

Equally it is not hard to see that the set in which lexical NP's denote is small. Again excluding deictic items (*this, that, I, we mine*) and deictic/anaphoric items (*he, they*) we observe that lexical NP's are either proper nouns, and so denote individuals, or else belong to a small finite set of essentially logical constants (*everyone, noone, someone,* etc.). Basically then the measure of the learning and use problem for lexical NP's is given by $n + c$, n the number of individuals and c the number of lexical logical constants. Note that even if further logical elements are found among NP_{lex} and they could denote freely in the AI property sets, there are only 2^{n+1} such, so even in this case we may infer from our definition that $Den_I NP_{lex}$ is small. Thus we suggest:

GEN 2: For C large, the set in which non-deictic lexical elements of C denote is small

Note that Det_k's for $k > 1$ further support GEN-2. At best there are a handful of logical constants (*more ... than ...*) among the (non-deictic) lexical Det_2's. So the magnitude of the learning problem here is given by a constant c, c the number of lexical det_2's. And even if further work revealed the existence of logical Det_k's freely interpreted in the AI set, the number of such would still be technically small: 2 raised to the power $\binom{n+2^{k+1}-2}{n}$. (Thanks to Johan van Benthem for determining this figure for us.)

There is one open problem concerning GEN-2 however, namely the size of $Den_I AP_{lex}$. To be sure the absolute AP's denote in a set of size 2^n so their denotation set is small. But how many additional functions are needed to provide denotations for lexical AP's such as *tall?* At the moment we do not know.

4. A GENERALIZATION OF LEXICAL FREEDOM

The distinction we have drawn between L-free and L-restricted categories is rather naturally seen as a special case of a more general distinction (pointed out to us by Peter van Emde Boas). The basic idea behind lexical freedom is that complex expressions in a category may extensionally denote things which the simplest expressions of that category cannot denote. Generalizing, given a category C, may we continually denote new things as the complexity of expressions in C is increased, or rather is there a complexity bound beyond which new expressions will not let us denote anything that could not already be denoted?

To formulate the question more precisely, let us represent the complexity of an expression by its *length*, as measured by the number of lexical items in it (which is reasonable, given the essentially context free grammar for our expressions in K&F). Now, for C a category and k a positive integer, write C_k for the set of expressions in C of length $\leq k$. And recall from Def 1 that for a universe I of individuals, $Den_I C_k$ is the set of possible interpretations of elements of C_k relative to the universe I. Then,

Def 2: k is an *extensional bound* for a category C iff for all sets I
of individuals and for all $k' > k$, $Den_I C_{k'} = Den_I C_k$

If C has no extensional bound it will be called *unbounded*, otherwise it is *bounded*, and the least such bound will be called *the bound for* C.

Note that any L-free category is bounded; it's bound is the length of the syntactically simplest expressions in C (e.g. 1, if C has proper lexical expressions). But if C is not L-free it does not follow that it is unbounded. So our precise question becomes: Which L-restricted categories are unbounded? Part of the answer is given by:

Thm 1: Det_1 is unbounded

The theorem follows as an easy corollary to the following two theorems from K&S:

(9)   *The Finite Effability Theorem*
For each conservative function f over a finite universe of individuals there is an expression d in Det_1 which denotes f under some acceptable interpretation of L.

(10)   *The Finite Ineffability Theorem*
For any finite subset D of Det_1 there is a finite universe I of individuals such that some conservative functions over I are undenotable by any d in D.

(Note that in (9) we construct the determiner expression d once f is given; in (10) we fix the determiner expressions D in advance.)

Thm 1 follows from (9) and (10) with the additional assumptions that Det_{1ex} is finite, that there are only finitely many ways of forming complex Dets, each one of which only introduces finitely many new expressions. These latter assumptions are satisfied by any reasonable grammar of English Dets. It then follows that for each positive integer k, $(Det)_k$, the set of Det_1's of length $\leq$ k, is finite. So let k be arbitrary. Then by the Ineffability Theorem, there is a finite universe I for which there are conservative functions undenotable by any element of $(Det)_k$. But by the Effability Theorem any of those functions is denotable, and thus denotable by a Det_1 of length greater than k. Thus $Den_I(Det)_k$ is a proper subset of some $Den_I(Det)_{k'}$, for some k' greater then k, proving the theorem.

We might note that the basic reason that the Ineffability Theorem for Det_1 holds is that the set of possible Det_1 denotations increases so much more rapidly than the denotation sets for the lexical items occurring in a Det_1. E.g. let $d = (d_1, \ldots, d_k)$ be a single Det_1 of length k. An upper bound on the set of possible denotations for d is given by the cross product for those of the d_i occurring in d. And as K&S show, this product, call it d(n), is sufficiently small compared to 2^{3^n}, the number of possible Det_1 denotations in a world of n individuals, that the limit of $d(n)/2^{3^n}$ goes to zero as n increases. And this implies that for sufficiently large finite n, $d(n)$ is smaller (in fact as much smaller as we like) than 2^{3^n}. Whence there are possible Det_1 denotations which are not possible denotations for our fixed d. The proof remains essentially unchanged when d is replaced by a finite set D of Det_1's.

Further, though we lack a complete formal proof, it seems likely that NP ($= Det_0$) is also unbounded. As a first step towards showing that NP is unbounded, we note that we have a Finite Effability Theorem for NP. In fact we have a stronger result:

Thm 4:   For every finite universe I of individuals there is an interpretation m of L such that every element of $Den_I NP$ is denotable under m. That is, there is a subset D of NP such that $m[D] = Den_I NP$.

The essential step in Thm 4 relies on the lemma below, also used in the proof of Finite Effability for Det_1.

Lemma   There is a fixed subset D of NP such that for any countable set K of individuals, $m[D] = K$, for some interpretation m of L.

We may choose D in the lemma to be $\{np_k : k \geq 0\}$, where $np_0 = $ *John* and $np_{j+1} = $ *the oldest friend of* np_j, all j. It is clearly possible, given a denumerable sequence $J_1, J_2, \ldots$ of individuals, that J_2 is the oldest friend of J_1, and that in general J_{j+1} is the oldest friend of J_j.

As a consequence of the lemma, all of any finite number of properties are denotable (under a fixed interpretation). To denote a property q for example, construct the CN *individual who is either np_i or np_j or* $\ldots$, where the finite disjunction of np's is taken over those in D which denote just the individuals with q. Call this CN cn_q. Equally we may denote q' (the property of being a non-q) by the CN *individual who is not [np_i or np_j or* $\ldots$], where again the np_i's are just those denoting individuals with q. Call this CN *non-cn_q*. Then the unit set $\{q\}$ is the denotation of *every cn_q and no non-cn_q*. Call this NP NP_q. Then any finite set Q of properties is denoted by the finite disjunction of the NP_q's for q in Q. And this gives us the Finite Effability Theorem for NP (as well as CN).

The basic step remaining in the argument that NP is extensionally unbounded is to show that for any fixed d in NP, the number of possible ways of interpreting d increases less rapidly than 2^{2^n}, the total number of possible NP denotations. If we can establish this point, then given any d in NP, we can choose n large enough (but still finite) that some property sets are undenotable by d under any acceptable interpretation. And what holds of a single such d will extend as per the proof in K&S to any finite subset

D of NP, yielding a Finite Ineffability Theorem for NP. Then the proof that NP is unbounded follows exactly that for Det_1.

The basic argument that finite ineffability holds for NP proceeds as follows: We argue that for any finite set I of individuals and for any given NP d, $Den_I d$, the set of possible interpretations for d, is small, that is, it is of size $2^{f(n)}$, where n is the cardinality of I and f(n) is a mere polynomial function in n. (In fact a polynomial of degree ≤ 3.) So let I and d be arbitrary as above. Then d is representable as a concatenation of k lexical items $(d_1, \ldots, d_k)$, and an upper bound on $|Den_I d|$ is given by the product of the $|Den_I d_i|$ and is small if each $|Den_I d_i|$ is small, since a product of numbers of the form $2^{f(n)}$ is itself of the form $2^{g(n)}$, for g(n) a polynomial in n.

Now suppose first that none of the d_i's is of category AP. Then for each d_i, either d_i lies in a small category, in which case $|Den_I d_i|$ is small, or d_i is a lexical NP or Det_k, in which case again, as previously shown, $|Den_I d_i|$ is small, or else d_i is a logical constant (e.g. *and*, etc.) in which case $|Den_I d_i|$ = 1 and so contributes nothing to $Den_I d$. Thus $|Den_I d|$ is small when d contains no AP's.

This argument does not go through however if some d_i is an AP, since we do not know how many functions are possible lexical AP denotations. However by investigation (see the list of Dets in K&S and K&M) of the ways in which AP's may occur in NP's we may conclude that, surprisingly perhaps, AP's contribute nothing to the total number of ways of (extensionally) interpreting an NP.

To see this point, consider first an occurrence of an AP as a modifier, as in *every tall student*. Though there are an unknown number of ways of interpreting *tall*, *tall student* occurs here as a CN and there are at most 2^n ways of interpreting a CN, whether lexical or complex. Since there is only one way of interpreting *every*, there are at most 2^n ways of interpreting *every tall student*, just the same as the number of ways of interpreting *every student*. Thus we may say that the AP *tall* does not occur essentially in *every tall student*. That is, it contributes nothing to the set of possible ways of interpreting *every tall student* over and above what is inherent in *every student*.

Moreover, though the point is not completely obvious, we claim that all occurrences of AP's within NP's are inessential in this sense.

Obviously enough, AP's occurring within other modifiers, such as relative clauses (*student who is tall, student who is a tall carpenter*) contribute nothing to the total, since the relative clause is itself a modifier and thus the entire CN's only admit of at most 2^n possible interpretations.

Following however the generous syntax in K&S, we do find apparently "free" occurrences of AP's within Dets, as exhibited in (11) below:

(11)   a.   Only the liberal but not the conservative (delegates voted for Smith)

    b.   Neither the tall nor the short (students were chosen)

    c.   More tall than short (students passed the exam)

    d.   (John's biggest) cows

    e.   (More of the liberal than of the conservative) (delegates ...)

Here K&S consider that the AP has combined with the Det to form a complex Det. These occurrences of AP's do contribute (an unknown) degree of freedom with regard to the range of possible interpretations for the Det's they form, but still contribute nothing to the range of possible full NP interpretations, as can be seen by inspection of cases. Thus the NP's in (11) exhibit the same range of interpretations as their counterparts in (12) where the AP's do occur as modifiers.

(12)   a.   Only the liberal delegates but not the conservative delegates ...

          b.   More tall students than short students ...

          c.   The (biggest (cow which John has))

Clearly for example, $Den_1(12a)$ is small, being $2^n . 2^n = 2^{2n}$, since the only freedom of interpretation is given by the two CN's *liberal delegates* and *conservative delegates*, 2^n in each case, everything else being a logical constant. Analogous claims hold for (12c) and (12d).

    We conclude then that the range of possible denotations for any NP over a finite universe is small. And if D is a finite set of such NP's its set of possible denotations is bounded by the product of its elements and is thus also small. We may infer then that for n sufficiently large, 2^{2n}, the size of the set of denotable property sets, is larger than the set of possible denotations for any antecedently selected (finite) set D of NP's. We conclude then that, like Det_1, NP is an extensionally unbounded category. As we form increasingly complex NP's we may increasingly denote new sets of properties.

    We are not however in a position to extend our argument and draw similar conclusions for the remaining large categories, Det_2 and AP. As regards Det_2 we lack a Finite Effability Theorem, and the one given for Det_1 in K&S does not immediately extend. And as regards AP, we also lack a Finite Effability Theorem, but we are optimistic that further research will yield one. $Den_I AP$ is defined as the boolean closure of $Den_I AP_{lex}$. Consequently for I finite, if every element of $Den_I AP_{lex}$ can be denoted, then any element of $Den_I AP$ can be denoted simply by forming finite boolean combinations of elements of AP_{lex}. But whether every element of $Den_I AP_{lex}$ can be denoted is an open question. We have after all only a fixed (finite) number of lexical AP's and these are not independently interpretable, e.g. we cannot interpret *short* and *tall* independently. So chosing n greater than the number of lexical AP's would more than guarantee that the number of restricting functions would exceed the number of lexical AP's. However, we may well be able to form sufficiently many complex AP's which are not absolute. E.g. *very tall, very very tall, ..., somewhat tall,* etc. seem not to be absolute. Whether these processes are sufficiently productive and permit sufficient freedom as regards their interpretation to guarantee that all of finitely many elements of $Den_I AP_{lex}$ can be denoted (under a fixed interpretation) awaits further research.

NOTES

1.   For simplicity of presentation we shall treat P_1's and P_n's in general as interpreted by total functions rather than ones that are only defined on proper subsets of the set of individuals. We do not think that generalizing predicate interpretations in this way will affect our results.
2.   For convenience we present the set I as a primitive of the model. On most approaches to formal semantics I would not be a primitive. E.g. on most approaches we would take a non-empty set E of entities as primitive. Then for each b in E we define I_b, or the *individual generated* by b, to be the set of subsets of E which have b as an element (that is, the set of principal ultrafilters over E). On the approach taken in Keenan & Faltz (1985) we take a complete atomic algebra P as primitive (It is the set of possible CN denotations) and define the individuals as the filters generated by the atoms of P. These two approaches yield isomorphic results and differences among them are irrelevant for our purposes here.
3.   Tom Wasow (pc) points out that a student *taller than Bill* and *a taller student than Bill* are not logically equivalent. The latter requires that Bill be a student and the former does not. We may interpret *taller ... than Bill* as a function whose value at a property p is the same as that which interprets *taller than Bill* at p provided p is a property of Bill. Otherwise its value at p is the zero property (that one which no individual has). Interpreted thus *taller ... than Bill* would be a kind of "restricted" case of an absolute AP though not strictly absolute. Adding such functions to our set of possible AP denotations will not, we feel, alter the claims made about AP's in later sections. We do not however add them, as their distribution is so restricted. E.g. it is unnatural to say *every taller student than Bill,* etc. We prefer an analysis then on which *a taller ... than Bill* is thought of as a complex Det_1, but do not pursue this analysis here.
4.   An alternative generalization here, more appealing perhaps to logicians, is:

GEN 1': First order categories are lexically free, higher order ones are not.

Certainly the denotation sets for L-free categories may be represented, up to isomorphism, as relations (of various degrees) on the set I of individuals of the model. Denotation sets for L-restricted categories on the other hand are only representable as relations on the power set of I. Taking this characterization of first vs. higher order, GEN 1' seems supported. Moreover, Johan van Benthem points out that, under a suitable characterization of "order", GEN 1 and GEN 1' are essentially equivalent.

APPENDIX

A. The general definition of automorphism invariance (AI)

Let h be a permutation of the universe I. (That is, h is a one to one function from I onto itself.) Extend h to $\{T, F\}$ by setting $h(T) = T$ and $h(F) = F$. Call such a function a basic automorphism. Now extend h to an automorphism on all denotation sets as follows:

(i) if h has been extended to a set A, then for each subset B of A, set
     $h(b) = \{h(b): b \in B\}$
(ii) if h has been extended to each of $A_1, A_2, \ldots, A_k$, extend h to their cross product by setting $h(a_1, \ldots, a_k) = (h(a_1), \ldots, h(a_k))$, all a_i in A_i.

As any denotation set is defined by taking power sets, subsets, or cross products beginning from I and $\{T, F\}$, h as extended is easily seen to be an automorphism of any denotation set (when restricted to that set). Note we use h abusively for the basic automorphism as well as its extension.

Now, an element f in any denotation set is *automorphism invariant* iff for all basic automorphism h, $h(f) = f$.

It is easily proven for the class of models we consider (K&S) that any expression e which meets the condition that for all models (I, m) and (I, m') m(e) = m'(e) always denotes an AI element of its denotation set. The converse may fail, and does. E.g. *several* may denote differently in different models with the same universe, but it always denotes an AI element of its denotation set.

REFERENCES

Bartsch, R.: (1975), 'Subcategorization of Adnominal and Adverbial Modifiers' in *Formal Semantics for Natural Language*, E. Keenan (ed) CUP.

Barwise, J., & Cooper, R.: (1981), 'Generalized Quantifiers and Natural Language' *Linguistics and Philosophy* 4.1 pp 159–219.

Kamp, J.A.W.: (1975), 'Two Theories about Adjectives' in *Formal Semantics for Natural Language*. Reidel, Synthese Language Library. Dordrecht, Holland, 1985.

Keenan, E., & Moss, L.: (1984), 'Generalized Quantifiers and the Expressive Power of Natural Language' in *Generalized Quantifiers* J. van Benthem & A. ter Meulen (eds). Foris Publications, Dordrecht, Holland.

Keenan, E., & Stavi, J.: (1981): 'A Semantic Characterization of Natural Language Determiners' to appear in *Linguistics and Philosophy*.

Montague, R.: (1970), 'English as a Formal Language' reprinted in *Formal Philosophy* R. Thomason (ed) 1974. Yale University Press, New Haven, original.

Montague, R.: (1973), 'The Proper Treatment of Quantification in Ordinary English' in *Approaches to Natural Language* J. Hintikka, J. Moravcsik, P. Suppes (eds). Reidel, Dordrecht, Holland.

Thijsse, E.: (1983), 'Laws of Language: Universal Properties of Determiners as Generalized Quantifiers' Doctoraalsciptie Rijksuniversiteit Groningen, Holland.

Westerstahl, D.: (1984), 'Logical Constants in Quantifier Languages' to appear in *Linguistics and Philosophy*.

Chapter 3

Quantification as a Major Module of Natural Language Semantics*

Sebastian Löbner

1. QUANTIFIERS

Quantification has been a challenge to the formal semantics of natural language since the very beginnings of this discipline. It has caused Russell to talk of a fundamental discrepancy between surface and underlying logical form of sentences, a dilemma for compositional semantics that began to be overcome not earlier than 1970 when Montague first presented his "Proper Treatment of Quantification in Ordinary English" (Montague 1974). Recently a major new attempt to cover more of the quantificational phenomena in a uniform manner, including logical and non-logical quantifiers, was undertaken by Barwise and Cooper (1981).[1]

Up to now all major approaches have been confined to the semantics and syntax of certain noun phrases that can be considered correlates or relatives of the quantifiers of predicate logics. In particular, the interest centred on singular count noun NPs. This might be explained by the preoccupation of formal semanticists with first order predicate logics and of linguists in general with languages such as English which exhibit a number and mass/count distinction.

Taken as a semantic phenomenon, however, quantification is by no means restricted to the cases investigated so far. It can be found in various syntactic categories, the most obvious cases being adverbs of quantification like *always* or *nowhere*, but also modal verbs, verbs with infinitive, gerund, or clausal complements, certain adjectives and several sorts of adverbs. I shall present several examples below, that may illustrate the grammatical variety of natural language quantification in the case of English. Of course, if one once starts to try to delineate the whole field in question one will soon encounter cases which are traditionally not at all covered by the term *quantification*. Having no other term at hand, I use it to refer to a seemingly very comprehensive range of phenomena which are syntactically and grammatically rather diverse but semantically closely enough related to form a class of their own.

* This paper was written under DFG-project Wu 86/6 "Quantoren im Deutschen".

1.1. Duality

I follow the tradition of Montague and Barwise & Cooper in considering quantifiers semantically as one place second order predicates which take again one place predicates as arguments.[2] Any such operator has the property of possessing a correspondent d u a l operator of the same type. In fact, any quantifier is part of a duality square, as shown in the following diagram:

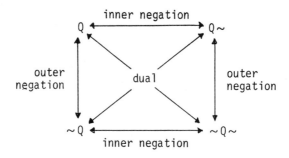

Diagram 1

The dual of a quantifier is defined as the outer negation of the inner negation. Accordingly there are three further operators given with any quantifier: its inner negation $Q\sim$, its outer negation $\sim Q$, and its dual $\sim Q \sim$.[3] Note, that the scheme is absolutely symmetrical and commutative. It is closed in itself and any of the four operators generates the whole scheme.[4] In case of self-dual quantifiers the square collapses into a binary opposition. We shall not deal with this special subclass of operators here. They are, in a way, atypical, since applied to them inner and outer negation have the same effect. In case of self-dual natural language quantifiers it is questionable whether there is any second order level involved at all.

Duality is a fundamental concept in connection with quantification, but has been neglected almost completely in the relevant linguistic literature. It is a fact that natural language quantifiers usually exist alongside others out of the same duality square. Very seldom the whole square is lexicalized but, normally, at least two elements are. Thus, any correct analysis of one element out of a duality square should at the same time hold for the other elements (provided duality can be established independently). This helps considerably judging the validity of one's analytical results.

The general duality scheme is not to be confused with the well-known Aristotelian square of opposition given in diagram 2. I have chosen the universal quantifier for Q and maintained the arrangement of diagram 1. Of course the existential quantifier could be replaced by the universal quantifier exploiting the duality relationship, but it does not matter how the four

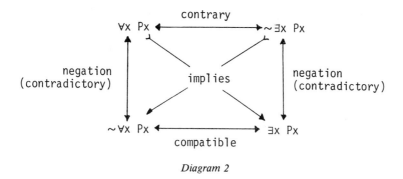

Diagram 2

statements in the square of oppositions are formulated. The relationships in the Aristotelian diagram only make complete sense if empty universes are excluded. Otherwise, again, the square collapses into a binary opposition, destroying the original structure. The essential difference between the Aristotelian square and the duality square is that the concepts of inner and outer negation and duality are third order concepts, in contrast to the second order concepts of compatibility, contrariness, and implication that constitute the square of oppositions. To see this, consider the following definitions, where A and P are any two predicates in the widest sense, including propositions (as predicates over possible worlds, situations, or whatever), and c (for "case") is a variable for whatever the predicates apply to.[5]

(1)   DEFINITION:

$$A \text{ is } \textit{compatible} \text{ with } P \quad \text{iff} \quad \exists c(A(c) \,\&\, P(c))$$
$$A \quad \textit{implies} \quad P \quad \text{iff} \quad \forall c(A(c) \rightarrow P(c))$$
$$A \text{ is } \textit{contrary} \text{ to } P \quad \text{iff} \quad \sim\exists c(A(c) \,\&\, P(c))$$
$$[A \text{ does } \textit{not imply} \quad P \quad \text{iff} \quad \sim\forall c(A(c) \rightarrow P(c))]$$

The fourth relationship of non-implication is also involved in the constitution of the Aristotelian scheme because the asymmetry of the implication relationship is crucial in order to distinguish the elements that are opposed diagonally and also to distinguish contrariness from contradictoriness. The four concepts defined in (1) themselves form a duality square with respect to the predicate P. For example, being compatible with A and being implied by A are dual second order predicates. (Needless to say, they constitute another Aristotelian square too, implication implying compatibility and so on.) Note further, that the Aristotelian square does not exhibit all the symmetries of the duality square.

Although in some cases the Aristotelian oppositions hold for the elements of a duality square, the two schemes are in principle logically independent from each other. The following two examples illustrate this point.

On the one hand, there are instances of the Aristotelian scheme without duality, due to the lack of any second order level. Take any two real first order predicates which exclude each other, together with their respective negations, and you can establish a square of oppositions, as shown in diagram 3.

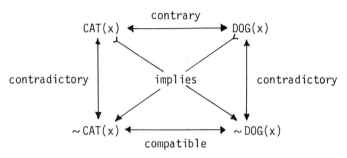

Diagram 3

On the other hand, there are dual operators for which the Aristotelian relations do not hold, such as *already* and *still*. *Still* and *already* span the duality scheme of diagram 4, when conceived as operators taking durative propositions. (I shall suggest an analysis below which will substantiate the duality claim involved.)

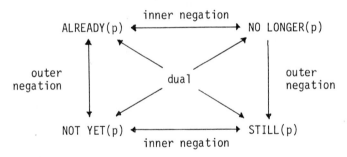

Diagram 4

The Aristotelean relations of compatability, contrariness, and implication are not even defined between the respective elements, because the statements on the left have different presuppositions from those on the right, and hence have truth values in different sets of cases. The Aristotelian concepts do not make sense in such a constellation.

1.2. Quantifiers and determiners

To come back to the general semantic conception − it is, however, not quantifiers, in the sense used here, that are the crucial operators underlying quantification, but determiners in the sense of Barwise & Cooper (1981). Barwise and Cooper postulate that any natural language quantifier has the property to "live on" a certain set:

(2)   DEFINITION: A quantifier Q *lives on* the set A iff
                      for every set P: Q(P) iff Q(P ∩ A).[6]

This set constitutes the relevant domain of objects under consideration. The standard restricted quantifiers of predicate logic, for example, live on their respective domain of quantification. This feature of natural language quantifiers shows that there is generally another predicate involved. It is therefore reasonable to consider two-place operators, namely determiners, instead of the one place quantifiers. Determiners take two predicates, one for the domain of quantification and one for the predicate quantified. Insertion of the domain predicate yields a quantifier in the sense defined above. Duality always involves the second argument, the predicate quantified.

I do not use the term *determiner* in a syntactic sense. Syntactically the roles of determiner, domain predicate, and predicate quantified can be distributed in many different ways. In case of nominal quantifiers of the form determiner (in a syntactic sense) plus noun, the determiner functions as a determiner in the semantic sense, the noun serves as the domain predicate, and the rest of the sentence — as long as it does not contain any higher operators — serves as the predicate quantified. There are, on the other hand, many cases of quantifiers that cannot be decomposed into determiner and domain predicate, such as *everything*, *nobody, sometimes* or pronominal *all*. The adverbs mentioned above, like *already*, are of the same kind, along with modal verbs and other more remote instances of quantification. Polar adjectives exhibit yet another constellation.

In what follows, I shall list several examples of natural language quantification, discuss some representative cases and finally try to extract a universal form which might underlie all cases of quantification considered.

2. SOME EXAMPLES

In the following examples the determiners and quantifiers are given in groups of four, each constituting a duality group. The elements of each group are listed in a fixed order to which I shall refer as type 1, 2, 3, and 4 respectively. The analysis I am going to suggest will yield type 1 throughout as existential quantification, type 2 as universal quantification, type 3 as the negation of type 1 and type 4 as the negation of type 2. Accordingly, type 1 and 2 are dual, as well as type 3 and 4.[7]

In the groups of four only those elements are listed which are lexicalized. Dots indicate elements that can be composed by means of a negative for either inner or outer negation. A stroke indicates a gap that cannot be filled with any expression of the required meaning in the given syntactic construction. I first present the examples as a whole and discuss them later in more detail.

(A1)　He likes $\left\{\begin{array}{l}\text{SOME}\\ \text{ALL}\\ \text{NO}\\ \cdots\end{array}\right\}$ books by Günter Grass.

(A2)　She spends $\left\{\begin{array}{l}\text{SOME}\\ \text{ALL her}\\ \text{NO}\\ \cdots\end{array}\right\}$ money on cat food.

(A3)　He $\left\{\begin{array}{l}\text{SOMETIMES}\\ \text{ALWAYS}\\ \text{NEVER}\\ \cdots\end{array}\right\}$ manages to be friendly.

(A4)　In China you can buy Coca-Cola $\left\{\begin{array}{l}\text{SOMEWHERE}\\ \text{EVERYWHERE}\\ \text{NOWHERE}\\ \cdots\end{array}\right\}$.

(A5)　If she is tired, she reads $\left\{\begin{array}{l}\text{comics (TOO)}\\ \text{ONLY comics}\\ \text{NO comics}\\ \cdots\end{array}\right\}$.

(B1)　It is $\left\{\begin{array}{l}\text{POSSIBLE}\\ \text{CERTAIN}\\ \text{IMPOSSIBLE}\\ \cdots\end{array}\right\}$ that that man will be reelected.

(B2)　That man will $\left\{\begin{array}{l}\text{POSSIBLY}\\ \text{CERTAINLY}\\ \text{IN NO CASE/WAY}\\ ?\end{array}\right\}$ be reelected.

(B3)   Statement A4.1 is $\begin{Bmatrix} \text{SATISFIABLE} \\ \text{TAUTOLOGICAL} \\ \text{CONTRADICTORY} \\ \text{DISPUTABLE} \end{Bmatrix}$.

(B4)   I $\begin{Bmatrix} \text{THINK IT (IS) POSSIBLE} \\ \text{BELIEVE} \\ \text{RULE OUT} \\ \text{DOUBT} \end{Bmatrix}$ that the butler is the murderer.

(B5)   His claim $\begin{Bmatrix} \text{is COMPATIBLE with} \\ \text{IMPLIES} \\ \text{is CONTRARY to} \\ \ldots \end{Bmatrix}$ yours.

(B6)   He will $\begin{Bmatrix} \text{ACCEPT} \\ \text{CLAIM} \\ \text{REFUSE} \\ \text{RENOUNCE} \end{Bmatrix}$ compensation.

(B7)   She $\begin{Bmatrix} \text{LET him pay} \\ \text{MADE him pay} \\ \text{KEPT him from paying} \\ \ldots \end{Bmatrix}$ the bill.

(B8)   He $\begin{Bmatrix} \text{CAN} \\ \text{MUST} \\ \ldots \\ \text{NEED NOT} \end{Bmatrix}$ accept that deal.

(B9) $\begin{Bmatrix} \text{GO} \\ \text{GO} \\ \text{DON'T GO} \\ - \end{Bmatrix}$ to that party.

(B10)   The doctor $\left\{\begin{array}{l}\text{ALLOWed}\\\text{ORDERed}\\\text{FORBADE}\\\cdots\end{array}\right\}$ him to eat meat.

(B11)   You have the $\left\{\begin{array}{l}\text{RIGHT}\\\text{DUTY}\\-\\-\end{array}\right\}$ to vote.

(C1)   The dollar is $\left\{\begin{array}{l}\text{ALREADY}\\\text{STILL}\\\text{NOT YET}\\\text{NO LONGER}\end{array}\right\}$ high.

(C2)   This house is $\left\{\begin{array}{l}\text{big ENOUGH}\\\cdots\\\cdots\\\text{TOO big}\end{array}\right\}$ for us.

(C3)   It is $\left\{\begin{array}{l}\text{BIG}\\\text{SMALL}\\\cdots\\\cdots\end{array}\right\}$ and has $\left\{\begin{array}{l}\text{MANY}\\\text{FEW}\\\cdots\\\cdots\end{array}\right\}$ rooms.

(C4)   In the weather forecast they said it will $\left\{\begin{array}{l}\text{CONTINUE to rain}\\\text{START raining}\\\text{STOP raining}\\\cdots\end{array}\right\}$.

2.1.1. Plain quantifiers

The examples of group A are obvious correspondents of the standard predicate logic quantifiers. In spite of considerable efforts there is not yet any theory which covers singular and plural count noun and mass noun quantification in a fully satisfactory way, although recent works such as Link (1983) promise a breakthrough to a uniform treatment. Nevertheless plural and mass noun quantification should be kept in view whenever quantificational phenomena are studied. One remark might be in place concerning (A5), the group around *only*. This word can occur in a noun preceding position but it is not a determiner in the syntactic sense. This is obvious because it can only occur in what looks like a determiner position when the following noun (in fact noun phrase) can be used without any determiner. *Only* can at best be considered preceding NPs in certain cases. It is, in fact, a focussing particle that can take NPs as well as all sorts of other expressions as focus elements. *Only* has two meanings which can roughly be paraphrased as "nothing but" and "no more than" and can give rise to ambiguity, though they might be closely related and even be instances of a uniform general meaning.[8] In example (A5) the intended reading is the "nothing but" variant. In this reading *only* functions as an inversion of *all*: it changes the roles of the domain of quantification predicate and the predicate quantified. The same holds for the other elements of the group, as is shown by the following equivalences:

$$(2) \quad \text{She reads} \left\{ \begin{array}{l} \text{comics (TOO)} \\ \text{ONLY comics} \\ \text{NO comics} \\ \text{NOT ONLY comics} \end{array} \right. \approx \left. \begin{array}{l} \text{SOME of what} \\ \text{ALL} \\ \text{NONE of what} \\ \text{NOT ALL} \end{array} \right\} \text{she reads is comics.}$$

Accordingly, duality applies to the predicate provided by the noun, because this is the predicate quantified. This could be more easily demonstrated if there were a proper noun negation. Take the following sentences for a demonstration of the dualities in this group:

(3)   NOT ONLY members are allowed. = *Non*members are allowed (TOO).
       ONLY *non*members are excluded. = NO members are excluded.

2.1.2. Possibility and necessity
The examples (B1) – (B11) all belong to the realm of possibility and necessity. It is generally agreed that these two concepts are instances of existential and universal quantification respectively, with a range of possibilities as domain of quantification which is given by certain characteristic conditions. The domain of quantification is usually implicit but can be made explicit by means of adverbial or conditional constructions:

(4)   *If you want to catch the train*, you must leave now.

(5)   *According to the recent polls* it is possible that he wins the elections.

The modal verbs form several duality groups. Another one would be *may/*

must/must not/need not. It all depends on the range of alternatives considered. Often an epistemic and a deontic reading of the modal verbs is distinguished. Kratzer (1977) has shown that there are as many readings — in this sense — as there are possible ranges of possibilities, and how to treat them all in a uniform way.

Some readers might be surprised by the double type assignment for the imperative in (B9). The imperative is usually used for commands, that is type 2 statements. But there seem to be cases, where it can be used to express a permission rather than a command. Imagine a young girl asking her reluctant mother to allow her to go to a party. Finally the mother could give in, saying (B9) in the type 1 interpretation.

In epistemic logic, *believe* is usually treated alongside *know*. The two verbs, however, do not belong to the same duality group defined with respect to the embedded proposition. Both verbs are of the same type 2 according to the consistency criterium discussed in the next section. The standard uses of the verbs require consistency of the respective propositions. You cannot at the same time believe p and not-p, similarly you cannot know both p and not-p. If two operators are dual they can not however both fulfil the consistency requirement unless they are identical i.e. self-dual.[9] But clearly neither *know* nor *believe* are self-dual. Hence, they must belong to two different duality schemes because they are neither identical, nor inner or outer negations of each other, nor duals. It seems that they are operators of the same kind but drawing on different evidence. There is a principal difference between those facts one can know and those one can at best believe, depending on whether one has authentic access to the relevant information. Some languages, such as Japanese, draw a clear distinction between these two sorts of facts. For example, the Japanese do not express the fact that one himself is happy in the same way as the fact that somebody else is happy. The latter is expressed obligatorily in the sense of somebody seeming or looking happy (cf. Kuroda 1973 for details).

The remaining four groups of quantifiers, presented in examples (C1) – (C4) will be discussed in detail below.

2.2. Type assignment and type assymmetry

One generalization that is obvious from the examples cited above is a clear asymmetry among the four types of quantifiers as to their lexicalization. Type 1 is lexicalized throughout and so is type 2, but there are many languages which exhibit considerable gaps in the lexicalization of type 2. Japanese and Chinese, for example, use complex expressions in most cases of universal quantification. Type 3 is synthesized in some cases of English. With respect to type 3, Indoeuropean languages seem to be exceptional in that they possess proper lexical units such as *no, never, none, neither, nothing*, etc. and even in these cases the respective words are historically compounds containing a negative prefix. Type 4 is lexicalized with a single word only in four examples out of twenty above. In two cases (B8 and C1) negative polarity items are used to fill the gap.

The absence of type 4 in the lexicon has been stated under more limited perspectives by other authors before. Barwise and Cooper (1981) postulate as a natural language universal that there are no determiners of type 4. I shall discuss their postulates in more detail after introducing independent criteria for the type assignment. Horn (1972) makes a similar claim referring to a wider class of expressions including modal verbs, modal adverbs and adjectives, and connectives besides the usual quantifiers.

Any asymmetry hypothesis, of course, is as strong as the type assignment is independent. We therefore need independent criteria for the distinction of the respective types. This is a nontrivial task because of the total symmetry of the duality scheme. Even if we could start from the Aristotelian square of oppositions there would still be no way of distinguishing quantifiers from their inner negations (note the left-right symmetry of the configuration in diagram 2). Intuitively, however, there are differences associated with the type distinctions prior to any analytical understanding.

First, there is a feeling that type 1 and type 2 are positive whereas type 3 and type 4 are negative. This distinction can be expressed in terms of what Barwise and Cooper call monotonicity (1981:184).

(6)   DEFINITION: A quantifier Q is *monotone increasing (mon↑)* iff Q(P) and $P \subset P'$ implies Q(P').   Q is *monotone decreasing (mon↓)* iff Q(P) and $P \supset P'$ implies Q(P').

In other words, in case of monotone increasing quantifiers the quantified predicate can be weakened salva veritate, whereas it can be further restricted in case of monotone decreasing quantifiers. As is easily checked, type 1 and type 2 quantifiers are mon↑ as opposed to the mon↓ quantifiers of type 3 and type 4. In case of the temporal presupposing quantifiers in (C1) and (C4) not all alternative predicates P' can be used but only those the presuppositions of which are fulfilled. The direction of monotonicity is necessarily reversed both by inner and outer negation because negation reverses implication. Hence duals have the same monotonicity direction (if any) and cannot be distinguished by means of this criterion. It is extremely useful though, because it can be used even in those cases which do not exhibit a splitting of the quantifier into determiner and domain of quantification predicate.

There are several possibly interrelated ways to distinguish between duals. One very simple criterion is the possibility that a quantifier applies to both a predicate and its negation. I feel tempted to call quantifiers which exhibit this possibility weak and those which do not strong. But as these terms are defined differently and only approximately extensionally equivalent by Barwise and Cooper (1981) let me call them tolerant and intolerant instead.

(7)   DEFINITION: A quantifier Q is *tolerant* iff Q(P) and Q($\sim$P) is possible at the same time.   A quantifier is *intolerant* iff Q(P) excludes Q($\sim$P).

Thus, a quantifier is intolerant if and only if it implies its dual. Obviously this criterion is applicable in exactly those cases where the quantifiers fit into the Aristotelian scheme of oppositions, and therefore is of no use for presuppositional quantifiers. It works, however, for all examples of the groups A and B above. A very simple proof.[10] shows that if a quantifier is intolerant then it is either self-dual or its dual is tolerant. Thus the tolerance criterion separates duals (while it is obviously blind as to the distinction between quantifiers and their inner negation). Intuitively, it separates universal quantifiers which are intolerant from the tolerant existential quantifiers. In case of universal quantifications the whole domain of quantification − or at least the greater part of it − has to be checked; they are difficult to verify, but easy to falsify, whereas for existential statements the converse is true. *Some, several, many* give rise to tolerant quantifiers, whereas *all, most,* and *no* lead to intolerance, provided empty universes are generally excluded, which is a reasonable assumption in this context, because if the quantifier lives on the empty set even the contraries *no* and *all* become indistinguishable. This criterion was first used by Laurence Horn (1972), though he does not use my terms.

Horn, investigating a wide range of logical operators which can be conceived as defining values on abstract scales − including quantifiers, modal verbs, modal adjectives and adverbs, connectives and others − states that for tolerant operators the outer negation can be lexicalized, but the inner negation can not. This statement aims at ruling out type 4 quantifiers, but needs the additional condition that it applies only to type 1 or monotone increasing operators.

Barwise and Cooper postulate two universals that exclude type 4 determiners from the lexicon of natural languages (with regard to NP quantification). One is their "monotonicity correspondence universal" (1981: 186) according to which "there is a simple NP which expresses the mon↓ quantifier $\sim$Q if and only there is a simple NP with a weak non-cardinal determiner which expresses the mon↑ quantifier Q." Weak monotone increasing quantifiers in the realm of nominal quantification are exactly the tolerant monotone increasing ones. Thus, according to this universal, the outer negation counterparts of type 2 determiners are ruled out, because type 2 quantifiers are strong (intolerant).

The other constraint relevant here is their "persistent determiner universal" (1981: 193): "every persistent determiner of human language is mon↑ and weak." In our terms: every persistent determiner of human language is type 1. Persistent determiners are those which are monotone increasing with respect to the domain of quantification predicate. Informally this means, that a

(8)   DEFINITION: A determiner D is *persistent*   iff   D(A, P) and
       A ⊂ B implies D(B, P).   D is *antipersistent*   iff   D(A, P) and
       A ⊃ B implies D(B, P).

true statement Q(P), "living on" the domain of quantification A, remains true if the domain of quantification is enlarged: adding new individuals or quantities to those which are already considered cannot provide any counterevidence. This holds for simple existential quantifiers like the numerals, *some, several, a few, numerous* and the like which state positively and non-exclusively that there is a certain quantity of positive instances of the predicate quantified. The property of persistency does not hold of determiners which may express a certain ratio between the amounts of positive and negative evidence, such as *few* and *many* in their proportional readings. Apparently, the inner negation counterparts of persistent determiners are themselves persistent, while outer negation changes persistency into antipersistency, i.e. downwards monotonicity with respect to the domain of quantification predicate.[11] Thus, persistency provides another criterion for the separation of duals. But not all determiners are either persistent or antipersistent. For determiners which are not highly degenerate, persistency implies tolerance.[12] For that reason only type 1 and type 4 determiners can be persistent. The persistent determiner universal, then, rules out type 4 because it is generally monotone decreasing.[13] I shall come back to the property of persistency below, after the discussion of phase quantifiers (C1 – C4). So far we have got a type assignment for the A and B cases by means of independent criteria, which allows to state the asymmetry hypothesis concerning the lexicalization of natural language quantifiers:

(9)   CONJECTURE: Natural language quantifiers can be classified in-
       to four types. Type 1 contains all existential quantifiers (maybe
       among others), type 2 contains all universal quantifiers, type 3 all
       negated existential quantifiers, and type 4 all negated universal
       quantifiers. The type assignment is unique. Natural language ex-
       hibits significant differences with respect to the extent of the lexi-
       calization of the four subclasses and to the average complexity of the
       expressions used in the four subclasses. The number of lexical items
       decreases, and the complexity of the expressions increases from type
       1 through type 4 with each step.

I have not, so far, provided criteria for the last four examples which group them together with the other ones. Instead of subclassifying the operators of these examples with general criteria I shall provide an explicit analysis for them.

3. PHASE QUANTIFICATION

3.1. Analysis of the examples

3.1.1. already, still, not yet, no longer

For reasons which will become apparent later I refer to the last four examples as phase quantifications. Let me start with the group of operators around *already*. There is a considerable amount of literature about this topic, but I am not going to discuss any other approaches because of the limited space here.

In the following analysis I treat only those uses of *already* and the other three adverbs, in which they can be understood as operators taking time-dependent durative propositions. Statements containing these adverbs are evaluated with respect to a certain temporal reference point $t°$, at which it is already/still/... the case that p. The adverbs carry with them certain presuppositions. Before I discuss them, let me first establish the duality relationships between the four operators.

Whatever the exact presuppositions of *already p* are, they are the same as those of *not yet p*. Dialogues as the following show that *already* and *not yet* are used as outer negations of each other, in the strong, presupposition preserving sense of negation:

(9)   Has the train already arrived? – No, not yet.

(10)   The train has not yet arrived. – You're wrong, it is already here.

In order to check the relationships concerning inner negation, let us assume for the sake of simplicity that *she is asleep* is the negation of *she is awake* (a simplification which will not affect the validity of the subsequent analysis). Then, the sentences (11) and (12), and (13) and (14) mean the same, respectively:

(11)   She is already asleep.   = already p.

(12)   She is no longer awake.   = no longer ~p.

(13)   She is not yet asleep.   = not yet p.

(14)   She is still awake.   = still ~p.

Consequently, *no longer* is used as the inner negation of *already*, and *not yet* functions as the inner negation of *still*.[14] *Still*, then, is the inner negation of the outer negation of *already*, i.e. its dual. From this it follows that *still* is also the outer negation of *no longer*, which is apparently the case:

(15)   Is he still angry? – No, no longer.

This yields the duality relations of diagram 4 above.

I assume that *already(p, t°)* and *not yet(p, t°)* have the same presupposition, that there is a phase of not-p which has started before t° and might be followed by at most one phase of p which reaches till t°. Then the point of the alternative "already p or not yet p" is whether the endpoint of the presupposed preceding negative phase is reached until t° or not. Starting from such a negative phase before t°, t° may fall into that very phase – in case of *not yet(p, t°)* – or else it falls into the following positive phase. Both statements are undefined if there is no negative preceding phase to start with. The semantics of *already* are rather subtle. *Already(p, t°)* states the transition from ~p to p in the immediate neighbourhood of t°, not more, "immediate neighbourhood" being meant in the topological sense (ruling out the relevance of any transition points earlier than the latest one). Pragmatic requirements of relevance change that topological closeness condition to a metrical one in most cases: the farther ago the transition point lies the less probable is the relevance of a statement that the transition has taken place.[15] Hence the feeling that *already(p, t°)* is normally used when p has just begun, and *not yet(p, t°)* when ~p is about to end. *already(p, t°)* is wrong if the previous state of ~p continues to prevail at t°. In many cases the expectation that this is so may be the reason for uttering *already(p, t°)*. But contrary expectations need not necessarily play a role for such statements. Nothing is wrong about a sentence like:

(16)   As I/you expected, the train has already/not yet arrived.

The meaning of *already* and its counterpart *not yet* is shown informally in diagram 5, the two arrows starting from t° symbolizing the two possibilities that t° either falls into the positive or the negative semiphase.

Being the dual of *already*, *still* carries a presupposition which derives from that of *already* by means of the negation of the embedded proposition:

(17)   presupposition of *no longer(p, t°)*
    = presupposition of *still(p, t°)*
    = presupposition of *~ already(~ p, t°)*   (by duality)
    = presupposition of *already(~ p, t°)*

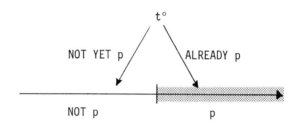

Diagram 5

Thus, the sentences *still(p, t°)* and *no longer(p, t°)* presuppose that there is a phase of p which has started before t° and might be followed by at most one phase of not-p till t°. *Still(p, t°)* is true if that phase of p includes t°, while *no longer(p, t°)* states that that phase has ended before t° and t° lies within the negative phase following it. Graphically we get the following picture of the meanings of the latter two operators in the spirit of diagram 5:

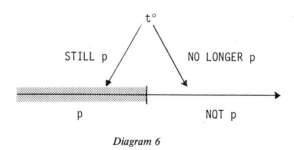

Diagram 6

Inner negation results in exchanging the positive and the negative semiphases, while outer negation concerns the decision whether the parameter t° falls into the first or the second semiphase. The middle point, in both cases is meant to belong to the positive phase. The starting and the end point of the whole interval considered are to be excluded.

3.1.2. *Enough* and *too*
As a pair of related operators *enough* and *too* take as operands any scaling adjectives or adverbs.[16] Scaling adjectives provide a specific scale of values,

possibly context-dependent, e.g. a scale of size in case of *big* and *small*.
Enough presupposes a range of admissible values on the scale with a lower
bound, *too* a range of admissible values with an upper bound. *A is ADJ
enough* means that the value for A on the scale provided by ADJ lies above
the critical lower bound of admissibility (and is hence admissible), whereas
A is too ADJ means that the value for A lies above the critical upper bound
of admissibility and is hence not admissible. The meanings of the operators
of the *enough*-group are thus completely analogous to those of the *already*-
group. There is even a proper paraphrase relationship between both cases:

(18)   a is quick ENOUGH   = a is ALREADY admissible in speed
        a is NOT TOO quick   = a is STILL admissible in speed
        a is NOT quick ENOUGH = a is NOT YET admissible in speed
        a is TOO quick   = a is NO LONGER admissible in
                                             speed

Of course the operators on the right side are not interpreted temporally in
this case. Diagram 7 displays a picture of the respective meanings:

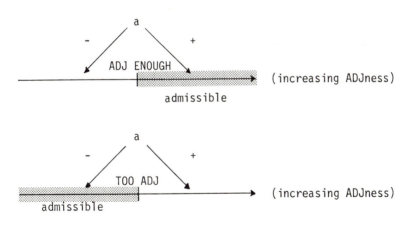

Diagram 7

We only need to replace the time scale by the scale provided by the adjective
or adverb and its polarity and the proposition p by the admissibility
predicate. The duality relationships obtain with respect to the implicit admissibility predicate and can therefore not be demonstrated at the surface.
The otherwise inexpressible inner negation is expressed by the pair
enough/too. If the adjective or the adverb in the focus is replaced by its antonym, the scale and the admissibility range remain the same but the order
is reversed. The result is an exchange of the first and the second semiphase
together with the corresponding relocation of the parameter: what is an

admissible value remains an admissible value. The effect, thus, is that of inner plus outer negation: *big enough* and *small enough* are duals and so are
too big and *too small*. For that reason the following equivalence holds,
which looks like a duality but is none:

(19)   a is big enough   = a is not too small

The expression on the right is the dual of *a is not too big* and hence the inner
negation of *a is too big*, which in turn is the inner negation of the left side,
according to (18). The following diagram is an illustration of the
equivalence (19).

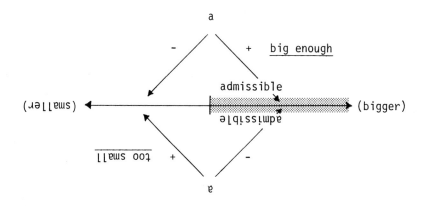

Diagram 8

3.1.2. Scaling adjectives

Scaling adjectives (and adverbs) themselves represent another example of
this type of meanings, adding a whole syntactic class to the realm of natural
language quantification. I regard the predicative use of adjectives as basic
in the following. Scaling adjectives refer to a range on a scale into which the
value of their argument falls. *A is big* says that the size of a falls into a range
of possible values on the scale of size which are considered high. Scaling adjectives and adverbs require a tripartition of the respective scale[17], consisting in a marked lower third, a neutral middle part, and a marked upper
third as shown in diagram 9. The choice of the scale itself and the exact partition of the scale into marked and unmarked values depend on the context
in a complex way which need not concern us here.

   Pairs of antonymous adjectives are asymmetrical in several regards.
There is one, intuitively positive, which exhibits more general possibilities
of use, in contrast to the other, which is more specific. *Big*, for example,

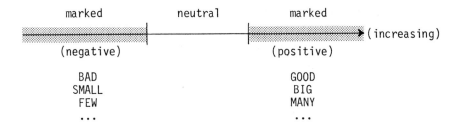

Diagram 9

being the positive pole, can be used in a neutral sense in connection with *how* or *so*, while its negative antonym *small* keeps its specific meaning in such phrases. Likewise the corresponding nouns referring to the dimension in a neutral way, such as *size, length, thickness*, and so on belong to the positive pole, often being derived from it, whereas the derivations from the negative pole cannot be taken neutral: *shortness, narrowness,* etc. In many cases no nominal derivations exist at all. These are only two differences out of several more which point to the same direction: the negative antonyms are more restricted, or more specialized, in use. This tendency is another aspect of the general type asymmetry observed above, as the positive antonyms will be analyzed as type 1 and the negative ones as type 2. Type 3 adjectives are rare and type 4 adjectives do not seem to exist at all.[18]

The meaning of scaling polar adjectives, again, is an example of phase quantification, the quantified predicate this time being the property of having a marked value on the given scale. Positive antonyms state that the value lies higher than what is considered unmarked and negative ones state that the value lies lower than that.

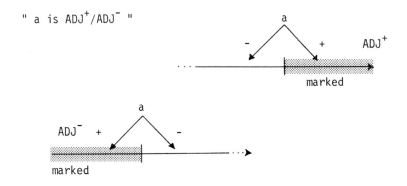

Diagram 10

Thus, antonymous scaling adjectives are duals with respect to the implicit markedness predicate.

One instance of this sort of quantifiers of particular interest is the pair *many* and *few*. They behave essentially like scaling adjectives: they can be used both predicatively and attributively, they take the same modifiers (*very, enough*[19], etc.), they have comparative and superlative forms, and they admit definite determiners preceding them in their attributive use. Semantically, they are intersective and relative – *many children* applies to those collections of children of a relatively high number just the same way as *intelligent child* applies to those children of a relatively high intelligence. The only difference between *many* and *few* on the one hand and adjectives like *thick* on the other is that the latter are distributive, whereas the former are collective. Used as quantifiers in the sense of Barwise & Cooper – the noun following *many* or *few* representing the domain of quantification and the VP the predicate quantified – the resultant meaning of (*many/few N*)$_{NP}$*VP* is that the number of those "Ns" to which the VP applies is relatively high or low, respectively, i.e. in set-theoretical terms the cardinality of the intersection of the extensions of the noun and the VP is marked as high or low. It is left to the context to provide the criterion for markedness. The so-called proportional and absolute meanings[20] need not be distinguished semantically. Needless to state, that *many* is type 1 and few is type 2. The two operators are therefore not negations of each other[21], which is correct. They are contraries with a non-empty range of neutral cases possible between "many" and "few".

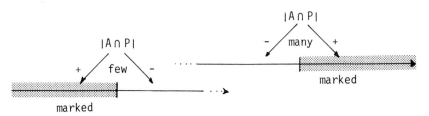

"many/few As are P"

Diagram 11

3.1.4. *continue, begin, stop*

In what follows I treat these verbs for the sake of simplicity as propositional operators, again taking durative propositions as arguments. The fact that these verbs are quantifiers, too, suggests that verbal aspect belongs to the realm of quantification, because they just represent the standard aspects *durative, ingressive*, and *perfective*. Again, the type asymmetry observation is confirmed by the fact that there is no aspect of *not-beginning*.

The duality relationships here can easily be checked. If something stops, the contrary begins, and vice versa. Hence, *begin* and *stop* are inner negations of each other. Furthermore, *stop* is the outer negation of *continue*, as a given state either stops or continues. This renders *continue* and *begin* duals.

The verbs under consideration, too, refer to an implicit time parameter t°. In contrast to the adverbs *already, still, not yet,* and no *longer* – which tell something about the recent past – these verbs tell something about the close future, how things go on from t° with respect to the proposition embedded[15]. The time stretch under consideration again is a double phase of not-p and p which contains t°. In case of *continue(p, t°)* and *stop(p, t°)* the first semiphase is p and has started before t°. If t° is the last point of this semiphase, *stop(p, t°)* is true, otherwise *continue(p, t°)* holds.

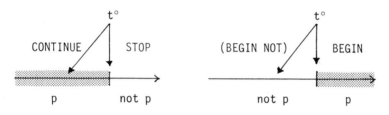

Diagram 12

The correspondence of these verbs and the adverbs around *already* becomes apparent if the course of events till t° for the latter ones and the course of events from t° on for the former ones is compared, as in the next diagram:

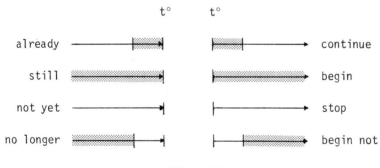

Diagram 13

Of course, in case of the statements on the right side the future course of events can only be treated as possible not as factual, because of the general asymmetry of past and future.

3.2. The general definition of phase quantification

The preceding four groups of examples can all be formalized in a uniform way. The formalization I present is not part of any particular framework and can certainly be given in alternative, maybe better, forms.

The four groups of operators semantically have two operands. They take a predicate quantified which defines a positive phase or range of values on a scale. The scale is the time scale in case of the *already*-group and the aspectual verbs, and the scale provided by the adjective or adverb in the other two cases. Adjacent to the positive phase defined by the predicate quantified, there is a negative contrast phase, either preceding or following the positive phase. It does not matter if there is a zone of indetermination between the positive and the negative phase.

The resulting double phase is fixed on the respective scale – which might contain several such double phases – by the additional condition that it has to contain a parameter point, t° or a in the examples above. This parameter point is the second operand. The four types of quantifiers now differ in presupposing that either the positive or the negative semiphase comes first and in stating that the parameter point falls into the first or into the second semiphase, thus resulting in four possible cases. (Minor modifications apply to the case of the aspectual verbs *begin* and *stop*.)

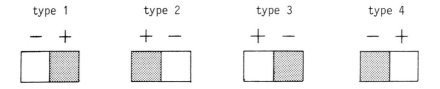

Diagram 14

Let me motivate the formalization I want to propose with a procedural description of the meanings of the four operator types. You start from within the first semiphase, no matter where but, say, from its leftmost point. This phase is either negative (type 1 and 3) or positive. You run along the scale till you reach the parameter point – which has to lie within the double phase – and check on the way whether you enter any second semiphase. If so you have true cases of type 1 or 4. Since the parameter point itself has to lie within the double phase, the starting point has to be the infimum of the l a s t positive or negative phase that starts before the parameter point. Let me call this point GSI for "greatest smaller *infimum*". The formal definition is:

(20) $GSI(P, a) =_{df} \inf\{x \mid x < a \ \& \ P(x) \ \& \ \forall y(x < y \leq a \ \& \ P(y) \rightarrow$
$\forall z(x < z < y \rightarrow P(z)))\}$

Obviously, GSI(P, a) is defined if and only if the following condition is fulfilled:

(21) $\exists x(x < a \ \& \ P(x) \ \& \ \forall y(x < y < a \ \& \ P(y) \rightarrow \forall z(x < z < y \rightarrow P(z))))$

The third conjunct, however, is redundant in case of simple durative predicates p. The existential presupposition for GSI(P, a) therefore reduces to

(22) $\exists x(x < a \ \& \ P(x))$

The use of the presuppositional term GSI renders it possible to put presupposition and assertion in one formula. In that way the duality relations become completely transparent. I shall give two equivalent formulations in order to show the latter as well as the parallelism of the phase quantifiers and the standard quantifiers of predicate logic. Type 1 can be taken as the statement that in the domain of quantification − i.e. between the relevant GSI and the parameter point − there are positive cases of the predicate quantified. From this it follows by the definition of GSI, that the parameter point itself falls into the positive semiphase. Type 2 can be expressed as universal quantification: all points within the domain of quantification fall into the positive semiphase.

(23)   general format of phase quantification:

     type 1: $\exists x(GSI(\sim p, a) \leq x < a \ \& \ p(x))$
     type 2: $\sim \exists x(GSI(\ \ p, a) < x \leq a \ \& \ \sim p(x))$ (dual of type 1)
     type 3: $\sim \exists x(GSI(\sim p, a) < x \leq a \ \& \ p(x))$ (outer negation)
     type 4: $\exists x(GSI(\ \ p, a) < x \leq a \ \& \ \sim p(x))$ (inner negation)

(24)   type 1: $\exists x(GSI(\sim p, a) < x \leq a \ \& \ p(x))$ (existential
     type 2: $\forall x(GSI(\ \ p, a) < x \leq a \rightarrow p(x))$ (universal)

Note, that the inner negation of the predicate quantified affects both occurrences of *p*. The definition applies immediately to the first three cases (*already/...*, *enough/ ...*, ADJ$^+$/...):

(25)

	scale	order $<$	predicate p	parameter a
already(p, t°)	time	earlier	p	$t°$
a is ADJ enough	ADJ^+ ness	less ADJ	admissible in ADJ^+ ness	a
a is $ADJ^{+/-}$	ADJ^+ ness	less ADJ^+	marked in ADJ^+ ness	a
many/few A are P	numbers	less	marked in number	$|A \cap P|$

A format very similar to (23) applies to the interpretations of the aspectual verbs. They differ slightly in that the domain of quantification is the phase that reaches from the parameter point up to the smallest greater supremum of the appropriate phase. I will not develop the exact formulation here because it is not needed for the following considerations.

Monotonicity and persistency

With this interpretation at hand the criteria of monotonicity and persistency become applicable to the phase quantifiers, too, and correspond to well known meaning properties of these operators. Recall that a determiner is persistent if it is immune against extending the domain of quantification. Any extension of the domain of quantification – which of course has to be kept within the limitation of the given doublephase as a whole – means a shift of the parameter point to the right, while any further restriction of the domain of quantification corresponds to a shift of the parameter point to the left. This way, the persistency of type 1 and type 4 accounts for the validity of the following inferences:

(26) $\begin{Bmatrix} \text{already} \\ \text{no longer} \end{Bmatrix} (p, t°) \ \& \ t^1 < t° \Rightarrow \begin{Bmatrix} \text{already} \\ \text{no longer} \end{Bmatrix} (p, t')$

(27) a is $\begin{Bmatrix} \text{ADJ enough} \\ \text{too ADJ} \end{Bmatrix}$ & b is ADJer than a $\Rightarrow$ b is $\begin{Bmatrix} \text{ADJ enough} \\ \text{too ADJ} \end{Bmatrix}$

(28) a is $\begin{Bmatrix} ADJ^+ \\ \text{not } ADJ^- \end{Bmatrix}$ & b is ADJ^+er than a $\Rightarrow$ b is $\begin{Bmatrix} ADJ^+ \\ \text{not } ADJ^- \end{Bmatrix}$

Antipersistency accounts for the reverse properties of the type 2 and type 3 operators.

Monotonicity, or right monotonicity, to follow van Benthems[24] terminology, makes good sense likewise. The property of upward monotonicity means immunity of the operator against any extension of the predicate quantified. Obviously, it is the "positive" type 1 and type 2 operators which have the parameter point falling into the positive semiphase that allow the phase p to be replaced by a greater phase p′ that contains p. Likewise the type 3 and type 4 operators do not allow the same change but allow for a restriction of the positive semiphase because that results in an extension of the negative one. Extension of a semiphase in the temporal cases means embedding it into a more comprehensive interval. In the cases involving adjectives it means loosening or tightening the criteria of markedness or admissability. The following inferences – all to be taken within the conditions presupposed – reflect the property of upward monotonicity for type 1 and type 2 operators:

(29)   She is $\left\{ \begin{array}{l} \text{already} \\ \text{still} \end{array} \right\}$ fast asleep. $\Rightarrow$ She is $\left\{ \begin{array}{l} \text{already} \\ \text{still} \end{array} \right\}$ asleep.

(30)   He is $\left\{ \begin{array}{l} \text{tall for a basket ball player.} \\ \text{short for a jockey.} \end{array} \right\} \Rightarrow$ He is $\left\{ \begin{array}{l} \text{tall} \\ \text{short} \end{array} \right\}$ for a man.

(31)   This is $\left\{ \begin{array}{l} \text{enough} \\ \text{not too much} \end{array} \right\}$ for three days. $\Rightarrow$

This is $\left\{ \begin{array}{l} \text{enough for two days.} \\ \text{not too much for a week.} \end{array} \right\}$

According to the phase quantifier interpretation offered here, *many* is monotone increasing and persistent, *few* being monotone *in*creasing and antipersistent. Persistency and antipersistency here corresponds to upward and downward monotonicity respectively for these quantifiers taken as generalized quantifiers in the sense of Barwise and Cooper's.[23]

3.3. The standard restricted quantifiers as phase quantifiers

We have seen so far that the phase quantifiers are special instances of restricted quantifiers. If we assume that the various possibility and necessity operators of the example group B above are cases of restricted quantifiers, too – which seems highly plausible[24] – this result enables us to state the lexicalization asymmetry hypothesis for a broad class of natural language expressions, and furthermore to associate the properties of persistency and monotonicity with the four types of operators throughout. Of course, this means a substantial constraint upon possible natural language quantifiers, supposed it be valid for further cases too not yet investigated under this perspective.

What is more informative about natural language quantification, however, is the fact that, conversely, the general cases of restricted quantification, too, fit into this considerably specific scheme – though at the cost of a slight generalization. This generalization, however, has its own merits. The standard restricted quantifications as given in (32) can be equivalently

(32) $\exists x(x \in A \ \& \ x \in P)$
         $\forall x(x \in A \rightarrow x \in P)$ equivalently: $\sim \exists x(x \in A \ \& \ x \in \bar{P})$

expressed using second order quantifiers over subsets of the domain of quantification instead of first order quantifiers over its elements, rendering the formulations in (33). Note that it is essential that only non-empty subsets of the range of quantification are considered, and that duality still holds with respect to the predicate P, which is now considered to apply to its subsets.

(33) $\exists X(\emptyset \subset X \subseteq A \ \& \ X \subseteq P)$
         $\forall X(\emptyset \subset X \subseteq A \rightarrow X \subseteq P)$ equivalently: $\sim \exists X(\emptyset \subset X \subseteq A \ \& \ X \subseteq \bar{P})$

Now, the empty set $\emptyset$, figuring as the excluded lower bound in the restrictive condition in (33) is the unique infimum of any set whatsoever with respect to the partial ordering of set inclusion. So it is the GSI for any set P as well as for its complement $\bar{P}$. Definition (20) above yields

(34) $GSI^*(P, A) = \inf_{\subseteq}\{ X \mid X \subset A \ \& \ X \subseteq P \ \& \ \forall Y(X \subset Y \subseteq A \ \& \ Y \subseteq P \rightarrow$
                        $\forall Z(X \subset Z \subset Y) \rightarrow Z \subseteq P))\}$

The third condition is redundant, because it holds for any sets A, P, X whatsoever.
   By this we get

(35) $GSI^*(P, A) = \inf_{\subseteq}\{ X \mid X \subset A \ \& \ X \subseteq P \}$

which is obviously the empty set if the term is defined at all, i.e. if the domain of quantification is not itself empty, a condition we presuppose throughout. (32) can therefore equivalently be reformulated as:

(36) $\exists X(GSI^*(\bar{P}, A) \subset X \subseteq A \ \& \ X \subseteq P)$
         $\forall X(GSI^*(P, A) \subset X \subseteq A \rightarrow X \subseteq P)$

(36) differs from the general phase quantification scheme in two respects. First, the predication relation here is not set membership but set inclusion. This seems to be a harmless step. One should be flexible at this point. Set

membership is only an adequate interpretation of predication in case of distributive predicates applied to individuals. The more general schemes in (33) and (36) can also be applied to collective predicates. In a similar way, mass noun quantification might require a further generalization of the predication relation, replacing set inclusion by a less specific part-of-relation. Thus, this generalization is not only harmless but even necessary.

The second deviation from the phase quantification scheme is the replacement of the underlying strict ordering with the partial ordering of set inclusion. For that reason I used the term *GSI** instead of *GSI*. This modification is indeed substantial because intuitively an essential feature of what I called phase quantifiers is that they work on scales. Is there any way to conceive the restricted standard quantifiers as phase quantifiers in the narrower sense? The answer is yes, and the way it is possible is more than merely a mathematical possibility.

The set theoretical formulae expressing the standard restricted quantifications either in the individual or in the subset mode depict a static conception of quantification: "*There are* elements/subsets of the domain of quantification A to which the predicate P applies." Such a picture is natural in a semantic framework which has in view the truth conditions of sentences and does not consider the way truth or falsity comes about. This would be the task of a procedural semantics. Apart from being particularly appealing in case of quantification, procedural descriptions of meanings could provide criteria to choose among alternative formulations of truth conditions which are equivalent when viewed from their results but not from the way they come about. (32), (33), (36) and the following interpretations of quantificational statements are examples of formulations which suggest different evaluation procedures for the same results.

Any procedure to determine the truth value of a restricted quantificational statement will in one way or the other contain a step by step checking of the domain of quantification with respect to the relevant predicate P. This presupposes — or induces, if you like — an ordering among the elements of the domain of quantification. (From Barwise & Cooper's "determiner universal" (1981: 179) we learn that every natural language quantifier lives on its domain of quantification, hence no other elements of the universe are relevant for the evaluation procedure.) If we restrict our considerations to the case of finite domains of quantification[25] it is a trivial fact that the domain can be linearly ordered, in particular it can be ordered in such a way that the elements which exhibit a certain property come first. Using the well-ordering theorem this result can be carried over to arbitrary domains of quantification. Diagram 15 shows such an ordering for the finite case, each little square representing an element of A.

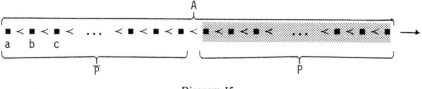

Diagram 15

If one runs through the elements of A from left to right, at the same time one runs through an ascending chain of subsets of A, starting from the empty set and gradually adding one element after the other till A is complete. The scale of elements of A in diagram 15 thus defines a scale of ascending subsets of A, represented by the dots in the next diagram.

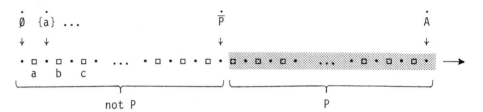

Diagram 16

I have marked the set names with a point in order to emphasize their role of being points on a linearly ordered scale. Any set can be conceived of in two different ways: as the unordered collection of its elements, and as the result of the enumeration of its elements. In the latter sense any set A marks a point on a scale of all individuals, namely the point where this set is completed. This ambivalence is directly related to the ordinal-cardinal ambivalence of natural numbers, the cardinal view corresponding to the unordered collection conception and the ordinal view to the enumeration conception. Using the ordinal set conception we can gain complete uniformity of the usual restricted quantification and the phase quantification format. This is expressed in the following formula. I use $<$ for the ordering among sets conceived as points. The application of P to a point X, written P[X] means that the point where the set X is completed falls into P, which implies that X contains elements with the property P.

(36) $\exists \dot{X}(\mathrm{GSI}(\sim P, \dot{A}) < \dot{X} \leqq \dot{A} \;\&\; P[\dot{X}])$
        $\forall \dot{X}(\mathrm{GSI}(\;\;P, \dot{A}) < \dot{X} \leqq \dot{A} \rightarrow P[\dot{X}])$

Conceived in this way, the standard restricted quantifiers exhibit a striking similarity with the adverb *already* and its associates. *Already(p, t°)* means: start somewhere in the phase of not-p that immediately precedes t°, go to t°, and you will enter a phase of p − or shorter: the time till t° reaches into a phase of p. *Some A are P* means analogously: start with elements of A for which P does not hold (if there are any), run through A, and you will enter P − or shorter: A reaches into P.

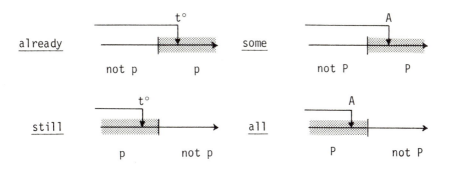

Diagram 17

One might object that this result seems artificial in that it uses an ordering which cannot be considered given in all cases, or even worse, that it is in conflict with an essential property of the quantifiers considered namely their being immune against a permutation of the elements of the respective universe.[23] This is right. The respective ordering, however, does not play an essential role. The only condition it must fulfil is the one, that the universe is divided into two halves and that the elements of one half precede those of the other half. This in turn requires not more than the possibility to distinguish between the two subsets properly. Thus the actual requirement is much weaker than it seems to be at the first glance. On the other hand, the cases of phase quantifications discussed before do not make full use of the underlying total ordering, either. It just happens, that time is totally ordered. There are uses of the *already*-group in German with spatial interpretation, working perfectly in the, of course not linearly ordered, natural three-dimensional space. A sentence like

(37)   Basel liegt schon in der Schweiz.
        "Basel lies already in Switzerland."

is to be interpreted as: "Walk along any relevant path to Basel and you will cross the border of Switzerland", a relevant path being any path starting outside Switzerland (the spatial region specification "Switzerland" representing a spatial predicate) and ending with Basel (conceived as the parameter point), crossing the border to Switzerland at most one time. This case resembles very much the general restricted quantification case.

3.4. Phase quantification and semantic automata

Johan van Benthem in his talk at this conference presented a new semantical approach to quantification which seems promising for the solution of the problems considered here. He suggests describing the meanings of (nominal) quantifiers by means of automata.[26] The universal and the existential quantifiers, e.g., are represented by two state finite automata with one accepting state, working on a binary alphabet. Their input consists in a tape with one entry for each element of the domain of quantification, the entry being 1 if the predicate quantified holds for that element and 0 if it does not hold. Let me call the accepting state "YES" and the refuting state "NO":[27]

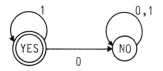 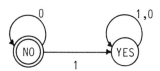

Diagram 18

The two automata are dual: you get the one out of the other if you exchange YES and NO (outer negation) and all 0s and 1s (inner negation). The two automata can be replaced by even simpler indeterministic finite automata:[28]

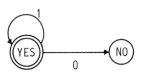 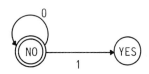

Diagram 19

They work for every ordering of the domain of quantification whatsoever, but clearly represent a simple notion of border-crossing (from P to not-P or the other way round) as their crucial element. Interpreted continuously, they can be considered to represent the meanings of *already(p, t°)* and *still(p, t°)*, supposing they start from the relevant GSI and end at t°. E.g. the universal automaton yields *still*: start with the truth-value YES and keep to it as long as you stay in p, but change irreversibly to NO as soon as you encounter not-p. Something similar to these automata could serve to represent the meanings of phase quantifiers in general, provided two things:

(i)   a definition of generalized automata that work on continuous scale in-

tervals divided into phases out of a finite choice of states, instead of working on tapes with discrete entries,
(ii) a way to treat presuppositions properly.

The latter problem opens very interesting perspectives. The operator *already*, for one, is presuppositional. It selects certain time intervals to which it can apply either positively or negatively, precluding others, namely those which do not start with a negative half or which have more than one change between positive and negative sub-phases. This behavior could be modeled by indeterministic automata that are defined for the relevant input intervals only, yielding no truth value if they encounter other data. In this way, there could be a very elegant solution available for the problems concerning the projection of presuppositions in quantificational contexts. Apparently, automata of the kind involved here can be inserted as subroutines into others, replacing the input 1 by the acceptance of a subautomaton and 0 by its refutation. (Note, that 1 and 0 anyway stand for the complex procedures of verifying the predicate quantified for the object under consideration.) Presupposition projection, now, can just be left to the functioning of the machine as a whole. It will fail to calculate a truth value in case of presupposition failure on any of its internal levels. Or to put it the other way round: the presupposition of a complex expression will be represented by the input selective behavior of the complex automaton representing its meaning.

REFERENCES

Barwise, Jon, & Cooper, Robin: (1981), 'Generalized Quantifiers and Natural Language.' *Linguistics and Philosophy*, 4-2, 159–219.
Benthem, Johan van: (1984), 'Questions about Quantifiers', *Journal of Symbolic Logic*, 49-2, 443–466.
Benthem, Johan van: (this volume), 'Semantic Automata'.
Blau, Ulrich: (1983), 'Three-Valued Logic of Precise, Vague, and Presupposing Quantifiers' in Ballmer, Thomas, and Pinkal, Manfred (eds.) *Approaching Vagueness*, North-Holland, pp. 79–129.
Eijck, Jan van: (1985), *Aspects of Quantification in Natural Language*. Doct. Diss., Univ. of Groningen.
Hopcroft, J., & Ullman, J.: (1979), *Introduction to Automata Theory*, Reading (Mass.), Addison-Wesley.
Horn, Laurence R.: (1972), *On the Semantic Properties of Logical Operators in English*, Ph.D. Thesis, Los Angeles, U.C.L.A.
Horn, Laurence R.: (1978), 'Remarks on Neg-Raising'. In Cole, Peter (ed.): *Syntax and Semantics*, Vol. 9, New York, Acad. Press, 129–220.
Kitcher, Philip: 1978, 'Positive Understatement: The Logic of Attributive Adjectives' *Journal of Philosophical Logic*, 7-1, 1–17.
Kratzer, Angelika: (1977), 'What *must* and *can* must and can mean' *Linguistics and Philosophy*, 1-3, 337–355.

Kratzer, Angelika: (1981), 'The Notional Category of Modality' in Eikmeyer, Hans-Jürgen, and Rieser, Hannes (eds.) *Words, Worlds, and Contexts*, Berlin and New York, de Gruyter, pp. 38–74.

Kuroda, S.-Y.: (1973), 'Where Epistemology, Style, and Grammar Meet: A Case Study from Japanese' in Kiparsky, Paul and Anderson, Stephen (eds.): *A Festschrift for Morris Halle*. New York, Holt, 377–391.

Link, Godehard: (1983), 'The Logical Analysis of Plurals and Mass Terms: A Lattice-Theoretical Approach' in Bäuerle, R., et al. (eds.): *Meaning, Use, and Interpretation of Language*. Berlin, New York, de Gruyter, 302–323.

Montague, Richard: 1974, 'The Proper Treatment of Quantification in Ordinary English' in Thomason, R. (ed.): *Formal Philosophy. Selected Papers of Richard Montague*. New Haven, Yale University Press, pp. 247–270.

Reichenbach, Hans: (1947), *Elements of Symbolic Logic*. New York, Dover Publ.

NOTES

1. Van Eijck (1985) gives a comprehensive survey and discussion of the work about quantification done by linguists, logicians, and philosophers.

2. This general conception of quantification will be modified below in a way that will, however, be compatible with the considerations following now.

3. Formally, $Q\sim$ is $\{\,P\,|\,Q(\bar{P})\}$, $\sim Q$ is $\{\,P\,|\sim Q(P)\}$, and $\sim Q\sim$ is $\{\,P\,|\,Q(\bar{P})\}$.

4. I.e., the set $\{\,Q,\,Q\sim,\,\sim Q,\,\sim Q\sim\,\}$ forms an operator algebra with respect to the operations of inner negation, outer negation, and dual.

5. In case of diagram 4 take the predicate variable P for c.

6. The original formulation of the definition (cf. Barwise and Cooper 1981: 178) is slightly more complicated.

7. I will not discuss the regularities governing the way inner and outer negation is expressed. Horn (1978) provides evidence which strongly suggests that the type-assignment used here is relevant for the occurrence of NEG-raising, which complicates the matter considerably.

8. The concept of phase quantification developed below seems to provide the basis for a uniform treatment of both meaning variants as the same operator working on different scales.

9. Cf. the remark concerning the "tolerance" criterion below.

10. Let Q be intolerant, i.e. $Q(P) \Rightarrow \sim Q(\sim P)$. Now, either the reverse holds too, or it does not hold. If it holds, $Q(P)$ is equivalent with $\sim Q(\sim P)$, its dual, hence it is selfdual. If it does not hold there must be cases, where $\sim Q(\sim P)$ holds and $Q(P)$ does not hold. This, in turn, means, that both $\sim Q\sim$ and $\sim Q$ are tolerant.

11. Let D be persistent, then $D(A, P) \Rightarrow D(B, P)$ if $A \subset B$. But this is the same as $\sim D(B, P) \Rightarrow \sim D(A, P)$ if $A\subset B$. Hence, $\sim D$ is antipersistent.

12. Let D be persistent. If D is not highly degenerate there exist sets A, B, and P, and a universe containing them such that $D(A, P)$ and $D(B, \sim P)$ hold. From that it follows by the persistency of D that both $D(A \cup B, P)$ and $D(A \cup B, \sim P)$ hold, rendering D tolerant.

13. I do not offer any explanation for the asymmetry described. Horn (1972) suggests that type 4 is rare because it is unnecessary, due to the fact that type 4 usually is a conversational implicature of type 1. But I presume that an explanation along this line is too weak. Often, it seems, type 4 is not only not needed but actually a v o i d e d, cf. the numerous cases of NEG-raising with type 2 (but not type 1) quantifiers, which yields type 3 in place

of type 4 (Horn 1978), or the pseudo-type-4 adjectives mentioned in note 18 below.

14. This is reflected immediately by the use of the corresponding particles in German, *still* translating *noch*, and *not yet* translating *noch nicht*.

15. Note that $t°$ may be different from the time of utterance, due to tense, temporal adverbials or implicit dislocation. ($t°$ is what Reichenbach 1947: 288) calls the "point of reference".) Hence, the transition point need not be recent or imminent in absolute terms, i.e. with respect to the time of utterance.

16. *enough* can also be used in the sense of **much/many enough* without taking any adjective or adverb.

17. Cf. Kitcher (1978) for that point.

18. In German, there are a few examples of lexicalized adjectives which look like type 4 but nevertheless are used with a different (type 2!) meaning: there is *gut* (1), *übel* (2), *ungut* (3), and *unübel* (pseudo 4), the latter being used only in the combination "nicht unübel" meaning just "not bad". Likewise, there is *schwer* (1) (in the sense of *difficult*), *leicht* (2) (= *easy*), *unschwer* (3), and *unleicht* (pseudo 4) which means just the same as *leicht* in phrases like "... wie man unleicht erkennt". In such cases, type 4 meanings seem not only to be rare but somehow to be blocked off.

19. With the exemption that the role of **much/many enough* is played by *enough*.

20. Cf. Blau 1983.

21. For the contrary suggestion cf. Barwise and Cooper (1981: 208). They do however not commit themselves to that view.

22. Cf. van Benthem (1984).

23. *Many A are P* means many(A, A ∩ P) to Barwise and Cooper and many ($|A ∩ P|$, M) to me. $P \subset P'$ implies both $A ∩ P \subseteq A ∩ P'$ and $|A ∩ P| \leq |A ∩ P'|$.

24. Cf. Kratzer (1981) among others.

25. As van Benthem (1984) does.

26. Cf. Benthem (this volume).

27. The starting state is marked by a double circle.

28. These automata are indeterministic, according to the terminology of Hopcroft & Ulman (1979), in so far as they are not totally defined for the second state. They stop as soon as they reach the second state, no matter what the further input would be.

Chapter 4

Nondurative Closure of Events*

Henk Verkuyl

1. INTRODUCTION

In this paper, I shall try to contribute to a better understanding of the combinatorial mechanism that, in my view, determines what sort of aspect must be assigned to a sentence. In earlier work, I could not get on with the right formalism, that is, a formalism that in principle can explain things rather than only describe them. The generative theory in which I expressed myself, did not provide the right tools at the time, and even now it is rather difficult if not impossible to apply this theory to the phenomena involved, as its present scope is too limited to incorporate the many insights about quantification and temporal phenomena such as uniqueness, frequency, location, duration, and so on, recently developed in the field of logical grammar.[1] I will present my analysis of nondurativity in the framework of the theory of generalized quantification, though in a way which is compatible with the generative theory of phrase structure and its interpretation.

Essential seems to me the idea of a nondurative closure. The notion of a nondurative aspect pertains to events having a structure that is closed off in some sense by a "culmination point", so that these events are bounded. Given an interval and a passage through this interval by some entity, the notion of closure can be applied to its beginning, its end, and to the number of entities which "go through" the interval. In metaphorical terms: the structure of an interval allows for three possible kinds of "leaks". To illustrate this, the leading idea is that the non-durative aspect in sentences like *She gave me a book* is due to a semantic element, say B, inherent to the Verb, which combines with (takes) a semantic element, say A, inherent to some NPs such as *she, me, a book*, and so on. The absence of B can render the sentence durative as in *He kept me away from a book*, and B can be neutralized by negation as in *She did not give me a book*. The sentence *She gave me a book* is characterized by an optimal nondurative closure, which can (provisionally, of course) be represented by $A + B + A + A$ because all

* Acknowledgement: Some of this material was first presented at the Groningen ZWO − Workshop on the Linguistic Representation of time in 1983. I am grateful to Franciska de Jong, Leonoor Oversteegen and Co Vet for their comments on earlier versions and in particular to Dick de Jongh, Harry Sitters and Martin Stokhof for their stimulating help in constructing the conceptual machinery presented in this paper.

NPs in this structure have a semantic element in common which pertains to a specified quantity of some sort. Durative leakage, indicated by Δ, occurs in (i) *Unknown passengers gave me a book* $(\Delta + B + A + A)$, in (ii) *Unknown passengers gave a book to sailors* $(\Delta + B + A + \Delta)$ and in (iii) *Unknown passengers gave books to sailors* $(\Delta + B + \Delta + \Delta)$.

In the so-called "thematic analysis" proposed by Gruber (1976[1965]) and applied and extended in Verkuyl (1972; 1976; 1978) and Platzack (1979) to temporal properties of sentences, change is represented in terms of an (concrete or abstract) Theme i.e. an object or objects "moving" from some point (Source) to another point (Goal). The thematic analysis is essentially interval-based in the sense that Source pertains to the beginning of an interval, Goal to its end, whereas Theme pertains to the entity (or entities) "travelling" from Source to Goal. Leaks can occur only with respect to one of these three elements in a "thematic kernel". For example, in (i) the Theme-NP *a book* denotes a specified quantity of books, the Goal-P *me* a specified quantity of people, whereas the Source-NP cannot be delimited as to its denotation. In nonthematic analyses, sentences with an n-place B-predicate have n possible leaks.

In my approach, nondurativity is a marked phenomenon: durativity is the situation in which the conditions for nondurativity are not met. Nondurativity arises only if all conditions for closure are fulfilled. In this paper, I shall try to give the formal machinery to precisely describe and explain the combinatorial mechanism that is at work in nondurative sentences. Some basic material will be presented in section 2. In section 3, the attention is focused on the semantic element which is labelled 'Specified Quantity of A', abbreviated as [+ SQA].[2] Due to the so-called theory of generalized quantification it is now possible to give the exact conditions under which NPs can be given this label. In section 4, I shall characterize the semantic element B inherent to Verbs. It is labelled [+ ADD TO] and it is considered an operator that takes [+ SQA] to construct a nondurative aspect. I shall formally describe this combinatorial machinery in section 5, explaining why the nondurative event in sentences like *John ate three sandwiches* comes to a stop. In this way the notion of culmination which plays a central role in the literature on Aspect and Aktionsart is given a precise interpretation. Subsequently, section 6 contains the proposal to drastically reduce the ambiguity of sentences like *Three boys saw two girls*.

2. SOME BASIC ASSUMPTIONS ABOUT ASPECTS

I shall now present some of the data which led me to propose that the nondurative aspect is constructed from more basic semantic information scattered over the sentence. Consider the following sentences:[3]

(1)   a.   She walked
       b.   She walked a mile

(2)   a.   He ate sandwiches
       b.   He ate a sandwich

(3)   a.   She drank from the whisky
       b.   She drank a draught from the whisky

(4)   a.   He played
       b.   He played that sonata

(5)   a.   She knitted at one of my sweaters
       b.   She knitted one of my sweaters

(6)   a.   The patients here died of jaundice
       b.   The patient died of jaundice

All a-sentences have a durative reading. This means that they report about a certain temporal entity, say an event, which is not bounded. The b-sentences all pertain to events which are closed off by necessarily having a natural culmination point, in (1b) her having walked a mile, in (2b) his having finished a sandwich, etc.

The durativity of the a-sentences can be made visible by their capacity to take durational adverbials such as *for an hour, until four o'clock,* etc. A sentence like (7a)

(7)   a.   She walked for an hour
       b.   She walked a mile for an hour

pertains to an event which was actualized from the beginning of a certain temporal measuring unit until its end. It is one event, which unrolls itself as it were along the time-axis. Sentence (1b) is marked, however, by its resistance to take *for an hour* as shown by (7b): (1b) does take the adverbial in some way, but this results in an enforced iterative reading: (7b) says that for an hour it was repeatedly the case that she walked a mile (if one wants to interpret (7b) at all). At any rate, a single event reading is virtually excluded unless one is going to benevolently stretch the event in question. Much discussion is possible with respect to the question how our knowledge of the world interferes with our readiness to force a stretched single event reading upon sentences like (7b), but I will not go into this question here.[4] My elucidation of the terms 'durative' and 'nondurative' serves only to refresh memory: there is a lot of literature on the opposition I am discussing here.[5]

In (1)–(6) the nondurativity of the b-sentences must be ascribed to different factors: a finite measure phrase in (1), an indefinite singular NP rather than a bare plural in (2), a lexically filled head rather than an empty head of a partitive construction in (3), a definite NP rather than an empty place in (4), an indefinite singular NP rather than the *at*-construction containing this NP in (5), and finally a definite singular NP as against a definite plural NP in (6). These cases represent only a small sample, but they suffice here.[6]

Things are complicated by scope differences as demonstrated by (8):

(8)   a.   The patient died of jaundice for months
       b.   For months the patient died of jaundice

       c.   The patients here died of jaundice for months
       d.   For months the patients here died of jaundice

Both (8a) and (8b) express the repeated death of the patient. That is, it makes no difference whether *the patient* is in the scope of *for months* or whether the reverse is the case. If we interpret *the patients here* as pertaining to an open set – whoever was patient here – (8c) and (8d) are perfect, expressing durativity. So again, scope does not matter.

However, *the patients here* can also refer to a closed set of patients, a delimited group introduced in the domain of interpretation. In that case (6a) is nondurative and one might expect that (8c) and (8d) are blocked just like (8a) and (8b). As far as I can judge, however, it is only (8c) that is blocked in this way, whereas (8d) is not blocked. The scope position of the adverbial with respect to *the patients here* in (8d) seems to make a finite group reading of this NP implausible. The point I would like to make can be made more clear by (9) and (10):

(9)   a.   Een uur lang fotografeerde hij dit kind
             For an hour he photographed this child

       b.   Dit kind fotografeerde hij een uur lang
             This child he photographed for an hour

(10)   a.   Een uur lang fotografeerde hij veel kinderen
             For an hour he photographed many children

       b.   Veel kinderen fotografeerde hij een uur lang
             Many children he photographed for an hour

These sentences show that there is a certain relation between the type of determiner occurring in a NP invoking nondurativity and the position of this NP. Both (9a) and (9b) have an iterated reading without a remarkable difference in meaning. However, (10a) does not make much sense in Dutch: one can imagine a situation in which a photographer was asked to photograph each member of a very large group of adults and children, which will take hours, and (10a) reports that he concentrated on the children for an hour. In this setting, (10a) improves, but nevertheless the presence of *veel* remains problematic for the interpretation and can only be interpreted as 'relatively many with respect to other things'. At any rate, (10a) cannot mean that he photographed many individual children repeatedly, whereas (10b) has a forced iterative interpretation, in which it holds for many individuals c from a set C of children that c was photographed repeatedly. Occurring in the scope of *een uur lang* (for an hour), the NP *veel kinderen* (many children) seems to be deprived of the possibility to refer to a delimited set of children that can be the unit for a repetition, i.e. the unit that is quantified over. The front position of *veel kinderen* (many children) in (10b) seems to promote the delimited group reading which is necessary to invoke a nondurative reading. I have no explanation for this phenomenon, but will return to it at the end of the following section.

3. SPECIFIED QUANTITY OF A

The theory of generalized quantification not only seems to provide the formal machinery for describing more precisely the conditions under which nondurativity arises, but it also seems to have explanatory force, as I hope to show.[7] My purpose in this section is to give a precise formulation of the notion of Specified Quantity of A (SQA), thus determining the necessary conditions for nondurativity.[8]

In the theory of generalized quantification determiners can be treated as relations between sets of individuals. Assuming a model $M = \langle U, \| \ \| \rangle$, where U is the domain of discourse and $\| \ \|$ an interpretation function, a determiner Det is interpreted as a functor D_U which relates a set A to a set B. For example, *all children are sleeping* is analysed as $D_U AB$, where $D_U = \|all\|$, $A = \|child\|$ and $B = \|sleep\|$ (In this example I ignore plural and tense, so the interpretation operates at a more abstract level). The denotation of an NP like *all children*, viz. $\|all \ children\|$, is considered a quantifier Q, which is a subset of Pow(U), the power set of U. In other words: Q is a collection of subsets of U.

To simplify the exposition, I shall discuss sentences of the form (11) with the help of a specific model (12), say M_1, with an U consisting of four individuals, its power set Pow(U), and $A = \|N\|$, $B = \|VP\|$, and $Q = \|NP\|$. M_1 is a model in which $A = \|child\| = \{b, c, d\}$ and $B = \|be \ photographed\| = U$. That is, there are three children in U and all elements of U are photographed but only three of them are children.

(11)   [$_{NP}$ Det [$_N$ children]] [$_{VP}$ were photographed]

(12)   a. U = { a, b, c, d}
        b. Pow(U) = {Ø, { a}, { b}, { c}, { d}, { a, b}, { a, c}, { a, d},
                    { b, c}, { b, d}, { c, d}, { a, b, c} { a, b, d},
                    { a, c, d}, { b, c, d}, U}
        c. A = ‖child‖ = { b, c, d}
        d. B = ‖be photographed‖ = { a, b, c, d}
        e. Q = ‖Det N‖

Let us now consider a sentence like (13), in which Det is the universal *all* and let us accept (14) as its proper definition (cf. Barwise & Cooper 1981; Zwarts 1981, 1983). |V| indicates the cardinality of V.

(13)   All children were photographed

(14)   a. ‖all N‖ = { X ⊆ U| ‖N‖ ⊆ X};   Presupposition: |‖N‖| > 0
        b. ‖all children‖ = {{ b, c, d}, U}

The denotation of *all children* in M_1 is given in (14b). The relation $D_U AB$ is defined such that B must be a member of Q to make sentences like (13) true. That is, if ‖*be photographed*‖ ∈ ‖*all children*‖, then sentence (13) is true in M_1. In (12d), ‖*be photographed*‖ = U and (14b) shows that U ∈ Q, so (13) is true in M_1. Given the fact that in M_1 |A| = 3, subsets of A with a cardinality smaller than 3 are not captured by definition (14a), because they do not satisfy the requirement that A ⊆ X. In a model, say M_2, in which ‖*child*‖ = { b, c, d} and ‖*be photographed*‖ = { a, b, d}, Q remains, of course, the same as in (14b). But { b, c, d} ⊄ { a, b, d}, so this model does not satisfy the condition that A ⊆ B. Hence (13) is not true in M_2. This is quite satisfactory indeed, as it is clear that one cannot use (13) truthfully if not all children were photographed.

   The information |‖N‖| > 0 in (14a) restricts the models to which (14a) applies: it rules out interpretations in those models in which the set denoted by N contains no members. In that case, Q is undefined; if there is no child in U, one cannot correctly use (13), as argued in De Jong & Verkuyl (1985). In (14a), |‖N‖| > 0 is given as a presupposition.[9]

   Consider now (15) and (16) in M_1:

(15)   Enkele kinderen werden gefotografeerd
        (Several children were photographed)

(16)   a. ‖enkele N‖ = { X ⊆ U| |X ∩ A| ≥ 2}
        b. ‖enkele kinderen‖ = { { b, c}, { c, d}, { b, d}, { a, b, c},
                    { a, b, d}, { a, c, d}, { b, c, d}, U}

Sentence (15) can express that a proper subset of a set of children was photographed, but it can also say that the whole set of children was photographed and that this set was rather small. In this latter interpretation, I am inclined to think of contrast: (15) speaks about a certain activity as compared with other activities. To account for this vagueness, the determiner *enkele* (several) is defined as in (16a), which leads in M_1 to the denotation given in (16b). Definition (16a) simply says that for $Det_U AB$ to hold the intersection of A and B contains some members. It does not say anything about the inclusion relation between A and B. In M_2, (15) is true because $A \cap B = \{b, d\}$ and $|\{b, d\}| = 2$. Note that (15) is true in M_1 as well, because $U \in Q$. Hence (13) and (15) have the same denotation in M_1 because the cardinality of the intersection $A \cap B$ is small by an (absolute) standard. (The question whether 3 is small or not is not a linguistic question, for that matter). So, (16a) provides for a correct description of the ambiguous (or vague) meaning of (15) and for the possible overlap with (14a) in models like M_1 as well.

My last example illustrates the interpretation of sentences like *No children were photographed* applied to M_1. Assuming that (17a) is the proper definition of *No N*, giving (17b) as the denotation of the NP, this sentence is false in M_1, because $U \notin \|$no children$\|$.

(17) a. $\|No N\| = \{X \subseteq U \mid A \cap X = \emptyset\}$
      b. $\|No children\| = \{\emptyset, \{a\}\}$

Suppose that we have a model M_3 with U and $\|child\|$ as in (11), but with $B = \|be photographed\| = \{a\}$. In that case the sentence becomes true, because $\{a\} \in Q$ since $A \cap B = \emptyset$. The same applies to $B = \emptyset$.

I shall now discuss two sets of quantifying NPs in terms of definitions like (14a) and (16a) on the one hand and (17b) on the other hand: members of the first set contribute to the construction of the nondurative aspect whereas the second set contains those NPs which necessarily lead to a durative aspect. In earlier work, I captured the common factor responsible for nondurativity by the label SPECIFIED QUANTITY OF A (SQA) indicating with it that a SQA-NP refers to a specific individual or to a bounded, restricted set A of individuals or to a restricted portion of matter A (1972: 59ff.). At the time, I was not able to propose a satisfying apparatus to formally deal with the factor SQA. Retrospectively, it is easy to see why: a basically syntactic approach cannot adequately deal with the assemblage of the nondurative aspect. From the explanatory point of view, a more precise treatment along the lines of the theory of generalized quantification seems more promising.

In (18) a (noncomplete but representative) list of Dutch determiners is given. In column 2 I have given their English equivalents.[10] The first two columns of (18a) – (18t) contain NPs whose presence is a necessary condition for the nondurative cases; the two columns of (18u) – (18z) contain NPs whose presence is a sufficient condition for durativity. The former NPs are to be marked as [+ SQA] under the appropriate conditions. I use the symbol $A^\#$ to denote a specific subset of A and informally described as 'specified quantity of A'; i.e. $A^\# \subseteq A$. So if an NP is marked as [+ SQA] its N denotes a set A which is a superset of $A^\#$. It is this $A^\#$ that I am interested in because it triggers nondurativity, given the right conditions. $Q = \|NP\|$, $A = \|N\|$, and $B = \|VP\|$ in a specific model, as before. The X in the definitions of (18) is a variable for subsets of U which are members of Q due to the definition. For example, the X of (18n) ranges over the subsets of U which are elements of Q in (16b).

Let us say that the cardinality of a given set V is bounded (or fixed) if $|V| = n$ ($n \in \mathbb{N}$ and $n > 0$) where n is either communicated by the speaker and/or hearer or is taken as fixed without having to know the exact numerical value. That is, speaker (and addressee) assume in the latter case that the V about which they speak is bounded at the moment of speech (as if one takes a picture of that situation fixing this situation). Our knowledge of the world says that the set of childen is an open set in the sense that members of this set fall out because they die or enter into adulthood and that new members enter every minute because they are born. Nevertheless, in normal conversation there seems to be a fixation in the sense that in using sentences like (14) applied to a set $\|child\|$ whose cardinality is unknown, one restricts $\|child\|$ to the set of all children that exist or are taken into consideration at that moment, a set which is closed off at the moment of speech, so that its cardinality is finite, or to a subset of it. In other words, normally we work with finite models, as it were induced by the finiteness of $|A|$ and $|A \cap X|$ (cf. B & C 1981: 163). In terms of (18), this means that most quantifiers presuppose a bounded U, so that $|A \cap B|$ in a specific model can be determined. Actually, only (18z) incorporate in their definitions the information that the cardinality of U is not bounded (it seems as if even U itself is not determined), as indicated by U^*.

I shall now briefly discuss the quantifiers listed in (18). There are several categories. In general, the cases (18a) – (18t) all express the fact that $|A \cap X|$ must be finite which is shown in column 5. The definitions imply that in a specific model where $B = \|VP\|$ the intersection $A \cap B$ has a finite cardinality. The quantifier in (18a) is defined such that $|\cap X \in \|Det\ N\|| = 1$ to assure that we speak about one member of A leaving open the possibility that there are other members of A in U. The quantifiers (18b) – (18i) all have in common that $A \subseteq X$, which implies that $A \cap X = A$. In (18b) – (18e), the cardinality of A has a numerical value which is communicated by the speaker to the hearer, so it follows that the cardinality of the intersection is finite in every model. In (18f) – (18i), the cardinality of A also has a numerical value, but the precise number is not given

(18)

	1 Dutch	2 English	3 Definitions of Q.	4 Presupposition	5 Implication w.r.t. $|A \cap X|$
a.	dat N	that N	$\{X \subseteq U \mid \{a\} \subseteq X\}$	$|A| \geq 1$	$= 1$
b.	Bertrand	Bertrand	$\{X \subseteq U \mid A \subseteq X\}$	$|A| = 1$	$= 1$
c.	het kind(sg)	the N(sg)	$\{X \subseteq U \mid A \subseteq X\}$	$|A| = 1$	$= 1$
d.	(de) beide N	both N	$\{X \subseteq U \mid A \subseteq X\}$	$|A| = 2$	$= 2$
e.	de n N	the n N	$\{X \subseteq U \mid A \subseteq X\}$	$|A| = n$	$= n$
f.	de N(pl)	the N(pl)	$\{X \subseteq U \mid A \subseteq X\}$	$|A| \geq 2$	> 1
g.	elk kind	each N	$\{X \subseteq U \mid A \subset X\}$	$|A| \geq 1$	> 0
h.	elk van de N	each of the N	$\{X \subseteq U \mid A \subset X\}$	$|A| \geq 1$	> 0
i.	alle N	all N	$\{X \subseteq U \mid A \subseteq X\}$	$|A| \geq 1$	> 0
j.	alles	everything	$\{X \subseteq U \mid U \subseteq X\}$	$|U| \geq 1$	> 0
k.	de meeste N	most N	$\{X \subseteq U \mid |A \cap X| > |A \cap (U-X)|\}$	$|A| > 2$	> 2
l.	een N	an N	$\{X \subseteq U \mid |A \cap X| \geq 1\}$	–	> 0
m.	sommige N	some N (sm)	$\{X \subseteq U \mid A \subset X \,\&\, |A \cap X| \geq 1\}$	$|A| \geq 2$	> 1
n.	enkele N	several N	$\{X \subseteq U \mid |A \cap X| \geq 2\}$	–	> 1
o.	enkele v/d N	some of the N	$\{X \subseteq U \mid |A \cap X| \geq 2\}$	$|A| > 2$	> 2
p.	veel N	many N	$\{X \subseteq U \mid |A \cap X| = \tilde{n}\}$	–	> 0
q.	weinig N	few N	$\{X \subseteq U \mid |A \cap X| = \tilde{n} \,\&\, \tilde{n} > 0\}$	–	$\geq n$
r.	n N	n N	$\{X \subseteq U \mid |A \cap X| = n\}$	–	> 0
s.	iets	something	$\{X \subseteq U \mid \|\text{nonhuman}\| \cap X \neq \emptyset\}$	–	> 0
t.	n N (sg) N_A	n N (sg) N_A	$\{X \subseteq U \mid |A \cap X|_u \geq n\}$	–	$\geq n$
u.	geen N	no N	$\{X \subseteq U \mid A \cap X = \emptyset\}$	$|A| > 1$	$= 0$
v.	geen v/d N	none of the N	$\{X \subseteq U \mid A \cap X = \emptyset\}$	$|A| > 1$	$= 0$
w.	niets	none	$\{X \subseteq U \mid \emptyset \cap X = X\}$	–	$= 0$
x.	niemand	nobody	$\{X \subseteq U \mid \|\text{human}\| \cap X = \emptyset\}$	–	$= 0$
y.	$\emptyset$ N(pl)	$\emptyset$ N(pl)	$\{X \subseteq U^* \mid A \subseteq X \,\&\, |A \cap X| = \%\}$	–	cannot be determined
z.	Δ P de N(sg)	Δ P the N(sg)	$\{X \subseteq U^* \mid |A \cap X|_u \neq 0\}$	$|A|_u = \%$	cannot be determined

by the speaker though possibly presupposed because the cardinality of A can be known in the context. In general, the numerical value of quantifiers defined in (18f) – (18i) is fixed by the model. That is, though the cardinality of A may remain unknown, one can be sure that it is finite. Hence the cardinality of the intersection is also finite. In (18j), the definition of *alles* (everything) says that the quantifier is $\{U\}$. The intersection $X \cap U$ is finite, if U is finite.

In cases like (18k) – (18t), we observe that the intersection is fixed by definition. In all these cases A is not a subset of X as part of the definition. On the other hand, only *sommige* (some, sm) requires that A is a proper subset of X. The presupposition connected with *sommige* is that there is an A consisting of at least two members (cf. De Jong 1983). The difference between (18n) and (18o) is exactly this presupposition with respect to A. In (18p) and (18q), I ignore the information with respect to a certain norm which determines the height of the finite cardinality of the intersection. I have abbreviated this information with a $\sim$-sign. In (18r), *n* is taken as 'at least' *n*. In (18s), *iets* (something) is defined as any set X whose intersection with a set of non-human entities in U has a finite cardinality. In this definition, the quantifier is taken as referring to non-human discrete entities.

The concept of delimitation can be applied to mass nouns as well, though one needs a counterpart to the concept of cardinality. In (18t), I have extended the use of the cardinality sign | | to such cases as *vier liter water (4 litres of water), een slok whisky* (a draught of whisky), etc. by adding a subscript u. The *n* in the definition is not a dimensionless number, but it pertains to a measuring dimension u.[11]

The cases in (18u) – (18z) are NPs which cause durative leaks. Their presence is a sufficient condition for durativity. In (18u) – (18x) the cardinality of the intersection is zero. In (18w) the quantifier applies to all subsets X of U such that $X \subseteq \emptyset$, i.e. to $\{\emptyset\}$. An alternative definition would be $\{X \subseteq U | \|nonhuman\| \cap X = \emptyset\}$, depending on whether *niets* (nothing) can cover the absence of human beings or not. In that case (18x) would be complementary to (18w).

In (18y) and (18z) U is not bounded because Q cannot choose a specific model, so that the cardinality of the intersection $A \cap B$ cannot be determined. The %-sign indicates that the cardinality of a certain set cannot be determined. In (18y) both A and B in an intersection $A \cap B$ can be open sets to which no cardinality can be assigned because they are not fixed in the context. Sentence (2a) is durative because there is no bound for the set of sandwiches that are eaten or for the set of things that are eaten by him. The definition says that no specific model is given so that no finite cardinality of the intersection can be determined. In (18z), the quantifier [Δ Prep definite article N] applies to mass terms like *from the whisky* in (3a) and *at one of my sweaters* in (5a). As in Verkuyl (1972), I assume a dummy head of the partitive construction. However, the amount of $\|N\|$ cannot be determined.

Summarizing, the crucial difference between the cases in (18a) – (18t) on the one hand and (18u) – (18z) on the other, can be brought out most clearly with the help of column 5. The former category is characterized by the fact that the intersection $A \cap X$ has a finite cardinality, whereas the cardinality of this intersection in the latter category is zero or cannot be determined. In (19) these three situations are exemplified:

(19)   a.   The children were photographed (nondurative)
       b.   No children were photographed (durative)
       c.   Children were photographed (durative)

It is possible now to exactly indicate the circumstances under which an NP of the form Det N in (18) denotes a 'Specified Quantity $A^{\#}$ of A''.

(20)   a.   Definition: *Specified Quantity of A*
            An NP of the form Det N, where $\|N\| = A$ and where $\|Det\|$
            relates a set B to A in a specific model M_i denotes a specified
            quantity $A^{\#}$ of A in $U(A^{\#} \subseteq A \subseteq U)$ iff
            (i) U is bounded
            (ii) $A^{\#} = A \cap B$
            (iii) $|A^{\#}| > 0$.
       b.   Definition: *Unspecified Quantity of A*
            An NP of the form Det N denotes an unspecified quantity of A
            (i) if $A \cap B = \emptyset$
            (ii) if there is no number given by the definition of Q by which
                 the cardinality of the intersection is bounded.

It is important to realize that $A^{\#}$ is a set containing individuals, so it arises at a first order level, in a specific model. The following (formally trivial) property of $A^{\#}$ must be relevated here to stress that the property of denoting a specified quantity is connected with properties of the X chosen in a model. That is, $A^{\#} = \{x \in B \mid x \in A \cap B\}$, which says that the [+SQA]-feature attributed to an NP pertains to those parts of A which are involved in the predication.

$A^{\#}$ can also be characterized in terms of properties of Q, i.e. in terms of collections of sets. Consider (16b), in which $Q = \{\{b, c\}, \{c, d\}, \{b, d\}, \{a, b, c\}, \{a, c, d\}, \{a, b, d\}, \{b, c, d\}, \{a, b, c, d\}\}$. Given the fact that $A = \{b, c, d\}$, it can be shown that $A^{\#}$ is an element of the power set of A minus those sets that have a cardinality smaller than 2. That is,

$A^{\#} \in POW_{>1}(A)$ and $POW_{>1}(A) \subseteq Q$, where $POW_{>1}(A) = \{\{b, c\}, \{c, d\}, \{b, d\}, \{b, c, d\}\}$. In general, if \$ indicates the restriction on the intersection implied by the definition of Q, $A^{\#} \in POW_{\$}(A)$ and $POW_{\$}(A) \subseteq \|NP\|$.

I shall now discuss some apparent counterexamples to the definitions in (18). This list covers all nondurative cases exemplified in (1b)–(6b). However, as noted in (8) some NPs denoting a specified quantity also allow for an unspecified interpretation. This applies to cases like (21):

(21) a. The child is innocent
      b. All children are innocent
      c. The children are innocent, etc.

It seems as if only NPs defined as $\{X \subseteq U \mid A \subseteq X\}$ have this property. This would explain the correspondence with the unspecified interpretation of (18y) in *Children are innocent*.

In my view, the difference between the nongeneric *Det N* and the generic *Det N* is not expressible in terms of the truth conditions. I think that a θ-operator as proposed in Verkuyl (1981: 587) is necessary to express this difference. This operator inherent to the nongeneric cases is defined as in (22):[12]

(22) $\theta A[\alpha(A)] \leftrightarrow_{df} \exists! A$ such that A is deictically or contextually or anaphorically given and α is true of A.

The absence of this operator in the generic cases would eliminate the presupposition with respect to $|A|$ as given in (18) column 4. One can think of this elimination in two possible ways. Firstly, either $|A| = 0$ or the cardinality of A cannot be fixed because A is changing. In that case $\{X \subseteq U^* \mid A \subseteq X\}$ leads to the implication that $|A \cap X| = \%$, which brings the NPs in (21) close to (18y). Secondly, the cardinality of A cannot be fixed because one speaks about A stereotypically, that is, in the Kripke-Putnam way. If one speaks about members of a set generically, one speaks in terms of stereotypical members of A so that a quantificational interpretation is not a proper way of understanding what is said about A. In this view the presuppositions in column 4 warrant a quantificational treatment of the NPs in question. I shall not make a choice between these options here.

To ensure that nondurativity is linked with nongenericity I shall assume that a θ-operator is inherent to NPs whose interpretation is [+SQA]. In general, generic interpretations lead to a durative aspect. So, a sentence like (23a)

(23) a. The mafiaboss killed his rival with a knife
      b. For centuries the mafiaboss killed his rival with a knife

is durative if this sentence is taken generically, for example if one wants to say that it was a custom among mafiabosses for centuries to kill rivals with a knife, as in (23b). In my view, the present analysis takes into account that in using a generic sentence like (23b) every speaker knows that its nongeneric counterpart (23a) is nondurative, the difference being that the generic variant of (23a) in (23b) lacks a θ-operator.

The second problem with (20) is related to scope differences as observed in section 2. The members of (18a) – (18t) can be marked as [+ SQA], i.e. as defined by (20a). However, sentences like (8c) and (8d) show that the position of an NP with respect to the durational adverbial sometimes determines whether the [+ SQA]-feature may become effective. If an [+ SQA]-NP is not in the scope of the durational adverbial, it is fully effective; if an [+ SQA]-NP is in the scope of the durational adverbial only a subset of (18a) – (18t) can contribute to the nondurative aspect, as shown in (24), in which the noun *glas* (glass) is taken as a count noun.

(24)	a. # dat glas	
	b. # Bertrand[13]	
	c. # het glas	(the glass)
	d. # (de) beide glazen	((the) both glasses)
	e. # de drie glazen	(the three glasses)
	f. ?de glazen	(the glasses)
	g. ?elk glas	(each glass)
Een uurlang brak hij	h. ?elk van de glazen	(each of the glasses)
(For an hour he broke)	i. ?alle glazen	(alle glasses)
	j. ?alles	(everything)
	k. ?de meeste glazen	(most of the glasses)
	l. # een glas	(a glass)
	m. ?sommige glazen	(some glasses)
	n. ?enkele glazen	(several glasses)
	o. ?enkele van de glazen	(some of the glasses)
	p. ?veel glazen	(many glasses)
	q. ?weinig glazen	(few glasses)
	r. # drie glazen	(three glasses)
	s. ?iets	(something
	t. # een glas whisky	(a glass of whisky)

[+ SQA]-NPs not influenced by their position in the sentential structure are indicated by the symbol # where # means that the repetition reading triggered by A # is always enforced. In other words, the single event reading is always excluded in the presence of a durational adverbial, whether the NP is in the scope of this adverbial or not. The absence of the symbol # indicates that it is possible to "escape from" a forced repetition reading because a single event reading is available. The question mark indicates that the resulting sentence is somewhat peculiar or even unacceptable.

The criterion for not putting a #-sign in front of the NPs in (24) is whether it is possible to have a reading in which not one single glass belonging to the intersection $A \cap X$ is necessarily broken more than once. Some of the sentences in (24) allow for a reading, even a sort of iterative reading, but only by extending the domain such that objects other than glasses are taken into account, giving a (rather tortuous) contrastive interpretation.

I cannot go into the many subtleties connected with the interpretation of (24a) – (24t) and their counterparts in which the NP is in frontposition having the durational adverbial in its scope. In the latter cases the NPs (18a) – (18t) all have a #-sign, the generic readings of some of them excepted. The subtleties in question have to do with the fact that the repetition can operate at the set-level or at the membership-level, or both. That is a sentence like *Both men crossed the street for hours* can pertain to a situation in which both men together crossed the street repeatedly, but it can also apply to iterated individual crossings.

As said I have no explanation for the scope differences. Possibly the explanation for the phenomenon that many [+SQA]-NPs from (18a) – (18t) loose their [+SQA]-feature in contexts like (24), is that their being in the scope of durational adverbials prohibits quantification over individual members of the intersection so that it is not possible to fix the cardinality of the intersection. This would explain why only those members of (18a) – (18t) are marked with the #-sign in (24) whose presupposition warrants the exact cardinality of $|A|$.

In the literature, the communis opinio nowadays seems to be that nondurativity is a structural property of sentences rather than a lexical feature. In Verkuyl (1972) I proposed that nondurativity is to be assigned to S (without the durational adverbial), after having argued in earlier work that it must be assigned to VP. My move from VP-level to S-level was prompted by the observation that the subject-NP plays a decisive role in the construction of the aspect, as shown by the difference between e.g. (8b) and (8d). Nevertheless, the combinatorial mechanism constructing the aspect can be said to operate repeatedly in a sentential structure, as can be shown with the help of (25), in which I assume an SOV-order for Dutch, the word order of a language being immaterial to the process of composition, as far as I can see. The combination of $[_{VP}NP^2 + V]$ leads to a nondurative aspect at the VP-level if NP^2 is [+SQA] and B is the proper lexically defined semantic element, which is necessary to bring about nondurativity. This operation is, in terms of the theory of generalized quantification, a functional application, in this case a Det_U AB-operation as described above, forming a new B, which in its turn enters into a Det_U AB-operation at the S-level.

(25)

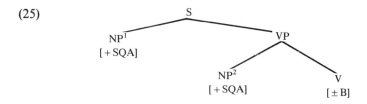

In other words, a structure like (25) has three opportunities to receive a durative interpretation: (a) B is not the appropriate feature; (b) NP^2 is [−SQA] as in (2a); (c) NP^2 is [+SQA], but NP^1 is [−SQA] as in *For hours nobody played that sonata.*

It is important to note that there is an asymmetry in the construction of the aspects reflected in (25). This asymmetry can be formulated as follows: (i) If the VP is durative, the subject-NP can never affect the aspect of the VP such that S becomes nondurative; (ii) if the VP is nondurative, the subject-NP can either keep this property unimpaired at S or it can change the aspect of the VP into a durative aspect at S. So, the role of the direct object and other complements of V in constructing the aspect seems different from the role of the subject. That is, *she* in (1a) *She walked* does not change the durative aspect of the VP into a nondurative one, whereas *a mile* in (1b) does have this effect.

4. ADD TO

In this section, I shall try to formally account for the notion ADD TO, as proposed in Verkuyl (1972; 1976). The basic idea of a nondurative closure is that a process of adding time particles, say intervals, to some interval which has already been generated can be cut off by the information labelled [+SQA]. Intuitively, this idea can be captured easily by comparing (1a) *She walked* with (1b) *She walked a mile.* In this case, the complex nondurative aspect in (1b) contains semantic information associated with *walk* and this information is present in both sentences. So, extending (1a) with *a mile* brings to a stop in (1b) what goes on indefinitely in (1a).

In Verkuyl (1978) it is argued that the meaning of verbs like *walk, drive,* and so on, can be associated with the concept of (homogeneously) proceeding in time. By doing this, one tries to account for the basic experience that time is flowing and that this experience can be accounted for by assuming that time is dense. Driving in a car is an event which takes time. While driving new time particles (say intervals) are added to what is behind us. The new time particles are added to a set of intervals which together constitute our drive. Any drive in this sense is experienced as dense. Nevertheless, we constantly switch to discreteness. Our proceeding in time can be counted by natural numbers, for example, in the case of natural days. So we are able to treat dense time as having a structure having gaps. By treating time as dense we proceed in terms of a structure isomorphic to the set of real numbers $\mathbb{R}$; by treating time discretely we proceed in terms of a less constrained structure, for example a structure isomorphic to $\mathbb{N}$ or possibly the set of integers $\mathbb{Z}$, where $\mathbb{N} \subset \mathbb{Z} \subset \mathbb{R}$. We shall write $\mathbb{N}^*$ to steer clear of the suggestion that the points embedded in $\mathbb{R}$ do necessarily have the same distance with respect to each other as is the case with $\mathbb{N}$. The addition of the asterisk to $\mathbb{N}$ (or $\mathbb{Z}$) has the effect of a more dynamic approach.

I think that it is important to realize that in our dealing with temporal phenomena in natural language $\mathbb{R}$ is not sufficient. Of course, the $\mathbb{N}$-structure is included, so to say, in $\mathbb{R}$-structure, but it is important to isolate these factors. The contraction principles I have in mind can be illustrated quite clearly by considering a situation in which a chess player moves his queen from d1 to d5. From the point of view of naive physics this move is dense: the queen can be shoven uninterruptedly from d1 to d5. From the point of view of chess positions, the move is discrete because the structure of the string d1, d2, d3, d4, d5 is isomorphic to the structure of the string 1, 2, 3, 4, 5 in $\mathbb{N}$. Important is that the basic elements, viz. the fields of the chess board, being points from a certain point of view, have an internal structure from other points of view. I shall call the phenomenon under consideration the $\mathbb{R} \rightarrow \mathbb{N}^*$-switch. Its main features are that subsets of a certain set can be contracted to (or treated as) points, and that the switch in orientation depends on the specific point of view of the speaker structuring the way in which he wants to talk about things and events. Mathematically, this idea comes very close to the so-called entier-function Ent having as its domain $\mathbb{R}$ and defined as follows: let p be an integer, then for all $x \in \mathbb{R}$ satisfying $p - 1 < x \le p$, the value $\text{Ent}(x) = p$ (Cf. Verkuyl 1978: 224ff; cf. also Kamp 1979 for time contraction).

Provisionally, the $\mathbb{R} \rightarrow \mathbb{N}^*$ – switch can be taken as an operation which assigns potential evaluation points $\Diamond S$ to $\mathbb{R}$-intervals, as sketched in (26). Following Oversteegen (1980) and Oversteegen & Verkuyl (1985), I assume a set S_T of possible and actual points of speech which function as points of evaluation with respect to $\mathbb{R}$-intervals E in a tense structure, where Reichenbach's point of reference R is taken as a possible point of speech and hence belongs to S_T. In (27) the Reichenbachian tense structure of (1a) *She walked* is given to illustrate the point in question. In short, assigning the past tense to the tenseless *She walk* amounts to converting (26) into (27).

(26)

She walk

(27)

$$\text{---}|\text{---}\bullet\text{---}\frac{E}{}|\text{-------------------}\bullet\text{---}\qquad\text{She walked}$$

$$\qquad\qquad S'\qquad\qquad\qquad\qquad\qquad S$$

E is represented as an interval. Tense structure (27) says that there is a point
in time S′ earlier than S at which *She is walking* is true. S′ is a possible point
of speech serving as a point of evaluation with respect to the truth of the
E described as *She is walking* (now = S′), and S is the point of speech which
is also a point of evaluation, with respect to (1a) itself. I assume that the
$\mathbb{R} \to \mathbb{N}^*$-switch generates a $\Diamond S$ which is actualized as S′ by adding the
tense structure to the tenseless nondurative sentence *She walk*. I shall read-
just some of the concepts introduced here in proceeding by assigning internal structure to E.

In the remainder of this section, I shall present some notions which may
lead to a precise characterization of what I mean with the ADD TO-operator
associated with the main verb of a sentence, assuming that the assignment
of tense must be incorporated in the treatment of aspect. Firstly, E sym-
bolizes a tenseless proposition and is represented by an interval I which is
a member of the set of intervals **I**. Furthermore it is necessary to define for
all subintervals X, Y of an interval:

(28)   Definition: $X < Y \leftrightarrow \forall x \in X\ \forall y \in Y(x < y)$

From this definition follows: $X < Y \to X \cap Y = \emptyset$. That is, if X precedes
Y, there is no overlap between X and Y. We can now assign substructure
to a certain interval:

(29)   Definition: *Periodisation of E*
P_E is a periodisation of E if P_E is a non-empty indexed
family $\{I_n\}_{n \in \mathbb{N}^*}$ of non-empty subsets of E, s.t.:

(i) $\bigcup_{n \in \mathbb{N}^*} I_n = E$

(ii) if $i < j$, then $I_i < I_j$

The basic idea of the ADD TO-operator associated with a Verb in Verkuyl
(1972) is that it brings about a periodisation of the E-interval introduced by
the Verb. Suppose that we associated with a Verb a semantic element, say
[+ ADD TO], which is part of the interpretation. Then we can say that
[+ ADD TO] can be interpreted in terms of the recursive application of a
successor function s, as defined in (30).

(30)   a.   Let I be the set of intervals and T be the set of time points.
Then $\| + \text{ADD TO}\| = $ the function s: $I \to I$ defined by: if
$I = (a, b)$, then $\exists c(s(I) = (b, c))$, and if a, b, c $\in$ T, then
$a < b < c$.

So s brings about a periodisation. That is, starting from an initial interval I_0 s generates a periodisation by taking $I_{n+1} = s(I_n)$. One can visualize the effect of this function, as in (30b), the right-hand side of which satisfies (29) with respect to the interval (a, c).[14]

(30)   b.

Given the fact that an E (if bounded) can be structured as a (finite) periodisation, we can make use of some set-theoretical properties of indexed families which do the job. In order to obtain the result we wish to have, we have to stipulate that S_T is a subset of a set S_{EV} of potential points of evaluation $\Diamond S$ some of which are actually taken as a point of evaluation by the tense of the sentence in question. This can be visualized as in (31):

(31)

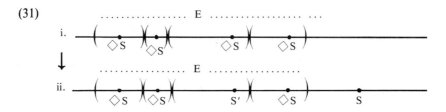

Our tense structure (27) returns in (31ii): one of the $\Diamond S$-points is replaced by S' and the point of speech S is added. So, (31ii) is a more elaborated version of (27) because it gives information about the internal structure of E.

How do we obtain (31ii)? Let us assume that (31i) represents sentence (1a) *She walked*, as far as its temporal structure without tense is concerned. The (arbitrarily chosen) periods constituting E (or part of E) are generated by the [+ ADD TO] feature associated with *walk*. Definition (29) guarantees set-theoretically that there is a function designating points that can be said to represent a period. That is, from every subinterval $J_i \in P_E$ one can pick out an arbitrarily chosen point which we call the representative r_i of J_i. The principle that warrants the existence of suchlike points is the Axiom of Choice which says that if E is a non-empty collection of non-empty subsets (in this case, the intervals generated by s), there is a function f assigning to each set J_i from E an element $f(J_i)$ such that $f(J_i) \in J_i$. The name r_i is short for $f(J_i)$. It follows that s creates a set of representatives r, which I shall call R_E. So, with each P_E there is associated a set of representatives R_E. In (31i) the representatives are represented by a dot.

We can now define a function $\alpha: R_E \to S_{EV}$ such that $\alpha(r_i) = \Diamond S_i$, where $i \in \mathbb{N}^*$ and such that if $x < y$, then $\alpha(x) < \alpha(y)$; so α is order preserving. This function accounts for the homogeneity of durative events as defined in Verkuyl (1978: 224ff.) and it introduces potential points of evaluation preparing, as it were, the E for its actualization in real time. In (31i) the result of applying α is made visible by the images $\diamond$S of the dots.

Summarizing, if a Verb is characterized by an [+ ADD TO]-features its interpretation is an unrestricted s which is supplied by α which introduces potential points of evaluation. Together they provide for the effect of homogeneity. The past tense in (31ii) selects one point of evaluation from the set S_T. This point S' plays a role in the tense structure, which also contains the point of speech S. In this way the interaction between the durative aspect contributing (31i) and past tense selecting (or designating) S' and introducing S, can be accounted for such that the idea of homogeneity of the event in question can be given a reasonably precise form.

5. [[+ ADD TO] + [+ SQA]]

In this section I shall present the combinatorial mechanism leading to the nondurative aspect in the VP of (25). It is reasonable to think of restrictions on the ADD TO-function s. I shall discuss two options. The first option is to assume that there is just one period due to restrictions on s. So we need a restriction on s of the following kind:

(32)   Let I be the set of intervals. Then the (restricted) function
        $s_E : I \rightarrow I$ is defined by: if I = (a, b), then $\forall c(s_E(I) = (b, c)$ and b = c).

That is, s produces just one interval, so P_E contains one member having one representative so that α generates just one potential point of evaluation. This would lead to the following characterization of the nondurative aspect at the VP-level:

(33)   Given (29), there is exactly one $\diamond$S $\in S_{EV}$ satisfying the condition
        that for all $J_i \in P_E$, $\alpha(r_i) = \diamond S_i$, and $|P_E| = 1$.

The virtue of this approach is that nondurativity can now be seen as a restrictive principle. However, the restriction of s to just one period seems too arbitrary: one would expect that the restriction on s is determined by the specific information carried by a constituent marked as [+ SQA], but actually this restriction was simply stipulated. So, I consider this option as inferior to the second option which does take into account the quantificational information conveyed by [+ SQA].

The basic idea underlying the second option says that $A^{\#}$ determines how many times the ADD TO-operation may proceed. The s function "is fed" periods as it were and $A^{\#}$ determines how many periods at the most can be fed to s. For example, in *He ate three sandwiches*, where $|A| = 3$, the restricted function can produce three subintervals of E (in each of which he ate one sandwich), or two intervals (one in which he ate one sandwich and one in which he ate two sandwiches) or just one interval (in which he ate them all together). Essential to this analysis is that one is not sure which choice the restricted function makes, but one is sure that it makes a choice and that the event thus necessarily terminates.

I shall now formalize this idea. Let us therefore consider (34): (34a) covers the lower part of (25); in (34b) the process of combining NP and V by functional application into a VP is given:

(34)   a.   b.

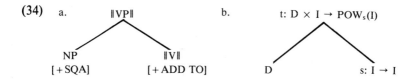

The successor function s (contributed by V) turns (at the VP-level) into a terminative function t not only having I as its domain but also a second domain, say D, supplied by the NP marked as [+SQA]. The co-domain of t is not I, but the set of initial segments $POW_w(I)$. I shall first explain the precise nature of D, and then characterize the co-domain of t, before defining the terminative function t itself.

D is not $A^\#$ but rather a collection of sets determined by the cardinality of $A^\#$. Given a finite set V with k members, the number $\varrho(k)$ of possible configurations p making up a partition of V is finite. $\varrho(k)$ applies to the number of ways in which a natural number k can be written as the sum of natural numbers. The finiteness of $\varrho(k)$ is an essential feature of the present analysis: we must be sure that our terminative function t is given a finite domain. Applied to an $A^\#$, having three members, say a, b, and c, $\varrho(3) = 3$, viz. (i) $1+1+1$; (ii) $1+2$; (iii) 3. The plus-sign in the number partition corresponds to event-splitting. So $1+1+1$ pertains to three singleton sets of entities each being involved by t in one of the three subevents of E, $1+2$ to two sets (one a singleton and the other one having two members), each of the sets involved by t in one of the two subevents of E, and 3 pertains to one set involved in one event. In this way of partitioning a set, order does not count, so $1+2 = 2+1$. Let $\langle x, y \rangle$ represent an ordered pair, then we can say that in the present approach, there is no difference between $\langle \{a\}, \langle b, c \rangle \rangle$ and $\langle \langle b, c \rangle, \{a\} \rangle$, or even between $\langle \{a\}, \langle b, c \rangle \rangle$ and $\langle \{b\}, \langle c, a \rangle \rangle$.

It is easy to see that the cardinality of the most elaborated configuration p is always k. So, it follows that if t operates on one of the $A^\#$-configurations that are determined by the number partition yielded by $\varrho(k)$, the domain of t is finite. Given a set marked [+SQA], i.e. a set with a finite cardinality, we know that there is a set $P_{A^\#}$ (D in (34b)) of all $A^\#$-configurations p each of which can be chosen by the function t. In the case of $A^\# = \{a, b, c\}$, $P_{A^\#} = \{\{\{a\}, \{b\}, \{c\}\}, \{\{a, b\}, \{c\}\}, \{\{b, c\}, \{a\}\}, \{\{a, c\}, \{b\}\},$

$\{\{a, b, c\}\}$. The cardinality of each $p \in P_{A^{\#}}$ is finite, because the cardinality of the p's in a $P_{A^{\#}}$ ranges from 1 to k.

As to the co-domain of t, one can observe that the operation combining $[+ADD\ TO]$ and $[+SQA]$ is rather complicated because t requires a collection $P_{A^{\#}}$ of sets p, whereas t actually operates on a given p chosen from the collection. This problem can be solved by not taking I as co-domain but rather a higher level set $POW_s(I)$ as defined in (35).

(35) $POW_s(I) = \{ J \epsilon POW(I) |\ J = \{I_0\} \vee J = \{I_0, I_1\} \vee$
$$J = \{I_0, I_1, I_2\} \vee \ldots \vee$$
$$J = \{I_0, I_1, I_2, \ldots, I_{k-1}\}\},$$
$$\text{where } I_{i+1} = s(I_i)$$

It is easy to see why $POW_s(I)$ is chosen as the co-domain of t if one looks back to diagram (31ii), where E is a set of intervals I, due to the application of (29): E can be defined as belonging to $POW_s(I)$.

Given the two domains $P_{A^{\#}}$ and I and the co-domain as defined in (35), we can now try to define the terminative function t. The function t has as its domain the Cartesian product of the sets $P_{A^{\#}}$ and I. What t must do, is to operate on an arbitrarily chosen member p from $P_{A^{\#}}$ producing the internal structure of the p which is selected. This is a configuration having as many subevents I as there are members of the set p which is (arbitrarily) chosen by t. Suppose that t (without our knowing so) operates on one of the $1+2$-configurations of $P_{A^{\#}}$, say $\{\{a\}, \{b, c\}\}$. Then, t will produce two periods I at the most, because the partition in question does not "feed" periods any longer. It is important to realize that we never know which partition is taken, though we are sure that one is taken. This accounts for the comfortable vagueness associated with sentences like *He ate three sandwiches*, as advocated by Kempson and Cormack (1981). The function t is defined such that one can be sure that the s inherent to V comes to a stop, because one can be sure that $|p|$ is finite, but one does not know which p is taken from $P_{A^{\#}}$.

(36) Definition: *terminative function t:*
$\|[[+ADD\ TO] + [+SQA]]\| =$
the function t: $P_{A^{\#}} \times I \rightarrow POW_s(I)$ s.t.:

$t(p, I_0) = \{I_0, I_1, \ldots I_{|p|-1}\}$, where $|p| \leq |A^{\#}|$.

Recall that the durative aspect in cases like (1a) *She walked* was attributed to both the successor function s producing intervals and the function α producing potential evaluation points. Our analysis makes it possible to characterize the nondurative aspect in terms of the combination of t and α, so that each subinterval of E being produced, has its own $\diamond S$, due to $\alpha(r_i) = \diamond S_i$, suggesting some homogeneity even in terminative events. However, one can also define the nondurative aspect in terms of (33) dropping the condition that $|P_E| = 1$, requiring along the line of Oversteegen and Verkuyl (1985) that α is a constant function. I leave this matter open for further research.

Finally, let us consider the upper part of diagram (25). As said, if the VP is durative, a subject $[+SQA]$-NP cannot accomplish a nondurative aspect at the S-level: *she walks* is durative even though *she* pertains to a $A^{\#}$. But what about a nondurative VP subjected to (36) and what about intransitive verbs like *explode, stumble, crash*, etc. and expressions like *be photographed*?

I think that it is reasonable to assume that every time a predicate — either simple via V in the lexicon — or compositionally formed at the level of VP or any other V-projection it is subjected to the $[+ADD\ TO]$-operation. So I assume that s can operate on the output of (36), thereby generating new intervals E, whose internal structure is determined either by the lexicon or by (36) or some other compositional function. To make clear what I have in mind, I shall illustrate this assumption with the help of (37):

(37)   a.   The bomb exploded
        b.   Three bombs exploded
        c.   Bombs exploded

It is clear that (37a) pertains to just one event, but this is not due to *explode*: (37b) can pertain to three events, though this is not necessary at all. So, the number of events 'explode' in (37) is determined by the $A^{\#}$ of the NPs in question. That is, s can operate on the VP *explode* starting to indefinitely generate intervals as in (37c), but the combination of the VP, tense and the subject-NP turns s into t in (37a) and (37b). What makes *explode* non-durative seems to be a lexical specification "petrifying" the internal structure of its E (Cf. Verkuyl 1980: 146). The same can apply to *be photographed*. In the case of VPs like *eat three sandwiches* in (38a) the petrification is due to the effect of (36):

(38)   a.   John ate three sandwiches.
        b.   Prisoners ate three sandwiches (in this old prison).

This nondurative VP is construed by (36), but its nondurativity can be lost by a $[-SQA]$-NP. In this case s can be said to operate again, but now at a higher level than as defined at the VP-level in (30). In (38) it is E rather than its subintervals that is taken as a counting unit forming a set of initial segments of type E. So, technically we must assume a terminative function t' in (38a) having as its domain the Cartesian product $P_{A^{\#}} \times POW_s(I')$, if one takes into account the levels of internal structure of intervals embedded in each other. I think that we can also assume a simplifying principle saying that one can maintain s and t as defined in (30) and (36), respectively. This principle seems to operate in the treatment of nouns like *hour, day*, and *week*. A week can be taken as a set of sets of hours, but one can also treat *hour* and *week* as belonging to the same type, directly pertaining to intervals. So, though there is some difference between the VP-functions s and t on the one hand, and their counterparts s ′ and t ′ at the S-level on the other hand, I think they are similar in a fundamental way.

6. CONCLUDING REMARKS

This account of the combinatorial mechanism constructing the nondurative aspect is very much is accordance with the fact that modifiers like *one by one, together*, or *in groups* can be taken as restrictions on the choice of the configurations p by t. That is, a sentence *The children were photographed one by one* picks out the $P_{A^#}$-configuration p having the same cardinality as $A^#$.

It is interesting to compare sentences like (39a) and (39b):

(39) a. The children were not photographed
      b. None of the children was photographed

Sentence (39a) is durative according to (20b). As observed in Verkuyl (1972), *not* blocks the construction of the nondurative aspect. This can be explained by assuming that *not* prevents members of A = ‖child‖ to be a member of the set B = ‖be photographed‖. In other words, *not* prevents $A^# = A \cap B$ from having members so that t cannot operate at all. The same applies to (39b) by definition (18v). Note also that sentences like (40)

(40)   John was eating three sandwiches

which have a Progressive tense form, can be analyzed as containing an operator *Prog* which postpones the application of t.

The present approach differs from many other proposals with respect to distributive and collective readings in that the Verb rather than the NPs is taken as the principal element in the analysis. Consider (41):

(41) a. 600 Dutch firms have 5000 American computers (Scha 1981)
      b. Three boys saw two girls (Gil 1982)
      c. Three men lifted a piano (Link 1984)
      d. Two examiners marked six scripts (Kempson & Cormack (1982)

All sentences in (41) have the structure NP_1-V-NP_2. The strategy mostly followed is to focus on the Cartesian product of the denotata of NP_1 and NP_2. By doing this, one seems not to be able to escape from the structures found in the real world (or a mental picture thereof). The differentiation between such structures corresponds to the differentiation between readings.

In my opinion, the treatment of atemporal phenomena in both linguistics and in logical grammar has largely been dominating the concept formation in these fields. The theory of quantification as developed by Frege and his followers and the linguistic treatment of quantificational expressions were predominantly atemporal until recently. Even though a lot of energy has been devoted to temporal phenomena such as temporal location, tense, aspect and so on, in the last twenty years, it appears very difficult to incomfortably take temporality as a mental point of departure. This explains the fact that the discussion about distributive, collective, and cumulative is neither systematically related to the notion of event-splitting nor to the notion of vagueness, as it should be. Scha (1981: 501), for example, assigns at least ten readings to (41a), Gil (1982) four classes of interpretations to (41b), as Link (1984) does to (41c), reducing them to three. The present analysis — though quite different as to the representational machinery — is more congenial to Kempson & Cormack's wish to drastically reduce the number of logical forms of sentences like (41d).

In the present approach it is the temporal V which is central to the quantificational interpretation rather than the a-temporal NPs, as illustrated by $A^{\#}$-configurations like $ac + d$, where the $+$-sign indicates the structuring of the universe U into events in which participants occur rather than into participants which constitute an event. That is, basic to my approach is the wish to treat the notion of event as superordinate to the notion of atemporal entities occurring in an event. This makes it possible to analyse (41c) in terms of an event which is actualized by making a choice (unknown to the addressee of (41c)) from a set L of possible lift-relations between members of a set of three men and a member of the set of piano's, where $L = \{ \{ \langle 3m, p \rangle \}, \{ \langle 2m, p \rangle, \langle 1m, p \rangle \}, \{ \langle 1m, p \rangle, \langle 1m, p \rangle, \langle 1m, p \rangle \} \}$.

In my opinion, it is linguistically ill-motivated to say that (41c) has as many readings as L has. Only if it is necessary to look into L, as conversation sometimes requires, are we entitled to look for a specific member of L by modification. Perhaps this is a terminological issue in the sense that a lot of people use readings where they should speak about possible actualisations (in a model), but if one speaks about sentences like (41c) in terms of ambiguity presented as a cake which can be cut into n readings, the danger is that one fails to see that it is essentially vagueness what is expressed by sentences like (41). The function t has been proposed to precisely account for this fundamental vagueness which is one of the essential features of natural language, not to be repaired either by the language user or — at a meta-level — by the grammarian.

BIBLIOGRAPHY

Bach, E.: (1980), 'Tenses and aspects as functions on verb-phrases'. In: Rohrer (ed.) *Time, tense and quantifiers*. Tübingen, 19–39.
Barwise, J., & Cooper, R.: (1981), 'Generalized Quantifiers and Natural Language'. In: *Linguistics and Philosophy* 4, 159–219.
Bennett, M.: (1981), 'Of Tense and Aspect: one analysis'. In: Tedeschi & Zaenen, 13–29.

Bennett, M., & Partee, B.: (1978), 'Toward the logic of tense and aspect in English'. IULC. Bloomington, Indiana.

Benthem, J. van: (1983a), 'Questions about quantifiers'. In: *Journal of Symbolic Logic'* 49, 443 – 466.

Benthem, J. van: (1983b), 'Determiners and Logic'. In: *Linguistics and Philosophy* 6, 447–478.

Bunt, H.C.: (1981), *The Formal Semantics of Mass Terms.* Amsterdam.

Carlson, L.: (1981): 'Aspect and quantification'. In: Tedeschi & Zaenen, 31–64.

Dahl, O.: (1981), 'On the definition of the Telic-Atelic (Bounded – Nonbounded) Distinction. In: Tedeschi & Zaenen, 79–90.

Dowty, D.R.: (1979), *Word meaning and Montague grammar.* Reidel vol. 7. Dordrecht/London.

Dowty, D.R.: (1982), 'Tenses, time adverbs and compositional semantic theory'. *Linguistics and Philosophy* 5, 23–55.

Gil, D.: (1982), 'Quantifier Scope, Linguistic Variation and Natural Language Semantics'. In: *Linguistics and Philosophy* 5, 421–472.

Heinämäki, O.: (1983), 'Aspect in Finnish'. In: C. de Groot & H. Tommola (eds.), *Aspect Bound. A voyage into the realm of Germanic, Slavonic and Finno-Ugrian aspectology.* Dordrecht, 153–178.

Hoeksema, J.: (1983), 'Plurality and Conjunction'. In: A.G.B. ter Meulen (ed.), *Studies in Modeltheoretic Semantics.* GRASS 1, 63–83.

Johnson, M.R.: (1981), 'A Unified Temporal Theory of Tense and Aspect'. In: Tedeschi & Zaenen, 145–175.

Jong, F.M.G. de: (1983), 'Numerals as Determiners'. In: H. Bennis & W.U.S. van Lessen Kloeke (eds.), *Linguistics in the Netherlands.* Dordrecht, 105–114.

Jong, F.M.G. de, & Verkuyl, H.J.: (1985), 'Generalized Quantifiers: the Properness of their strength'. In: J. van Benthem & A. ter Meulen (eds.), *Generalized Quantifiers: Theory and Applications.* GRASS 4, Dordrecht.

Kabakčiev, K.: (to appear), 'The article and the Aorist/Imperfect Distinction in Bulgarian: an analysis based on cross-language 'aspect' parallelism'. Dpt of Foreign Languages Univ. of Pleven.

Kamp, H.: (1979), 'Events, instants, and temporal reference'. In: R. Bäuerle, U. Egli, & A. von Stechow (eds.), *Semantics from Different Points of View.* Berlin etc., 376–416.

Kempson, R.M., & Cormack, A.: (1981), 'Ambuigity and Quantification'. In: *Linguistics and Philosophy* 4, 259–309.

Link, G.: (to appear), 'Plural'. In: D. Wunderlich & A. von Stechow (eds.), *Handbook of Semantics.*

Meulen, Alice ter: (1983), 'The Representation of Time in Natural Language. In: Alice ter Meulen (ed.), *Studies in Modeltheoretic Semantics.* Dordrecht, 177–191.

Milsark, G.: (1977), 'Toward an Explanation of Certain Peculiarities of the Existential Construction in English'. In: *Linguistic Analysis* 3, 1–29.

Mourelatos, A.P.D.: (1981), 'Events, Processes and States'. In: Tedeschi & Zaenen, 191–211.

Oversteegen, E.: (1980), 'Tijd aan banden'. Doctoraalscriptie Utrecht.

Oversteegen, E., & Verkuyl, H.J.: (1984), 'De temporele zinsstructuur van het Nederlands: twee tijdsbanden'. In: *Glot* 7, 257–297.

Platzack, C.: (1979), *The Semantic Interpretation of Aspect and Aktionsarten. A Study of Internal Time Reference in Swedish.* Dordrecht.

Scha, R. (1981), 'Distributive, Collective and Cumulative Quantification' In: J.A.G. Groenendijk, T.M.V. Janssen & M.B.J. Stokhof (eds.), *Formal Methods in the study of Language.* Amsterdam, 483–512.

Tedeschi, P.J., & Zaenen, A. eds.: (1981), *Syntax and Semantics 14; Tense and Aspect.* New York, etc.

Thijsse, E.: (1983), 'On Some Proposed Universals of Natural Language'. In: A.G.B. ter

Meulen (ed.), *Studies in Modeltheoretic Semantics*. GRASS 1, 19–36.

Verkuyl, H.J.: (1972), *On the Compositional Nature of the Aspects*. Dordrecht.

Verkuyl, H.J.: (1976), 'Interpretive rules and the Description of the Aspects'. In: *Foundations of Language* 14, 471–503.

Verkuyl, H.J.: (1978), 'Thematic relations and the Semantic Representation of Verbs Expressing Change'. In: *Studies in Language* 2, 199–233.

Verkuyl, H.J.: (1980), 'On the Proper Classification of Events and Verb Phrases'. In: *Theoretical Linguistics* 7, 137–148.

Verkuyl, H.J.: (1981), 'Numerals and Quantifiers in X̄-Syntax and their Semantic Interpretation'. In: J.A.G. Groenendijk, T.M.V. Janssen & M.B.J. Stokhof (eds.), *Formal Methods in the study of Language*. Amsterdam, 567–599.

Vet, J.P.: (1976), 'Aspecten: een kwestie van tijd'. In: *Spektator* 6, 137–155.

Vet, J.P.: (1980), *Temps, Aspects et adverbes de temps en français contemporain*. Geneve.

Vlach, F.: (1981), 'The Semantics of the Progressive'. In: Tedeschi & Zaenen, 271–292.

Zwarts, F.: (1981), 'Negatief polaire uitdrukkingen'. In: *Glot* 4, 35–132.

Zwarts, F.: (1981), 'Determiners: A Relational Perspective'. In: A.G.B. ter Meulen (ed.), *Studies in Modeltheoretic Semantics*, GRASS 1, 37–62.

NOTES

1.   In Verkuyl (1972) I adopted the so-called generative semantics variant of transformational generative grammar to deal with durativity and nondurativity, although I indicated there that the (now outdated) opposition between generative and interpretive semantics did not really bear on the issue, as shown in Verkuyl (1976) and in Platzack (1979).

2.   In Verkuyl (1972) I used the term 'Specified Quantity of X'. In view of the custom in the theory of generalized quantification to indicate the denotation of the head of the NP as A, I will replace X by A.

3.   In this paper my object language is Dutch. As there is a considerable overlap between Dutch and English as to the temporal properties of durative and nondurative sentences and with regard to quantified NPs I shall give my examples in English if there is no particular reason to present the Dutch equivalents.

4.   Our real world knowledge with respect to a sentence like (i) *He ate a sandwich for an hour* says that it (normally) takes some minutes to eat a sandwich. Consequently, we force ourselves into either a forced repetition or into stretching in order to solve the tension we feel with assigning a single event reading to (i). Note that even though one substitutes *for two minutes* for *for an hour* there remains a tension which is absent in *He ate for two minutes* (or *for an hour*). So it is this tension which constitutes the linguistically interesting property. If *he* in (i) refers to a mouse and *a sandwich* to a sandwich intended for humans, then our problem of assigning a single event reading to (i) is usually solved by interpreting (i) as a sentence having a progressive form. If *he* is a giant, then the enforced repetition reading is strongly favoured. These examples can be taken as illustrating that the language user is normally very ingenious in finding ways out in order to maintain communication.

5.   Dowty (1979, 1980); Bennett (1981); Carlson (1981); Dahl (1981); Johnson (1981), Kucera (1981), Mourelatos (1981), Vlach (1981); Ter Meulen (1983), Vet (1976; 1980) among many others. Unfortunately some of these proposals backslide into the Vendler quadripartition (states, activities, accomplishments, achievements) which is basically lexical semantics, that is, a description of real world knowledge (or a mental picture thereof). The thesis underlying the bipartition 'durative – nondurative' in Verkuyl (1972; 1976) and in this paper is that it is necessary for linguists to treat aspect at the level of structural semantics rather than at the level of lexical semantics (cf. Dahl 1981).

6. In languages having overt case and lacking articles the combinatorial mechanisms are, of course, quite different but semantically they can be reduced to the same principles. In Finnish, for example, aspectual difference can be expressed by a verb together with a partitive object (durative) and together with an accusative object (nondurative). Cf. Heinämäki (1983); Kabakciev (to appear) for Bulgarian.

7. Cf. Barwise & Cooper 1981; Van Benthem 1983a, 1983b; Hoeksema 1983; De Jong 1983; De Jong & Verkuyl 1985; Thijsse 1983; Zwarts 1981; 1983.

8. It is not my purpose to propose a representation fitting in a formal representational language such as Intensional Logic or Gallin's Ty2 or Logical Form of generative grammar. In this paper I restrict myself to a set theoretical representation only.

9. The standard interpretation of the universal quantifier in logical literature is not based upon the most regular use of *all* in natural language, but on its conditional use $\forall x[P(x) \rightarrow Q(x)]$ where $\|P\| \subset \|Q\|$ by induction or hypothesis.

In the literature, the condition with respect to the cardinality of A can be given either as a part of the truthconditions or as a presupposition. In the former case Q is taken as a total function (e.g. in Zwarts 1983), in the latter case as a partial function (e.g. De Jong 1983; De Jong & Verkuyl 1985). In this paper I shall follow the latter option.

10. The translation of the Dutch material into English is not without problems. For example, the Dutch *sommige* is to be translated as the weak nonuniversal sm (cf. Milsark (1977: 7). Note that the Dutch singular definite article has two forms: the neutral *het* (as in *het kind* (the child) and the masculine and feminine *de* (as in *de man* (the man) and *de vrouw* (the woman). Recall that this paper treats the Dutch cases. Most of the definitions in (18) can be found in the works mentioned in footnote 7.

11. In regular set theory the cardinality of a certain finite set V is a function | | assigning to each set V a natural number, i.e. the number of elements constituting V. So $|V| = n$. To extend the application of [+SQA] to mass nouns one could appeal to the so-called ensemble theory as proposed in Bunt (1981) in which the basic relation is $\subseteq$ rather than ϵ, the equivalent of cardinality being a measure function | | which applied to an ensemble V yields $|V| = \langle n, u \rangle$, where the function value consists of a rational number and the name of the unit which is part of a measuring dimension (length, volume, duration, etc.).

12. In Verkuyl (1981: 589) the NP *these three children* was represented as:
$\lambda P\Theta A[\lambda P[\forall x[P(x) \rightarrow child'(x)] \& |P| = 3](A) \& P(A)]$.

13. *Bertrand* is the name of a certain glass owned by my neighbour. In this case and in the regular use of the proper name I follow B&C (1981: 174) by taking it as a principal ultrafilter at the NP-level.

14. I remain neutral with respect to the question of whether (30) produces open or closed or closed-open or open-closed intervals, though I am inclined to assume the last option.

Chapter 5

Noun Phrase Interpretation and Type-Shifting Principles

Barbara H. Partee

0. INTRODUCTION

The goal of this paper is to attempt a resolution of the apparent conflict between two approaches to noun phrase (NP) interpretation, one being Montague's uniform treatment of NP's as generalized quantifiers and the other,
argued for by a variety of authors both before and after Montague, distinguishing among referring, predicative, and quantificational NP's (or uses
of NP's). I believe that the most important insights of both sides are basically correct and mutually compatible. To try to show this, I will draw on and
extend the idea of general type-shifting principles, argued for in Partee and
Rooth (1983), together with the idea of type-driven translation developed
by Klein and Sag (1985). I will draw heavily throughout on the many recent
studies of model-theoretic properties of various generalized quantifiers and
determiners, especially the work of Barwise and Cooper and of van Benthem. I believe that these tools can take us a good way toward explaining
the diversity of NP interpretations on the basis of general principles relating
syntax to semantics plus particular semantic properties of individual determiners, nouns, and NP-taking predicates.

I will retain from Montague's approach the requirement of a systematic
category-to-type correspondence, but allow each category to correspond to
a family of types rather than just a single type.[1] For an extensional
sublanguage I propose basic NP types e ("referential"), $\langle e, t \rangle$ ("predicative"), and $\langle \langle e, t \rangle, t \rangle$ ("quantificational"). While this last, the type of
generalized quantifiers, is the most complex, it is also the most general; we
can argue that all NP's have meanings of this type, while only some have
meanings of types e and/or $\langle e, t \rangle$. Part of our task will be to see to what
extent we can find general principles for predicting from the generalized
quantifier interpretation of a given NP what possible e-type and/or $\langle e, t \rangle$-
type interpretations it will have. This enterprise turns out to shed new light
on some old puzzles, such as the semantics of singular definite NP's like *the
king*, which turn out to be interpretable in all three types but with slightly
different presuppositional requirements in each.

Opening up the issue of type-shifting principles and attempting to investigate them systematically also turns out to suggest a new perspective on

the copula *be* and on the determiners *a* and *the*; I will suggest that this perspective may offer some help in explaining why certain semantic "functors" may be encoded either lexically or grammatically or not explicitly marked at all in different natural languages.

In sections 1 and 2 below I review a variety of proposals for interpreting various kinds of NP's and some of the evidence for the claim that there are NP interpretations of all three types mentioned above. The main proposals for type-shifting principles are the subject of section 3. Section 4 deals with the "Williams puzzle" introduced at the end of section 2; the proposed solution exemplifies the possibility of highly language specific type-shifting rules in contrast to the more general principles described in section 3. The paper concludes with a brief sketch of some possible implications of the perspective advanced here for the treatment of English *be* in section 5.

1. ALTERNATIVE TREATMENTS OF NP'S: SOME EXAMPLES

I begin by reviewing alternative interpretations for a number of different kinds of NP's, contrasting Montague's treatment with others that can be found in the literature. These are summarized in Table 1; comments follow.

Table 1.
MG Treatment of NP's and alternatives

NP	Translation	Type
(1) John	MG: $\lambda P[P(j)]$	$\langle\langle e, t\rangle, t\rangle$
	j	e
(2) he_n	MG: $\lambda P[P(x_n)]$	$\langle\langle e, t\rangle, t\rangle$
	x_n	e
(3) every man	MG: $\lambda P[\forall x[man'(x) \rightarrow P(x)]]$	$\langle\langle e, t\rangle, t\rangle$
(4) the man	MG: $\lambda P[\exists x[\forall y[man'(y) \leftrightarrow y = x] \& P(x)]]$	$\langle\langle e, t\rangle, t\rangle$
	(i) $\iota x[man'(x)]$	e
	(ii) $\lambda x[man'(x) \& \forall y[man'(y) \rightarrow y = x]]$	$\langle e, t\rangle$
(5) a man	MG: $\lambda P[\exists x[man'(x) \& P(x)]]$	$\langle\langle e, t\rangle, t\rangle$
	(i) man'	$\langle e, t\rangle$
	(ii) Kamp-Heim: x_i	e
	cond: $man'(x_i)$, x_i "new"	
(6) dogs	(i) Chierchia: $\cap$ dog'	e
	(ii) Carlson, in effect: $\lambda P[P(\cap dog')]$	$\langle\langle e, t\rangle, t\rangle$
	(iii) dog'	$\langle e, t\rangle$

Consider first the first three NP's in the table, *John, he_n*, and *every man*. One of Montague's best-known contributions to semantics was to show how these and other NP's could be given a uniform semantic type, by taking the type of all NP's to be $\langle\langle e, t\rangle, t\rangle$.[2] The fruitfulness of this idea is well-attested by now, and there are independent reasons for wanting to analyze at least some occurrences of proper names as generalized quantifiers, for instance when they occur in conjunctions like *John and every woman* and perhaps when they occur as antecedents of "bound variable pronouns".[3] But otherwise it would be more natural to treat proper names and singular pronouns as individual constants and variables respectively; this is indeed the more traditional view. Partee and Rooth (1983), in a discussion which focuses mainly on type assignments to extensional and intensional verbs, argue for a modification of Montague's strategy of assigning to all members of a given syntactic category the "highest" type needed for any of them. We proposed there that (i) each basic expression is lexically assigned the *simplest* type adequate to capture its meaning; (ii) there are general type-lifting rules that provide additional higher-type meanings for expressions, so that the uniform higher-type meanings Montague posited for a given syntactic category will indeed be *among* the available meanings for all expressions of that category; and (iii) there is a general processing strategy of trying lowest types first, using higher types only when they are required in order to combine meanings by available compositional rules. (For example, *John* would have to be "lifted" from j to $\lambda P[P(j)]$ to interpret the conjunction *John and every woman*.) According to that proposal, *John* and he_n would have basic interpretations of type e, and the interpretations Montague assigned to them would be predictably available by way of a general "lifting" rule. *Every man*, however, would have only the generalized quantifier-type interpretation. This dual treatment of proper names and pronouns is one piece of the more general picture we will develop here.

In the case of definite descriptions like *the man*, there are of course many issues of pragmatics to worry about that affect the question of what belongs to the semantic content of such expressions. What I want to do is consider several possible interpretations of different types and see whether they can be related by means of general type-shifting principles; if so, that might relieve us of the burden of trying to decide which is the "right" interpretation – perhaps they all are. One alternative to Montague's generalized quantifier interpretation of *the man* is the iota-operator analysis given in (4i), of type e. The iota-operator combines with an open sentence to give an entity-denoting expression, denoting the unique satisfier of that open sentence if there is just one, and failing to denote otherwise. (This interpretation could also be "lifted" to a generalized quantifier interpretation different from Montague's, agreeing with that given by Barwise and Cooper (1981).) Less familiar but at least implicit in some discussions is the possibility of a predicative reading for definites, as given in (4ii), which picks out the singleton set of (or the property of being) the unique man if there is just one and the empty set (or empty property) otherwise.

For indefinites, there again seem to be plausible interpretations of all three types: Montague's generalized quantifier interpretation incorporating an existential quantifier; an $\langle e, t \rangle$ interpretation equivalent to the bare common noun interpretation (the traditional translation of indefinites in predicate positions); and the treatment suggested in recent work of Kamp and Heim, which is not adequately represented by the rough translation into intensional logic given in (5ii) but which can, I think, fairly be said to treat indefinites as *e*-type variables accompanied by conditions on assignments to those variables.[4]

Bare plurals like *dogs*, in (6), were not treated at all by Montague; Carlson (1980) proposed that they be treated as proper names of kinds, and Chierchia (1982a, b, 1984) provides an enrichment of intensional logic including a nominalization operator mapping properties onto property-correlates in the domain of entities, treating the bare plural as one such nominalization.[5] Carlson's $\langle \langle e, t \rangle, t \rangle$ interpretation can then be reanalyzed in retrospect as in (6ii), as bearing the same relation to Chierchia's nominalized property $^\cap dog'$ as Montague's translation of ordinary proper names bears to their translation as individual constants. The simple $\langle e, t \rangle$ translation in (6iii) remains a plausible interpretation for bare plurals in predicate positions.

2. EVIDENCE FOR MULTIPLE TYPES FOR NP'S

So far I have just enumerated a number of cases where interpretations of differing types have been proposed for various NP's, without giving many arguments that a single NP may in fact have multiple interpretations. And indeed I do not intend to try to settle the question of how many distinct interpretations any given NP has and just what they are, although I will make some suggestions. In this section I will review some evidence for the plausibility of the claim that there are NP interpretations of at least types e and $\langle e, t \rangle$ as well as $\langle \langle e, t \rangle, t \rangle$, and in what follows I will try to show how interpretations of these types can be systematically related to one another.

2.1. Evidence for type e

The claim that proper names are basically of type e and only derivatively of type $\langle \langle e, t \rangle, t \rangle$ hardly needs defense, and there is almost as much tradition (though more controversy) behind the treatment of singular definite descriptions as entity-denoting expressions. However, there seemed to be no harm and considerable gain in uniformity in following Montague's practice of treating these NP's always as $\langle \langle e, t \rangle, t \rangle$, until attention was turned to the relation between formal semantics and discourse anaphora by the work of Kamp (1981) and Heim (1982). As illustrated in examples (7) and (8), not only proper names and definites license discourse anaphora, but in-definites as well; other more clearly "quantificational" NP's do not.

(7)   John/the man/a man walked in. He looked tired.

(8)   Every man/no man/more than one man walked in. *He looked tired.

The generalization seems to be that while any singular NP can bind a singular pronoun in its (c-command or f-command)[6] domain, only an *e*-type NP can license a singular discourse pronoun. The analysis of in-definites is particularly crucial to the need for invoking type *e* in the general-ization, since if it were only proper names and definite descriptions which licensed discourse anaphora, one could couch the generalization in terms of the retrievability of a unique individual from the standard Montagovian generalized quantifier interpretation (an ultrafilter in those cases).

2.2. Evidence for type $\langle e, t \rangle$

Certain verbs appear to take $\langle e, t \rangle$ arguments; some allow only adjective phrase complements (*turn introverted, *turn an introvert*), while others, like *become* and *consider*, allow both AP and NP complements. Particular-ly strong evidence for these NP's being of type $\langle e, t \rangle$ comes from their con-joinability with AP's in such positions, since I assume that true constituent conjunction requires identical types and I have seen no evidence for treating adjective phrases as either type *e* or $\langle \langle e, t \rangle, t \rangle$.

(9)   Mary considers John competent in semantics and an authority on unicorns.

Although not all verbs that seem to take $\langle e, t \rangle$ complements allow exactly the same range of NP's in such complement positions (see Reed (1982)), I will for simplicity take occurrence with *consider* as diagnostic for "predicative NP's", i.e. NP's that can have an $\langle e, t \rangle$ interpretation.

(10)   Mary considers that an island / two islands / many islands / the prettiest island / the harbor / *every island / *most islands / *this island / *?Schiermonnikoog / Utopia.

In general, the possibility of an NP having a predicative interpreta-tion appears to be predictable from the model-theoretic properties of its interpretation as a generalized quantifier; in fact we will argue below that *all* NP's in principle have an $\langle e, t \rangle$ interpretation, but some of them (like *every island, most islands*) yield unsatisfiable or otherwise degenerate predicates.

Williams (1983) notes that sentences like (11) provide counterexamples to

(11)   This house has been *every color.*

the above claim. We will take up such examples in section 4, arguing that in these cases the possibility of an $\langle e, t \rangle$ reading results from a language-specific and quite idiosyncratic property of the head noun of the construction, which affects the syntactic as well as the semantic properties of the resulting phrase.

3. TYPE-SHIFTING: GENERAL PRINCIPLES AND PARTICULAR RULES

3.1. A general picture

While I aim to uncover considerable systematicity in the phenomenon of type-shifting, I do not want to suggest that there is a single uniform and universal set of type-shifting principles. There are some very general principles which are derivable directly from the type theory, others which are quite general but which depend on the algebraic structure of particular domains (such as the $\langle \langle e, t \rangle, t \rangle$ domain), others which require the imposition of additional structure on the domain of entities or other domains, and still others which seem to be language-particular rules. (Note that lexical rules of the sort discussed by Dowty (1978, 1979) usually involve a change of type; those which employ zero morphology may be thought of as a species of language-particular type-shifting rules.) Even the most general type-shifting principles, such as the "lifting" operation that maps j (type e) onto $\lambda P[P(j)]$ (type $\langle \langle e, t \rangle, t \rangle$), need not be universal, but I would expect such a principle to be universally available at "low cost" or "no cost" for any language that has NP's of type $\langle \langle e, t \rangle, t \rangle$ at all.[7] Conversely, there might be type-shifting rules which are not of any formal generality but which are universal or at least very commonly employed because their substantive content has some high cognitive naturalness (such as perhaps the rule which turns proper names into common nouns denoting a salient characteristic, as in "He's a real Einstein"). The general picture I will sketch below will focus on formally definable type-shifting principles which I believe are linguistically exploited in English and at least potentially universal; I believe this perspective might be helpful for studying semantic universals and typology, but I have not carried out any serious cross-linguistic study.

In Diagram 1, the circles represent the three model-theoretic domains $D_{\langle e, t \rangle}$, and $D_{\langle \langle e, t \rangle, t \rangle}$, labelled by their types, and the arrows represent mappings between them, operations which map objects in one domain onto corresponding objects in another domain. I will say more about some of them below; others will be discussed in subsequent sections.

I should note here that while my focus in this paper is on type-shifting operations that can map NP-meanings onto other meanings for those same NP's, the same operations can of course be involved in rules which relate expressions in distinct syntactic categories as well. In particular, I consider $\langle e, t \rangle$ a "marked" type for full NP's in English (as opposed to the "unmarked types" e and $\langle \langle e, t \rangle, t \rangle$); it is the "unmarked" type for common noun phrases and verb phrases, and one of the possible types for adjective phrases and prepositional phrases, so we should not be surprised if the type-shifting operations mapping to or from type $\langle e, t \rangle$ show up even more in rules relating NP's to expressions of other categories than in rules providing multiple meanings for single NP's. On the other hand, not all languages make as clear a syntactic distinction between NP's and CN's as English does, and the naturalness of some of these type-shifting operations may help to account for that fact.

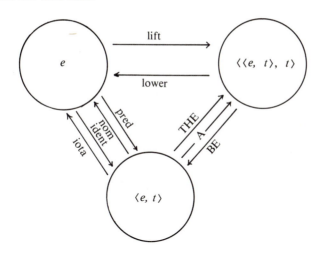

Diagram 1

lift:	$j \to \lambda P[P(j)]$	total; injective
lower:	maps a principal ultrafilter onto its generator; lower(lift(j)) = j	partial; surjective
ident:	$j \to \lambda x[x = j]$	total; injective
iota:	$P \to \iota x[P(x)]$ iota(ident(j)) = j	partial; surjective
nom:	$P \to \cap P$ (Chierchia)	almost total; injective
pred:	$x \to \cup x$ (Chierchia) pred(nom(P)) = P	partial; surjective

Many of the mappings come in pairs which are inverses. For example, the operation *lift*, which has been mentioned before, has an inverse *lower*. *Lift* maps any entity *a* onto the principal ultrafilter generated by *a*; in IL terms, it maps (the denotation of) j onto (the denotation of) $\lambda P[P(j)]$; in set-theoretic terms, it maps *a* onto $\lambda X[a \in X]$. *Lift* is total and injective ("in-to"). Its inverse, *lower*, is partial and surjective ("onto"), mapping any principal ultrafilter onto its generator. So *lower(lift(a))* = *a*, and if *lower* ($\mathcal{P}$) is defined, *lift(lower* ($\mathcal{P}$)) = $\mathcal{P}$.[8]

The pair *ident* and *iota* are similarly inverses. *Ident* is the total, injective operation mapping any element onto its singleton set; in IL terms, it maps j onto $\lambda x[x = j]$. *Iota* is its partial surjective inverse, mapping any singleton set onto its member; in IL, augmented by the iota operator, it maps P onto $\iota x[P(x)]$. (In an intensional system, we would want in addition or instead a version of *ident* mapping an entity onto the *property* of being that entity, and a version of *iota* mapping a property onto the unique individual having that property, if there is indeed just one, and undefined otherwise. In either case we would have *iota(ident(a))* = *a* and, when defined, *ident(iota*(P)) = P.)

The other pair of mappings between *e* and ⟨ *e, t* ⟩, *nom* and *pred*, are extensional misrepresentations of the operators "∩" and "∪" from Chierchia (1984).[9] *Nom* maps properties onto their entity-correlates if these exist (the Russell property, for instance, will be acceptable as a predicate but will not have any entity-correlate); this is the operation which on Chierchia's analysis is involved in nominalizing the common noun *dog* to form the bare plural *dogs* and the adjective *blue* to the proper noun *blue*, and in the formation of infinitives and gerunds from verb phrases. It is "almost" total, applying to all "ordinary" properties at least, and injective. Its inverse, *pred*, applies to those entities which are entity-correlates of properties, and returns the corresponding property. *Pred* is partial and "almost" surjective. Where defined, *nom* and *pred* are inverses. We will make use of these operators in our analysis of the Williams counterexample.

These three pairs of operators illustrate the heterogeneity of type-shifting principles I alluded to at the beginning of this section: *lift* is a matter of simple combinatorics that falls directly out of the type theory, and would have an analogue between types *a* and ⟨ ⟨ *a, b* ⟩, *b* ⟩ for any *a* and *b*. *Lower* is not independently definable in combinatoric terms since it does not apply to the whole of the higher domain, but is definable as the inverse of *lift* or independently in terms of generators of ultrafilters. *Ident* and *iota* are not merely combinatorial but are still "formal" insofar as they do not depend on any particular assumptions about the domain D_e. *Nom* and *pred* are more "substantive" in that they depend on the inclusion of properties or property-correlates among the entities.

There is also room for considerable diversity in how natural languages make use of such type-shifting principles, encoding them with lexical items (*iota* might be a candidate meaning for the definite article), via lexical rules (*nom* or *pred* for the rule relating *blue* as adjective to *blue* as proper noun, depending on which one takes as basic), syntactic rules (*nom* for the formation of bare plurals), or not encoding them at all (e.g. if *lift* is universal for proper nouns.) I will return to these linguistic issues at various points below. I should note here that *lower* is not necessarily part of the grammar of English at all, but is useful in the metatheory for predicting which NP's have *e*-type readings from their generalized quantifier interpretations.

3.2. Sample application: the king *in all three types*

By the criteria presented in section 2, singular definite descriptions like *the king* can occur in all three types.[10] Diagram 2 below shows mappings that could provide a possible account of this distribution and of the slight differences in meaning and presupposition that accompany the three uses. (The reader can fill in the caveats needed here about the wealth of research these suggestions need to be tested against and integrated with, etc.) Solid lines indicate total functions, dotted lines partial ones.

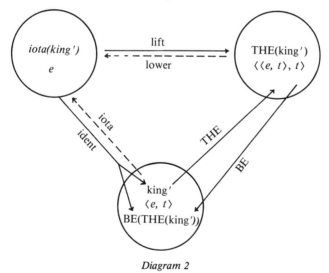

Diagram 2

Four of these mappings were described in the previous section: *lift, lower, ident,* and *iota*. *THE* is the total function which maps any set Q onto the generalized quantifier given by Montague's syncategorematic interpretation rule for the introduction of *the* (see entry (4) in Table 1). In subsequent work in Montague grammar, this operation is usually assigned as the meaning of the determiner *the* itself; it is expressed in IL as $\lambda Q \lambda P[\exists x[\forall y[Q(y) \leftrightarrow y = x] \& P(x)]$; in languages lacking an overt definite article, one would have to look for grounds for choosing between a syncategorematic treatment and the positing of a zero definite article. Since *THE* is a total function, there are no presuppositions required for the use of definite descriptions as generalized quantifiers.[11] If there is a unique king, *THE(king ')* denotes the set of all his properties; otherwise it denotes the empty set of properties, so that any sentence in which *THE(king ')* has maximal scope comes out simply false. *Iota(king ')*, on the other hand, is defined iff there is one and only one king; if we assume that *e* is the unmarked type for subject position,[12] and the preferred type for arguments of extensional verbs generally, this would help to explain the strong but not absolute preference for taking existence and uniqueness as presuppositions rather than as part of the content in subject and other argument positions.

So far, we have a contrast between an *e*-type meaning *iota(king ')* and an $\langle \langle e, t \rangle, t \rangle$ meaning, *THE(king ')*, traceable to two alternative meanings for *the*, namely *iota* and *THE*. These are related to each other by the fact that whenever *iota* is defined, i.e. whenever there is one and only one king, *lift(iota(king '))* = *THE(king ')* and *lower(THE(king '))* = *iota(king ')*, and furthermore whenever *iota* is not defined, *THE(king ')* is vacuous in that it denotes the empty set of properties. (*THE(king ')* will generally have a non-vacuous intension, of course, which is presumably why it is useful to have a presuppositionless version of definite descriptions.)

Now what about a possible predicative ($\langle e, t \rangle$) reading for *the king?* Suppose we start with the $\langle \langle e, t \rangle, t \rangle$ reading *THE(king ')*. We know that one way of getting from a denotation of type $\langle \langle e, t \rangle, t \rangle$ to one of type $\langle e, t \rangle$ is to apply the function denoted by Montague's PTQ translation of English *be*, $\lambda \mathcal{P} \lambda x [\mathcal{P}(\lambda y [y = x])]$. This is the function called BE in the diagram; I will say more to argue for its "naturalness" in the next section. For now let me just present the suggestion that we treat this operator not as the meaning of the word *be* but as a type-shifting functor that we apply to the generalized quantifier meaning of an NP whenever we find the NP in an $\langle e, t \rangle$ position.[13] The English *be* itself, I will suggest (following Williams (1983)), subcategorizes semantically for an *e* argument and an $\langle e, t \rangle$ argument, and has as its meaning "apply predicate", i.e. $\lambda P \lambda x [P(x)]$. This pair of proposals gives the same result as Montague's for phrases like *be the king, be a man, be John*, but distributes the meaning among the parts differently, in such a way that we now have a predicative reading for NP's in positions other than after *be* (which Montague's treatment did not provide), and we can now have the same *be* occurring with NP's and with predicates of other syntactic categories. I think this is an important advantage and will say more about it in later sections; let's return now to the implications of this proposal for the predicative reading of *the king*, which can be defined as *BE(THE(king '))*.

In IL terms, *BE(THE(king '))* works out to be

$\lambda x[king'(x) \& \forall y[king'(y) \to y = x]]$, or equivalently, $\lambda x[\exists y[king'(x) \leftrightarrow x = y]]$. This gives the singleton set of the unique king if there is one, the empty set otherwise. Since both *BE* and *THE* are total functions, this is always available as a possible $\langle e, t \rangle$ reading of *the king*; no presuppositions are required. Note that if there is *at most* one king, $king' = BE(THE(king'))$, i.e. this predicative reading of *the king* is the same as the common noun *king* in that case, since both pick out the empty set if there is no king and a singleton set if there is exactly one king. The fact that the common noun and the predicative definite description agree modulo this "at most one" presupposition may help explain why in English the definite article is sometimes but not always optional in predicative constructions, as illustrated in (12).

(12)   a.   John is { the president / president }
      b.   John is { the teacher / *teacher }

It appears that the definite article is optional in such constructions just in case the presupposition that there is at most one such-and-such in any context is virtually built into the language, so that the conditions for the equivalence of predictive *the president* and *president* can generally be taken for granted. While this somewhat functional account may help to explain the contrast between (12a) and (12b), it cannot be taken as a predicative explanation, since as we will see in the next section, predicative *in*definites like *a man* are always fully equivalent to the common noun, so it would seem even more natural for a language to omit redundant indefinite articles, as in French, than redundant definite articles.

    The double-headed arrow on the *ident* mapping reflects the fact that for *iota* to be defined there must be one and only one king, hence $king' = BE(THE(king') = ident(iota(king'))$. In fact, when *iota* is defined, the diagram is fully commutative: $king' = BE(THE(king')) = ident(iota(king')) = ident(lower(THE(king'))) = BE(lift(iota(king')))$, etc. This property of the mappings lends some formal support to the idea that there is a unity among the three meanings of *the king* in spite of the difference in type. There are of course alternatives that should be considered; the diagram would also be commutative if we replace the total function *THE* by a partial function identical to the composition *lift · iota*, so that there would be the same presuppositions for the meanings in every type, and no reading of *the king* lacking those presuppositions. I tend to believe there *is* a presuppositionless reading, but I doubt that clear arguments can be found within a purely extensional sublanguage.

3.3. A and BE as "natural" type-shifting functors

When we consider possible functions mapping from $\langle e, t \rangle$ to $\langle \langle e, t \rangle, t \rangle$ the obvious candidates are all the determiners, since that is exactly their type. Natural language data suggest that *a* (and plural *some*) and *the* are particularly natural, since they are often not expressed by a separate word or morpheme but by constructional features, or not expressed at all. Sometimes definites are marked but indefinites unmarked. Determiners like *every, many, most,* and numerals are always expressed by a word or morpheme, as far as I know. Sometimes an indefinite article is overt in referential positions, unexpressed in predicative positions. Can we find formal backing for the intuition that what *a* and *the* denote in English are particularly "natural" type-shifting functors? We have already done this to some extent for *the*; here we will consider *a*, and also strengthen the case for the naturalness of the functor *BE* introduced in the previous section.

Let *A* be the categorematic version of Montague's treatment of *a/an*: in IL terms, $\lambda Q[\lambda P[\exists x[Q(x) \& P(x)]]]$. We will focus first on the naturalness of *BE*,[14] then argue that *A* is natural in part by virtue of being an inverse of *BE*.

Fact 1:   *BE* is a homomorphism from $\langle \langle e, t \rangle, t \rangle$ to $\langle e, t \rangle$ viewed as Boolean structures, i.e.:

$$BE(\mathcal{P}_1 \sqcap \mathcal{P}_2) = BE(\mathcal{P}_1) \sqcap BE(\mathcal{P}_2)$$
$$BE(\mathcal{P}_1 \sqcup \mathcal{P}_2) = BE(\mathcal{P}_1) \sqcup BE(\mathcal{P}_2)$$
$$BE(\neg \mathcal{P}_1) = \neg BE(\mathcal{P}_1)$$

Fact 2:   *BE* is the unique homomorphism that makes Diagram 3 commute.
(There are other homomorphisms, and other functors that make the diagram commute, but no others that do both.)[15]

What exactly does *BE* do? Perhaps more perspicuous than Montague's IL formulation is its expression in set-theoretical terms: $\lambda \mathcal{P}[\lambda x[\{ x \} \in \mathcal{P}]]$.

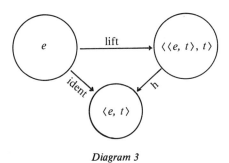

Diagram 3

That is, it applies to a generalized quantifier, finds all the singletons therein, and collects their elements into a set. The commutativity of Diagram 3 is then straightforward, since a generalized quantifier obtained by applying *lift* to an entity a will contain just one singleton, $\{a\}$. And as Keenan and Faltz (1978, 1985) showed, the full $\langle\langle e, t\rangle, t\rangle$ domain can be generated by applying Boolean operations to generalized quantifiers of that special sort (the "individual sublimations", in the terms of Dowty, Wall and Peters (1981).) So *BE* does indeed seem to be a particularly nice, structure-preserving mapping from $\langle\langle e, t\rangle, t\rangle$ to $\langle e, t\rangle$.

The semantic naturalness of the *BE* operator is of course independent of whether we take it to be the meaning of English *be*, analyzed as a transitive verb taking $\langle\langle e, t\rangle, t\rangle$ objects as in PTQ, or, as I proposed above, treat it as a (potentially universal) operator that is always available to turn an $\langle\langle e, t\rangle, t\rangle$ meaning into an $\langle e, t\rangle$ meaning. The choice between the analyses will depend heavily on syntactic considerations. In either case, *BE* is a total function, so we still have to explain why some NP's don't occur naturally after *be* or in other predicative positions. The explanation is that although *BE* is total, and preserves important structure of the $\langle\langle e, t\rangle, t\rangle$ domain, it also ignores a lot of structure by looking only at the singletons in any generalized quantifier. *Most men*, for instance, will never contain any singletons, so *be most men* will always be empty; similarly for distributive readings of plurals like *two men, several men,* etc. (Group readings of such plurals yield good predicative readings, which is predicted if groups or plural individuals are treated as entities, as in Link (1983).) *Every man* contains a singleton only if there is just one man; although it is probably too strong (certainly among logicians!) to claim that *every* presupposes "more than one", one and zero are degenerate cases, usually included only for the sake of generality, and to use *every man* predicatively you would have to *know* you were dealing with a degenerate case, in which case *the* or *the only* would be appropriate and more straightforward. Note that *BE*(no man$'$) = not(*BE*(a man$'$)); English seems to prefer the latter construction, Dutch the former, although I don't think either would be declared ungrammatical in either language.

In general it seems that the NP's that yield sensible predicative readings fall into two categories: those formed with "weak" determiners (Milsark (1977), Barwise and Cooper (1981)), which are intuitively the indefinites, and definite singular NP's. In the former case the predicative reading is tantamount to stripping *A* off the generalized quantifier reading and leaving the common noun meaning (since *BE* and *A* are inverses); in the case of definite singulars, the extensionality of the system discussed here would make the predicative reading tantamount to applying *ident* to the corresponding entity, probably an unsatisfactory analysis.[16]

Having established the naturalness of *BE* as a type-shifting functor from

$\langle\langle e, t\rangle, t\rangle$ to $\langle e, t\rangle$, one question that springs to mind is: For what possible *DET* meanings is it true that $BE(DET(P)) = P$?[17] One answer is A, as is familiar from the fact that in PTQ, *(be a man)'* comes out equivalent to *man'*; hence A meets one reasonable condition for naturalness by virtue of being an inverse of *BE*. (But *exactly one* is also an inverse for BE; the general requirement is that the singleton sets contained in *DET*(P) must be all and only the singletons of elements of P.)

Two other potentially significant properties of A are that it is symmetric and is monotonically increasing in both arguments; I conjecture that these are both "nice" properties. That's a vague claim, but I would expect to see it borne out in order of acquisition and in cross-linguistic distribution of determiners and of any other functor categories for which those properties are definable. The properties certainly distinguish A from *exactly one*, which has neither of them.

I would conjecture, in fact, that among all possible DET-type functors. A (which combines English *a* and *some*) and *THE* are the most "natural" and hence the most likely to operate syncategorematically in natural languages, or not to be expressed overtly at all, and that *BE* is the most "natural" functor from $\langle\langle e, t\rangle, t\rangle$ meanings to $\langle e, t\rangle$ meanings. On the formal side, this requires finding and arguing for further formal criteria for what makes a functor "natural", and showing that *A, THE,* and *BE* score high under such criteria. On the linguistic side, I would expect to see further evidence that the semantic force of *A, THE* and *BE* is often carried by constructional rather than lexical meaning.[18]

3.4. Mappings to and from type e.

In Montague's *PTQ*, no English expressions were analyzed as type e; on our approach, there is still no syntactic category uniformly interpreted as type e, but many NP's have type e interpretations as one of their possible interpretations. Lexical NP's, proper nouns and singular pronouns may be basically of type e and acquire $\langle e, t\rangle$ and $\langle\langle e, t\rangle, t\rangle$ meanings by *ident* and *lift* respectively. Non-lexical NP's with e-type interpretations are probably most easily accounted for as resulting from type-shifting operations applied to initially higher type interpretations, although it is possible that type-lowering has become grammaticized so that, for instance, *the* may have an interpretation as *iota* as well as (or instead of) an interpretation as *THE*. (It may not be easy to find arguments to decide whether the e-type interpretation of *the king* is best analyzed as *iota(king')* or as *lower(THE(king'))*.) We have already mentioned several mappings to and from type e: *lift* and *lower, ident* and *iota, nom* and *pred*. In this section we will say a bit more about *lower*, and particularly about the Kamp-Heim treatment of indefinites as type e. Then we will suggest that the type-shifting perspective fits well with recent proposals by Link and others for the treatment of mass and plural noun phrases using model structures which impose additional structure on various subdomains of the domain of entities.

3.4.1. Lower and indefinites. As described in section 3.1., *lower* applies to any generalized quantifier which is a principal ultrafilter and maps it onto its generating element in the e domain. This accounts for e-type readings of definite singular NP's like *the king, this dog, Bill's car* (and *John* and *he*, if these are not directly generated as type e.) It does not directly give e-type readings for definite plurals like *those three men*, a principal filter whose generator is a set, nor to indefinite singulars like *a man*, which on their standard treatment are not principal filters at all. The former case will be taken up when we discuss Link's treatment of plurals, the latter right now.

While Kamp's and Heim's proposals for the treatment of various kinds of noun phrases and anaphora suggest rather far-reaching changes in the semantic framework, Zeevat (ms. 1984) has recast central parts of their proposals in terms that help to localize the major innovations around the treatment of free variables and the mechanisms of variable-binding. Using Zeevat's notation, an "indexed indefinite" like $[a \; man]_n$ can be translated as in (13),

(13) $\lambda P[P(x_n^*) \wedge man'(x_n)]$

where the asterisk is a diacritic that plays a role in the non-standard rules for variable-binding. Alternatively, it could be translated as $\lambda P[P(x_n^*)]$ plus the condition $man'(x_n)$, if the condition is treated as a separate clause as in Heim (1982). In either case, as Heim has emphasized, the removal of the existential quantifier from the interpretation of indefinites makes their meanings much more like pronoun meanings, and apart from the complication that we are here dealing with variables, the meanings are similar to proper noun meanings like $\lambda P[P(j)]$, and *lower* can apply to give *a man* an e-type reading x_n^* (together with the condition $man'(x_n)$).[19]

3.4.2. Plurals and mass noun phrases. Link (1983) proposed additional structure within the domain of entities, including the recognition of a subdomain of "plural individuals" and a subdomain of quantities of matter, each with a certain amount of Boolean structure and with a mapping from the former to the latter; in terms of this structure Link is able to solve a number of puzzles in the semantics of plurals and mass nouns. To integrate his structure with the perspective suggested here, we can see that there is a natural pair of mappings relating Link's plural individuals in the e domain to sets of ordinary individuals, in the $\langle e, t \rangle$ domain; let us call these mappings *link* and *delink*, as in Diagram 4 below.

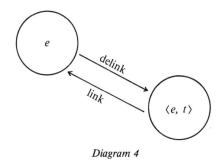

Diagram 4

Then *link*({ *a, b*}) = *a* ⊕ *b; delink(a* ⊕ *b)* = { *a, b*} . *Link* is total (singleton sets map onto the single individuals which are the atoms of the plural-individual structure) and injective; *delink* is partial and surjective.

With this possibility of easy shifting between the group (individual) perspective and the set perspective, we can readily generate *e*-type readings of definite plurals like *the three men*, in fact via several equivalent routes. If we start with a distributive reading like Barwise and Cooper's, taking the generator set of the principal filter (a new operation we call *genset*) would get us a set of (the) three men, whence *link* would get us a plural individual. Starting with the kind of group reading provided by Link, we could apply *lower* directly to get the same plural individual.

The behavior of the cardinals *two, three, . . .* can probably also be illuminated on this perspective; briefly, I would suggest that the primary interpretation of *three* is as an ⟨ *e, t* ⟩ adjective applying to plural individuals (here it means "exactly three"), which can be promoted to an ⟨⟨*e, t*⟩, ⟨*e, t*⟩⟩ prenominal (intersective) adjective by standard techniques. Then either by composition with *A* or by the Kamp-Heim treatment of indefinites it can become a determiner (group reading), picking up the explicit or implicit existential quantifier which would account for the "at least" reading normally associated with cardinal determiners. Lastly, the *delink* operation could naturally be extended to a corresponding operation on all "group" determiners to yield corresponding distributive determiners; an analogous operation was proposed in Michael Bennett's dissertation (Bennett 1974).

Pelletier and Schubert (forthcoming) discuss a wide range of problems in the syntax and semantics of mass expressions and provide an excellent critical survey of suggested solutions, offering some new proposals of their own. Drawing in part on the work of Link and of Chierchia discussed here, as well as earlier work by Parsons, Pelletier, ter Meulen and others, they sketch several alternative approaches which make use of implicit semantic operations. Some of these operators perform type-shifting operations, others have what we might call 'sort-shifting' effects within a single type; as noted earlier, the distinction is a very theory-dependent one that we don't wish to lay any emphasis on here. Much of the heaviest debate in the mass noun literature concerns the semantics of predicative mass expressions and the question of what they are true of: ordinary objects, quantities of matter, and/or substances or kinds. Pelletier and Schubert show how one can take various positions both on the number and nature of the ontological distinctions made in the model and on the number and nature of discrete senses of mass predicates relative to a given ontological background. A number of the proposals they describe involve sort-shifting operators which convert, for example, a mass predicate true of kinds (as in 'Red wine is *wine*') into one true of objects or quantities of matter (as in 'The puddle on the floor is *wine*') or vice versa. Their own proposals suggest the desirability of letting the 'unmarked' or default case for mass predicates be that a given mass predicate such as *beer* can apply indifferently to entities of a number of different sorts: quantities of beer, kinds of beer, conventional servings or kinds of servings of beer; objects coincident with or constituted by quantities of beer, and involving what we might call 'sort-restricting operators' as part of the semantics of constructions which limit the applicability of the predicate to some proper subset of these cases; these can be viewed as a special kind of sort-shifters which take a more general sort onto a subsort. Such a possibility does not exist for type-shifting operators in a type theory like Montague's but would in some more general theories of types and is therefore an interesting potential addition to the inventory of natural type-shifting operations.

Pelletier and Schubert, following Chierchia, also propose type-shifting operators converting mass predicates (typically expressed as common noun phrases) of these various sorts to mass terms denoting substances (typically expressed as determinerless full NP's) and vice versa. As in Chierchia, these are basically the same *nom* and *pred* operators that apply in the semantics of bare plurals and other nominalization phenomena.

And of course the ease of shifting between mass and count senses of the same common noun phrase has long been noted and illustrates the existence of other apparently very natural short-shifting operations that may or may not be grammaticized in different languages: count to mass via the Pelletier/Lewis "universal grinder" (put in a chair and you end up with chair all over the floor); mass to count with either a "conventional portion of" or "kind of" interpretation.

3.4.3. Structure in the e domain. All of the operations *nom* and *pred, link* and *delink*, and analogs for mass terms depend on the existence of richly structured subdomains in the domain of entities; these structures can be seen to be taking over some of the work previously done by the type theory. More of the same sort of shift can be seen in proposals for the semantics of comparatives which treat "degrees" as entities, and in proposals for an event-based ontology in which events are also entities. First-order theories put

virtually *all* of the burden on structure internal to the entity domain; Chierchia (1984) argues that linguistic evidence favors a semantics which is at least
second-order but not a fully recursive type system like Montague's. This
kind of investigation of trade-offs between strongly typed systems and less
strongly typed systems with multiple subsorts of entities is also being carried
out in the domain of programming languages; see Goguen and Meseguer
(1984), Meseguer and Goguen (1984) and Futasugi et al. (1985).[20] It is partly
because this kind of study opens up so many possibilities that have not been
explored that I feel in no position to argue for a "best" way of analyzing
particular constructions.

In closing this section, let me note that there remain NP's for which none
of our operations provide *e*-type readings; these, not surprisingly, are the
ones traditionally thought of as most clearly "quantificational": *no man,
no men, at most one man, few men, not every man, most men.*[21] *Every man*
could get an *e*-type reading via *lower* in case there is only one man; but
linguistically it never seems to act as a singular "referential" term, suggesting again (cf. section 3.3.) that it is at least pragmatically anomalous to
use *every* in a way that constrains it to just one. Such NP's can occur in *e*-
type positions only by "quantifiying in", which would account for the
traditional distinction between them and "referring expressions". On the
perspective advanced here, we can capture such traditional distinctions
without giving up the unification achieved by Montague's work, which we
still need in order to account for the possibility of conjunctions like "King
John and every peasant", which would be inexplicable on an analysis which
captured only the differences and not the common $\langle \langle e, t \rangle, t \rangle$ structure.

4. THE WILLIAMS PUZZLE

Anticipating the kind of proposal put forward in section 3.3., Williams
(1983) argued that the possibility of $\langle e, t \rangle$ readings for NP's can*not* be
predicted from the determiner, citing examples like (14), where virtually any
determiner can occur.

(14)   This house has been every color.

I believe this apparent counterexample and others like it can be explained
in terms of the idiosyncratic and language-particular behavior of the head
noun. In English (but not e.g. in Dutch) many "attribute" nouns allow this
kind of construction: *color, size, length, weight, age, price.* A relatively
"tolerant" context which accepts such nouns rather easily is "This dress is
the wrong ___", a more restrictive one is in the use of these "attribute NP's"
as postnominal modifiers, as in (15), where grammaticality judgments are

my own — there appears to be considerable individual variation on judgments about particular words, reinforcing the idea that this is a quite idiosyncratic lexical property.

(15)   a dress that size / that color / that length / that price /
       *that material / *that design / ?that pattern / *that origin.

In this construction we have a predicative ($\langle e, t \rangle$) use of an NP that does not correspond to the result of any of the type-shifting operations we have seen so far. To see what's going on semantically, consider the following pattern:

(16)   a.   This shirt is blue.
       b.   Blue is a nice color.
       c.   This shirt is a nice color.

In (16a), *blue* is an adjectival predicate ($\langle e, t \rangle$), predicated of the shirt. In (16b), we have the nominalized property *blue*, type *e*, and the expected $\langle e, t \rangle$ predicative use of *a nice color*; the entities in the extension of *color* are colors: blue, red, green, etc. — not shirts. Semantically, (16c) is quite different from (16b), and amounts to something like a combination of (16a) and (16b) with the color unspecified. Many languages do not allow this kind of predication to be expressed with a simple noun phase but require the equivalent of (17a) or (17b) below, construction types which also occur with some attribute nouns in English.

(17)   a.   This shirt is of a nice color.
       b.   This shirt has a nice color.

The possibility of using bare NP's as predicates in this way in English is reminiscent of the adverbial use of NP's studied by Larson (1985), which is also quite idiosyncratic: *that day, that way, *that manner.*

The crucial formal tool that allows a straightforward account of this special predicative use of attribute NP's is Chierchia's nominalization theory, which relates predicative properties like *blue* as in (16a) to their type *e* nominalizations as in (16b). Although Chierchia's theory takes properties as (intensional) primitives, I don't think it does any harm here to misrepresent the predicative property as type $\langle e, t \rangle$ for ease of exposition.

If we take adjectival *blue*, $\langle e, t \rangle$, as basic, the *e*-type proper noun *blue* can be translated in Chierchia's system as $^\cap blue'$; if we take the *e*-type noun as basic, the adjective is $^\cup blue'$; in either case the two are related by those inverse operators, the ones called *nom* and *pred* in section 3.1. Recall that *pred*, or "$^\cup$", is defined only for entities which are the "entified" counterparts of properties.

Color is a common noun, its type $\langle e, t \rangle$; entities in its extension are, as noted above, properties (*blue, red,* etc.). This is the semantic content of what I mean by "attribute noun": these nouns express properties of properties. In addition to knowing this semantic fact about the noun *color*, we must encode with a diacritic syntactic feature − say, $+A$ − the syntactic difference between "adjectival" attribute nouns like *color, size, weight* and *age* which do fit into constructions like those in (14), (15), and (16c) and other attribute nouns like *property, virtue,* and *origin* which do not. The combining stem *-thing* can function as a $+A$ attribute noun, as in the frequently puzzled-over construction in (18).

(18)   He is everything I hoped he would be (intelligent, non-sexist, vegetarian, etc.)

I am not sure what to call the syntactic category of this special predicative use of attribute NP's; here I will assume that they belong to a syntactic category *Pred* (semantic type $\langle e, t \rangle$) which includes predicative adjective uses of NP's, since these special attribute NP's can occur in constructions where other predicative NP's cannot, such as postnominal position as in (15) and in *there*-constructions as in (19) below (on some analyses these are the same fact):

(19)   a.   There's nothing here a good color.
        b.   There's no one here the right age.
        c.   *There's no one here a good teacher.
        d.   *There's nothing here the right answer.

To complete the analysis, I need just one syntactic and semantic rule and a couple of uncontroversial assumptions. The first assumption is that any NP whose head noun has the feature $+A$ also has the feature $+A$; this follows from most theories of feature inheritance.[22] The second is that the rule of quantifying-in[23] quantifies generalized quantifiers into e-type positions only, not into $\langle e, t \rangle$ positions. I will also assume a pro-form *that*ᵢ as an e-type $+A$ variable over (entified) properties; this corresponds to the use of *that* discussed by Ross (1969), illustrated in (20).

(20)   They said she was beautiful and { that she was / she was that }

The syntactic and semantic rule for attribute predicates can be formulated as follows:

> *Attribute Predicate Rule*
> *Syntactic Rule:* If $[_{NP} \, \alpha]$ is $+A$, then $[_{Pred}[_{NP} \, \alpha]]$
>   is a Pred.
> *Semantic Rule:* If $[_{NP} \, \alpha]$ translates as α', then
> $[_{Pred}[_{NP} \, \alpha]]$ translates as $^{\cup}\alpha'$.

Note that the semantic rule is defined only for NP's of type *e* and turns them into ⟨*e, t*⟩ predicates; so this rule applies to attribute NP's like *that color, the color Mary liked best, a color I once saw in a sunset, two colors* (group reading), and the pro-form *that*ᵢ, which all have *e*-type readings via the general principles discussed earlier, but not *every color*. The generalized quantifier reading of + A NP's is just like that of any other NP, and no special rules apply to them; we only need assume that only a + A NP can be quantified into a + A position. We can now illustrate the syntactic derivation and semantic interpretation of Williams' example (14).

(21)

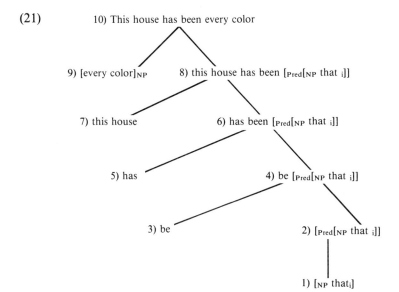

1) x_i (type *e*)
2) $^\cup x_i$ (type ⟨*e, t*⟩)
3) $\lambda P\lambda x[P(x)]$
4) $\lambda P\lambda x[P(x)](^\cup x_i)$ -----> $\lambda x[^\cup x_i(x)]$ (type ⟨*e, t*⟩)
5) $\lambda Q\lambda y[H(Q(y))]$ (here H is a past operator)
6) $\lambda Q\lambda y[H(Q(y))](\lambda x[^\cup x_i(x)])$ -----> $\lambda y[H(^\cup x_i(y))]$ (type ⟨*e, t*⟩)
7) h_1 (type *e*; I ignore the internal structure of this NP here)
8) $\lambda y[H(^\cup x_i(y))](h_1)$ ----> $H(^\cup x_i(h_1))$
9) $\lambda P[\forall x[color'(x) \longrightarrow P(x)]]$
10) $\lambda P[\forall x[color'(x) \longrightarrow P(x)]](\lambda x_i[H(^\cup x_i(h_1))])$ ----->
    $\forall x[color'(x) \longrightarrow H(^\cup x(h_1))]$

The last line gives the desired interpretation: for all x, if x is a color, at some time in the past this house has had the property $^\cup x$, the predicative version of the property x.

Semantically, this analysis depends heavily on Chierchia's treatment of nominalization; syntactically, it depends on having a syntactic derivation in which the *e*-type NP position contained within the derived Pred remains accessible to quantifying in, since I assume one cannot generally quantify into $\langle e, t \rangle$ positions. I believe that the same principles account for the exceptional relativization out of predicate position exemplified in (18).

A similar approach might account for another kind of case of quantified NP's appearing in predicate position, as in (22).

(22)   Olivier has been every Shakespearean king.

Here we have an ordinary noun as head, and various treatments are possible, depending on what one considers the best analysis of sentences like (23).

(23)   Oliver is Richard III.

If one analyzes both NP's as *e*-type, either treating this *is* as "is playing" or by admitting a *be* of identity, then this isn't really a predicative position and quantifying in is to be expected. I would suggest that we have the same *be* here as elsewhere, and that Richard III as a role is a non-rigid individual concept of (type $\langle e, t \rangle$) (see Janssen (1984) for related discussion), which can be turned into a predicate nominal, in this case [$_{PNOM}$[$_{NP}$ Richard III]], interpreted as $\lambda x[x = {}^\vee r]$. However, unless we map "roles" as individual concepts back into the entity domain in a move analogous to Chierchia's, we would still need to give a non-standard type analysis to *every Shakespearean king*.

5. ENGLISH BE.

In section 3.2. above we suggested that the semantic operation we called *BE* should be treated not as the meaning of English *be* but as a type-shifting functor freely applicable to generalized quantifier meanings of NP's to yield predicative readings for those NP's. We suggested further, following Williams (1983), that English *be* subcategorizes semantically for an *e* argument and an $\langle e, t \rangle$ argument, with a meaning paraphrasable as "apply predicate". (This treatment of *be* was adopted in the derivation (21) of example sentence (14).) We may want to say further that *be* imposes no sortal restrictions of its own, requiring that its $\langle e, t \rangle$ argument be predicable of its *e* argument. Depending on how inclusive the *e* domain is, one may want to go further and call *be* genuinely polymorphic, taking one *X*-type and one $\langle X, t \rangle$-type argument, for any type *X*.

If we accept Williams's argument that the arguments of *be* may occur in either order, we get the added benefit of automatically generating both readings of ambiguous pseudoclefts; this is discussed further in Partee (1986). An appropriate treatment of this "semantic transparency" of *be* should also be able to account for cases of control phenomena and other instances of "syntactic connectedness" (Higgins 1973) across *be*, provided the control phenomena are treated semantically; but this is a suggestion in need of considerable work before it becomes a serious proposal.

It may be going too far to think of *be* as making no semantic contribution of its own, although this is a fairly traditional view. On the proposals just sketched, there would be no difference in meaning at all between *cat* and *be a cat, asleep* and *be asleep*, etc. While this is also true of Montague's treatment and of most proposals that are expressible in first-order logic, it seems questionable. One should consider in this regard the insightful work of Stump (1985), who assigns to *be* a kind of sort-shifting meaning, turning predicates of stages (G. Carlson ontology) into predicates of individuals but otherwise still semantically transparent.

The syntax and semantics of the copula in English and other languages is of course a vast subject which I can't hope to do justice to in a few paragraphs. But it does seem promising that the present approach allows a treatment of *be* that accords well with traditional views suggested by the word *copula*, preserving the positive aspects of Montague's treatment of the *be* + *NP* construction while unifying that construction with other kinds of *be* + *Pred* construction.

6. CONCLUSIONS

Much work remains to be done to determine the appropriate way to incorporate the kinds of operators studied here into a theory of grammar. I have said very little about syntax or about constraints on the mapping of syntax to semantics in this paper. Most of the emphasis has been on the exploration of certain kinds of operations which I believe are at work somewhere in the semantics of English and many of them probably universally. Some of them may be built into the operation of specific rules, e.g. the *nom* operator in the semantics of rules of nominalization: some may apply freely whenever there is a mismatch between the simplest type of a given expression and the type needed for a particular occurrence of it to be well-formed, e.g. *lift* provides a simple *e*-type NP like *John* with a generalized quantifier meaning so that it can occur in conjunctions like *John and every other student*. Some may be language-specific, like the + A-rule discussed in connection with the Williams puzzle in section 4; others, like the free applicability of *lift* to provide generalized quantifier meaning to *e*-type NP's, may well be universal, at least among languages which have NP's with generalized quantifier meanings at all. Finding which are which, and undoubtedly uncovering new type-shifting and sort-shifting principles in the process, would appear to be an important and promising venture which will require close study of a wide range of languages.

Another general direction of research suggested by these beginnings that may be of interest beyond the study of semantics is the search for "cognitively natural" operations. As I suggested at various points above, I believe an interesting case can be made for regarding certain semantic operations or functions of a given type as more "natural" than others on various plausible criteria, vague as such a notion must be. I will close by reiterating the need for interdisciplinary collaborative efforts on this issue, empirical studies to help determine what kinds of operations and functions are particularly widespread in the world's languages, frequently occur syncategorematically, are acquired early, etc.; and formal studies to help us gain a better understanding of the possible structures of semantic domains and possible formal criteria of naturalness to apply to mappings between them. One can imagine such studies of "natural mappings" extending well beyond the sorts of cases studied here, and relating to such disparate issues as the role of symmetry in perception, the problem of projectible predicates ("grue" vs. "green"), the interpretation of metaphors, and the development of mathematical intuition. Wherever one can uncover richly structured domains and evidence of an important role being played by mappings between them, it should be possible to investigate the relative cognitive "naturalness" of various such mappings, and such studies should in principle help to advance our understanding of the contribution our "hardwired" predilections make to the way we make sense of the world we find ourselves in.

ACKNOWLEDGEMENTS

I am grateful to many sources of aid and encouragement in the development of this paper. The initial impetus came from Edwin Williams's persuasive arguments against a uniform category-type correspondence for NP's, as set out in Williams (1983); my first attempts to find a way to accept Williams's arguments without throwing out the indisputably fruitful uniform interpretation of NP's as generalized quantifiers were carried out in a seminar jointly taught in the Spring of 1984 by Emmon Bach, Hans Kamp, and me, and I am grateful to all its participants for valuable comments and suggestions, particularly Nina Dabek, Roger Higgins, Hans Kamp, and Edwin Williams. The idea of looking for "natural functions" between a domain and range of given sorts or types had been earlier suggested by work of

David Lebeaux on unifying the interpretation of the progressive in a seminar on tense and aspect which Emmon Bach and I had taught in the Spring of 1982. Further developments came during a six-week period in the Summer of 1984 as visiting scholar at Stanford's Center for the Study of Language and Information, where I presented a preliminary version of this paper. My research during the summer was supported in part by CSLI and in part by a grant from the System Development Foundation, the latter of which has also supported my subsequent research and writing up of the paper. I received invaluable help and encouragement from colleagues and students who accompanied me to CSLI, especially Gennaro Chierchia, Raymond Turner, Nina Dabek, Craige Roberts, and Karina Wilkinson, and from other local and visiting researchers at CSLI, including Ivan Sag, Ewan Klein, Paul Kiparsky, Ton Wasow, Joan Bresnan, Mark Johnson, and especially Jose Meseguer and Joseph Goguen, who introduced me to the literature on polymorphic types and to the algebraic perspective on type- (or sort-)shifting operations that I have only just begun to learn to exploit. Further important help came from Johan van Benthem before and during the 5th Amsterdam Colloquium where the main presentation of this paper was made. Other valuable suggestions and encouragement came from participants in the Amsterdam Colloquium, from participants in a workshop on mathematical linguistics at the University of Michigan, especially Richmond Thomason and Hans Kamp, from the audience at a subsequent colloquium presentation at the University of Connecticut, especially Howard Lasnik, and from participants in fall 1984 and spring 1985 seminars at the University of Massachusetts, especially Fred Landman, Emmon Bach, Ray Turner, Nirit Kadmon, and Frank Wattenberg, to whom I am also grateful for inviting me to present this work to a New England Set Theory meeting in December, a stimulating challenge in interdisciplinary communication which turned out to be a most enjoyable and productive experience. I hope I haven't misused any of the help I got along the way; I'm sure it will take more help from colleagues in several disciplines to overcome remaining inadequacies, fill in gaps, and extend this approach if possible to a comprehensive theory of syntactic categories and semantic types.

NOTES

1.   Since the requirement of a homomorphism from syntactic categories to semantic types is fundamental to Montague's approach, one cannot literally allow a single syntactic category to map onto more than one semantic type within that approach. There are various ways of reformulating my proposal to conform to the homomorphism requirement, e.g. by exploiting the common view of syntactic categories as feature bundles. Flynn (1981) argues for the inclusion of both X-bar and categorial identification in syntactic categories, and there is considerable independent motivation for such a move, e.g. in the cross-classification of X-bar categories

such as "PP", and "AdjP" and categorial grammar categories such as "predicate", "predicate modifier", etc.

Incidentally, nothing I say in this paper is meant to decide between the use of type theory and the use of sorted domains in a type-free or less strongly typed theory. I use type theory because it is more familiar to me; I don't really know how much difference it makes. Chierchia and Turner (in preparation) discuss this question.

2.   Here and throughout I am simplifying to a purely extensional sublanguage unless explicitly stated otherwise. That is one of the big gaps in this work that needs to be filled.

3.   See, for instance, Partee and Rooth (1983) on conjunction, Reinhart (1983) on bound-variable anaphora.

4.   See Chierchia and Rooth (1984), Zeevat (1984).

5.   This of course goes beyond the bounds of a purely extensional fragment; what I do in this paper is systematically misrepresent properties as sets, hoping that the differences between them will not affect the main ideas.

6.   See Bach and Partee (1980), Reinhart (1983).

7.   So I would predict that any language which has expressions like "every man" as a syntactic NP of semantic type $\langle\langle e, t\rangle, t\rangle$ will also allow proper names like "John" to be $\langle\langle e, t\rangle, t\rangle$, hence will allow conjunctions like "John and every man". Similarly, while children acquiring English may start out with only e-type NP's, once they acquire quantificational NP's they should soon show signs of promoting simpler NP's to the higher type as well.

8.   I am using expressions of Montague's intensional logic, with his conventions as to the types of variables, to denote corresponding model-theoretic objects, occasionally recasting things in set-theoretical vocabulary where it may add perspicuity. The type-shifting operations are defined on model-theoretic objects; we might find it useful to add their names as logical constants to the intensional logic or other intermediate representation language.

9.   See note 5.

10.   In a fuller treatment, the same should apply to definite plural and mass terms as well, like *the men* and *the water*.

11.   There could be (and would be unless something rules it out) a second generalized quantifier reading of *the king, lift(iota(king'))*. I'm not sure how one would get evidence for or against such an ambiguity.

12.   I believe one can interpret Frege (1892) as making such a claim about subject NP's.

13.   I assume that the grammar specifies various positions as e, $\langle e, t\rangle$, etc., via subcategorization and other rules. I believe that positions are not subcategorized as $\langle\langle e, t\rangle, t\rangle$ unless they are also intensional, like the object of *seek*, hence outside the scope of this discussion. In cases of ambiguity, I would predict that if any NP can be either e or $\langle e, t\rangle$ in a certain position, e would be the preferred choice not only because it is a simpler type, but also because e and $\langle\langle e, t\rangle, t\rangle$ are (I believe) unmarked types for NP's, while $\langle e, t\rangle$, the unmarked type for VP's, AdjP's, and many PP's, is a marked type for NP's. I don't know what to expect in cases of ambiguity between $\langle e, t\rangle$ type and $\langle\langle e, t\rangle, t\rangle$ type for a given NP in a given position, since there is then a conflict between simplicity of type and markedness as an NP-type.

14.   My thanks to Johan van Benthem for showing me that Montague's BE functor is indeed "natural", both intuitively and by various formal criteria, something I had never appreciated in spite of years of familiarity. This section was much weaker before he helped with it.

15.   Thanks to Johan van Benthem for the fact, which he knows how to prove but I don't, and to Hans Kamp who gave me further help in understanding it.

16.   This is yet another place where it seems evident that we want properties and not sets to play a basic role in what we are calling the $\langle e, t\rangle$ domain. The *predicate* reading of "the owner of this land" should neither presuppose that the land has an owner nor depend on who the owner is if there is one. Although intensionality will probably complicate the type-shifting picture, I believe it is indispensable for a satisfactory analysis.

17.   That is, we are asking what determiner-type meanings are inverses of *BE* in one direction. We cannot expect any determiner meaning to be an inverse in the other direction, i.e. to satisfy $DET(BE(\alpha)) = \alpha$ for all α, since *BE* loses information: $BE(\alpha) = BE(\beta)$ for any α and β that contain the same singletons.

18.   Moortgat (1985) gives evidence of *the, a*, and Carlson-type bare-plural readings in first elements of noun-noun compounds in English, Dutch, and German, where semantic NP-type readings are carried by syntactic CN's. The formation of bare plurals should also count as "natural", I would hope, but I am following Chierchia in viewing it as basically a nominalization operation ($\langle e, t \rangle$ to e) rather than a DET-type functor; its composition with *lift* would then be a DET-type functor.

19.   Johan van Benthem has warned me that the kinds of type-shifting functors I have been employing cannot be assumed to apply straightforwardly to variables, since we are not then dealing directly with model-theoretic objects in the same way. But I believe that the same principles *ought* to apply, and it would at least be straightforward if we included logical constants like *lower* and *lift* in an intermediate representation language such as Zeevat's reconstruction of Kamp's DRS language.

20.   My thanks to Jose Meseguer, Joseph Goguen, and Ray Turner for making me aware of related work in the semantics of programming languages. I'm not able to understand and appreciate much of the technical work in that field, but it seems clear to me that this is another problem area where interdisciplinary collaboration could have considerable payoff.

21.   Sometimes "most men" seems to have an *e*-type reading paraphrasable as "a group containing most men"; this seems even easier to get with "most of the men". See Doron (1983) for discussion of some of these issues and of differential availability of predicative $\langle e, t \rangle$ readings for partitive and non-partitive plural NP's. Plurals and mass terms raise many more semantic issues than can be touched on here; it would take at least another paper to examine a significant fraction of current work on mass terms and plurals in the light of the type-shifting perspective suggested here. See, for instance, Scha (1981), Hoeksema (1983), van Eijck (1983). Westerstahl (forthcoming), Pelletier and Schubert (forthcoming), Lønning (1984).

22.   NP's formed with the bound CN-stem *-thing* must also be able to be marked +A, perhaps optionally as illustrated in (18); there should probably be some general way of indicating that *-thing* has maximally permissive selectional features and corresponds to a maximally inclusive "sortal range" of entities.

23.   The same restriction could be applied to other proposed mechanisms for dealing with quantifier scope, such as Cooper-storage, quantifier-lowering, or QR (quantifier raising).

BIBLIOGRAPHY

Bach, Emmon and Barbara H. Partee (1980), "Anaphora and semantic structure", in J. Kreiman and A. Ojeda, eds., *Papers from the Parasession on Pronouns and Anaphora*, Chicago Linguistics Society, Chicago, 1–28.

Barwise, Jon and Robin Cooper (1981) "Generalized quantifiers and natural languages" *Linguistics and Philosophy* 4.2, 159–219.

Bennett, Michael (1974) *Some Extensions of a Montague Fragment of English*, UCLA Ph.D. dissertation.

Carlson, Greg N. (1980) *Reference to Kinds in English*, Garland Publishing Co., New York (update of Carlson 1977 Univ. of Mass/Amherst dissertation).

Chierchia, Gennaro (1982a) "Bare plurals, mass nouns, and nominalization" in D. Flickinger, M. Macken, and N. Wiegand, eds., *Proceedings of the First Coast Conference on Formal Linguistics*, Stanford University, Stanford, 243–255.

Chierchia, Gennaro (1982b) "Nominalization and Montague grammar: a semantics without types for natural languages'', *Linguistics and Philosophy* 5, 303–354.

Chierchia, Gennaro (1984) *Topics in the Syntax and Semantics of Infinitives and Gerunds*, Ph.D. dissertation, Univ. of Mass/Amherst.

Chierchia, Gennaro and Mats Rooth (1984) ''Configurational Notions in Discourse Representation Theory'' in Charles Jones & Peter Sells (eds.) *Proceedings of NELS 14*, Univ. of Mass./Amherst.

Chierchia, Gennaro and Raymond Turner (in preparation) ''Semantics and Property Theory''.

Doron, Edit (1983) *Verbless Predicates in Hebrew*, Ph.D. dissertation, Univ. of Texas/Austin.

Dowty, David (1978) ''Governed transformations as lexical rules in a Montague grammar'', *Linguistic Inquiry* 9.3, pp. 393–426.

Dowty, David (1979) *Word Meaning and Montague Grammar*, Synthese Language Library, D. Reidel Publishing Co., Dordrecht.

Dowty, David, Robert Wall and Stanley Peters (1981) *Introduction to Montague Semantics*, Synthese Language Library. D. Reidel Publishing Co., Dordrecht.

Flynn, Michael (1981) *A Categorial Theory of the Base*. Ph.D. dissertation, Univ. of Massachusetts/Amherst.

Frege, Gottlob (1892) ''Über Sinn und Bedeutung,'' *Zeitschrift für Philosophie und philosophische Kritik* 100 (25–50); trans. by Max Black as ''On sense and reference'' in *Translations from the Philosophical Writings of Gottlob Frege*, ed. by P. Geach and M. Black, Basil Blackwell, Oxford, 1960, 56–78.

Futatsugi, K., J. Goguen, J.-P. Jouannaud, and J. Meseguer (1985), ''Principles of OBJ2'', Report No. CSLI-85-22, CSLI, Stanford Univ., Stanford.

Goguen, Joseph and Jose Meseguer (1984), ''Equality, types, modules and (why not?) generics for logic (programming'', *Journal of Logic Programming* 1, 179–210. Also report CSLI-84-5, Stanford.

Heim, Irene (1982) *The Semantics of Definite and Indefinite Noun Phrases*, Ph.D. dissertation, Univ. of Massachusetts/Amherst.

Higgins, F.R. (1973), *The Pseudo-cleft Construction in English*, unpublished doctoral dissertation, MIT, Cambridge, Mass.

Hoeksema, Jack (1983) ''Plurality and Conjunction'' in Alice G.B. ter Meulen (ed.), *Studies in Modeltheoretic Semantics*, Groningen-Amsterdam Studies in Semantics 1, Foris: Dordrecht, 63–83.

Janssen, Theo M.V. (1984) ''Individual concepts are useful'' in Fred Landman and Frank Veltman (eds.) *Varieties of Formal Semantics: Proceedings of the Fourth Amsterdam Colloquium, September 1982*, Foris: Dordrecht.

Kamp, Hans (1981) ''A theory of truth and semantic representation'', in J. Groenendijk, Th. Janssen and M. Stokhof, eds., *Formal Methods in the Study of Language (Part I)* Mathematisch Centrum, Amsterdam, 277–322.

Keenan, E.L. and L.M. Faltz (1978) *Logical Types for Natural Language*, UCLA Occasional Papers in Linguistics, 3.

Keenan, Edward L. and Leonard M. Faltz (1985), *Boolean Semantics for Natural Language*, Dordrecht: Reidel.

Klein, Ewan and Ivan Sag (1985), ''Type-driven translation'', *Linguistics and Philosophy* 8, 163–201.

Larson, Richard (1985), ''Base-NP Adverbs'', *Linguistic Inquiry* 16, 595–621.

Link, Godehard (1983) ''The logical analysis of plurals and mass terms: a lattice-theoretical approach'', in R. Bäuerle, Ch. Schwarze, and A. von Stechow, eds., *Meaning, Use, and Interpretation of Language*, Walter de Gruyter, Berlin, 302–323.

Lønning, Jan Tore (1984) ''Mass terms and quantification'', in Jens Erik Fenstad, ed., *Report of an Oslo Seminar in Logic and Linguistics*, Preprint Series, No. 9, Matematisk institutt, Univ. of Oslo.

Meseguer, J. and Goguen, J.A. (1984), "Initiality, induction and computability", in M. Nivatt and J. Reynolds, eds., *Algebraic Methods in Semantics*, Cambridge Univ. Press.

Milsark, Gary (1977) "Toward an explanation of certain peculiarities of the existential construction of English", *Linguistic Analysis* 3, 1–29.

Montague, Richard (1970) "Universal Gammar" reprinted in Montague (1974) 222–246.

Montague, Richard (1973) "The proper treatment of quantification in ordinary English", reprinted in Montague (1974) 247–270.

Montague, Richard (1974) *Formal Philosophy: Selected Papers of Richard Montague*, edited and with an introduction by Richmond Thomason, Yale Univ. Press, New Haven.

Moortgat, M. (1985), "The mathematics of word structure", to appear in the Proceedings of the Conference on Categorial Grammars and Natural Language, Tucson, spring, 1985.

Partee, Barbara and Mats Rooth (1983) "Generalized conjunction and type ambiguity", in R. Bäuerle, C. Schwarze, and A. von Stechow, eds., *Meaning, Use, and Interpretation of Language*, Walter de Gruyter, Berlin, 361–383.

Partee, Barbara (1986), "Ambiguous pseudoclefts with unambiguous *be*", in S. Berman, J.-W. Choe, and J. McDonough, eds., *Proceedings of NELS 16, 1985*, GLSA, Univ. of Mass., Amherst, 354–366.

Pelletier, F.J. and L.K. Schubert (forthcoming), "Mass Expressions", to appear in D. Gabbay and F. Guenthner, eds., *Handbook of Philosophical Logic*, vol IV, Walter de Gruyter, Berlin.

Reed, Ann (1982) "Predicatives and Contextual Reference", *Linguistic Analysis* 10.4, pp. 327–359.

Reinhart, Tanya (1983), "Coreference and bound anaphora: a restatement of the anaphora questions", *Linguistics and Philosophy* 1983, 47–88.

Ross, J.R. (1969) "Adjectives as Noun Phrases," in D. Reibel and S. Schane, eds. *Modern Studies in English: Reading in Transformational Grammar*, Prentice Hall, Inc., Englewood Cliffs, New Jesey.

Scha, Remko (1981) "Distributive, collective, and cumulative quantification", in J. Groenendijk, T. Janssen, M. Stokhof, eds., *Formal Methods in the Study of Language, Part II*, Mathematisch Centrum, Amsterdam, 483–512.

Stump, Gregory (1985), *The Semantic Variability of Absolute Constructions*, Synthese Language Library, D. Reidel Publishing Co., Dordrecht.

Van Benthem, Johan (1983a) "Determiners and logic", *Linguistics and Philosophy* 6, 447–478.

Van Benthem, Johan (1983b) "The logic of semantics" in F. Landman and F. Veltman (eds.), *Varieties of Formal Semantics*, GRASS series, Foris, Dordrecht.

Van Eijck, Jan (1983) "Discourse Representation Theory and Plurality", in Alice G.B. ter Meulen (ed.), *Studies in Modeltheoretic Semantics*, Groningen-Amsterdam Studies in Semantics 1, Foris: Dordrecht, 85–106.

Westerstahl, Dag (forthcoming), "Quantifiers in formal and natural language", to appear in F. Guenthner and D. Gabbay, eds., *Handbook of Philosophical Logic*, vol. IV.

Williams, Edwin (1983) "Semantic vs. Syntactic Categories" *Linguistics and Philosophy* 6, 423–446.

Zeevat, Henk (1984) "A compositional approach to discourse representation", unpublished manuscript, Erasmus Univ., Rotterdam.

Chapter 6

Formal Semantics and Type-free Theories

Raymond Turner

The current paradigms in natural language semantics all employ set theories in which the axiom of foundation holds. This is true, for example, of both Montague Grammar and Situation Semantics. The first part of this paper is largely given over to some informal considerations which are meant to suggest that a foundation for semantics would be better served by a set theory in which the axiom of foundation fails. It will be argued, if perhaps implicitly, that some form of type-free set or property theory is necessary to do justice to the rich variety of phenomena in natural language which exhibit some form of direct or indirect self-reference. We shall concentrate on a group of phenomena wich, in one way or another, stem from the general linguistic process of nominalization. Kamp (1983) and Landman (1985) have pointed out other areas of semantics where some form of "type-freeness" seems both natural and necessary.

This paper then has two objectives. One is to indicate why formal semantics needs a type-free set or property theory and the second is to develop one.

1. THE SUBJECT/PREDICATE DISTINCTION

We shall adopt the traditional linguistic distinction between subject and predicate. Semantically, nouns or noun-phrases pick out objects and predicates or predicate-phrases are employed to say something about the object or thing so identified. As Strawson might put it: subjects fix the subject matter, and predicates do the saying.

The following pairs of sentences are taken to be in subject-predicate form.

(1)   a.   John runs.
          b.   Running is fun.

(2)   a.   John walks.
          b.   To walk is rare.

(3)   a.   Peggy and Toby are dogs.
          b.   Dogs are animals.

(4)   a.   The block is gold.

    b.   Gold is an element.

(5)   a.   The book is red.
       b.   Red is a colour.

(6)   a.   White gold is gold.
       b.   Gold is gold.

(7)   a.   John loves every dog.
       b.   To love every dog is impossible.

To provide the semantics for such subject-predicate sentences we introduce two domains: a domain D of objects and a domain F of properties. Noun-phrases are to receive their denotations in D and predicative phrases are to receive theirs in F. For neutrality we shall not assume that the elements of F are functions or sets. Rather properties are taken as sui-generis and are not necessarily to be understood in set-theoretical terms. Thus in order to provide the semantics for simple subject-predicate sentences we require the aid of a relation or function of predication.

$$p : F \times D \rightarrow \{0, 1\}.$$

Intuitively, $p(f,d) = 1$ means that d satisfies the property f. Such a relation is of course expressed by the copula in natural language.

Now consider the various pairs of sentences in this catalogue. An expression, which in the first sentence of each pair functions as a predicate is transformed in the second into something which functions as a subject. We shall refer to this general phenomenon (following Chierchia 1984) as Nominalization. This phenomenon seems quite pervasive in natural languages such as English and is intended to include Infinitives, Gerunds, Mass Terms, Adjectives, Bare plurals as well as simple cases of morphological nominalization.

There are two possible ways we might proceed in providing a semantic analysis of subject-predicate sentences involving nominalized predicative expressions. We might adopt a Fregean perspective and claim that the denotations of such nominalized predicates are objects, which are systematically correlated with the denotations of the predicates themselves. Alternatively, we might adopt the view that the predicative expressions and their nominalized counterparts have the same denotations.

If we adopt the first view, then one thing we must do is to provide an account of those intuitions which demand that the denotations of predicative expressions and their nominalized counterparts are systematically related. One way of achieving this is to assume the existence of a function

$$g : F \rightarrow D,$$

which associates, with the denotation of each predicative expression, the denotation of its corresponding nominalized form. Furthermore, the function g ought to be quite finely discriminating — we do not want too many properties to be associated with the same element of D. Indeed, we want distinct properties to be associated with distinct elements. This forces g to be injective. It is through the function g that some form of "self-application" is rendered possible.

In summary, we have the following model-theoretic set-up:

(1)   F — domain of predicates;

(2)   D — domain of objects;

(3) $g : F \rightarrow D$ — injective;

(4) $p : F \times D \rightarrow \{0, 1\}$

For pedagogical reasons, we shall make some simplifying assumptions. The injective nature of g certainly allows us, formally, to view F itself as a subset of D. This reduces the above to a framework which really reflects the second perspective. Furthermore, we shall assume that p is a function from the whole of $D \times D$ into $\{0, 1\}$. Conceptually, one can think of p as being false for all those pairs $\langle d_1, d_2 \rangle$, for which $d_1 \notin F$. Formally, it streamlines the theory a little — we can work with a single-sorted first-order language rather than a two-sorted one. These assumptions have no impact upon the generality of what follows; all of the theory applies to the enriched ontology with only minor modifications.

2. A FIRST-ORDER LANGUAGE WITH ABSTRACTION AND PREDICATION

These assumptions do, however, permit us to employ much simpler model-theoretic structures. They have the from:

$$P = \langle D, p \rangle$$

where D is a non-empty set and p is a function from $D \times D \rightarrow \{0, 1\}$, or equivalently a relation on $D \times D$. We shall employ the functional representation in the model theory.

Given such an ontology, the appropriate language in which to develop such a theory of abstraction and predication is that of first-order logic, enriched by the addition of a binary predication relation. More explicitly, in L, there are individual variables, $x_1, x_2, x_3, \ldots$, basic individual constants $c_1, c_2, c_3, \ldots$, and one binary relation symbol, p. The terms of the language include not only the variables and basic constants, but also terms of the form $\lambda x \cdot A(x, y_1, \ldots, y_n)$, where $x, y_1, \ldots, y_n$ include all the free variables of the wff A. In such a term, the x is bound and the $y_1, \ldots, y_n$ are free. The usual conventions regarding bondage and freedom apply. Where we are not interested in the other free variables of $A(x, y_1, \ldots, y_n)$ we shall just write $\lambda x \cdot A(x)$ with $y_1, \ldots, y_n$ understood. The atomic wff are of the form $p(t_1, t_2)$ where t_1 and t_2 are terms. More complex wff are formed by conjunction (A&B), disjunction (AvB), negation ($\sim A$), universal quantification ($\forall x A$) and existential quantification ($\exists x A$). We shall often employ the standard abbreviation of writing $\bar{y}$ for $y_1, \ldots, y_n$.

The ability to represent such complex relations as terms in the language is crucial to our analysis of nominalized predicates. English has the facility to nominalize almost any predicative expression. Without this facility we could not, for example, represent nominalized predicative expressions such as those in example (7). Note that, restricting the language to abstracting on one variable at a time, is not a real limitation. One can always form wff of the form

$$p(\lambda y \cdot p(\lambda x \cdot A(x,y), t), t'),$$

to obtain the effect of multiple abstractions, and predications. Thus, manyplace relations are indirectly representable in the language.

In order to provide the semantics of this language we assume that all terms are contained in D. This can be achieved by assuming that $D \supseteq N$, and then Gödel numbering all the terms. More precisely, each term of the form $\lambda x \cdot A(x, y_1, \ldots, y_n)$ can be represented as a primitive recursive function, f say, such that $[\lambda x \cdot A(x, d_1, \ldots, d_n)]$ is $f(d_1, \ldots, d_n)$. Then in such a term x is bound and the y_i are free. We shall also assume, again to simplify things as much as possible, that every element d of D is named by some term in the language – which we shall also denote by d. We shall refer to the set of closed terms of the form $\lambda x \cdot A(x, d_1, \ldots, d_n)$ as **Form**. We make, in general, only two assumptions regarding our models, namely that they validate:

(Ab1) ... $p(\lambda y \cdot A(^x_s), t) \leftrightarrow P(\lambda x \cdot A(^y_t), s)$
(Ab2) ... $p(\lambda y \cdot A(x, \bar{y}), u) \leftrightarrow p(\lambda z \cdot A(z, \bar{y}), u)$.

These are perfectly harmless; there is no problem in constructing models which satisfy them. Indeed, we could code the terms so that they were automatically true. The only proviso is in (Ab1): x must not occur free in t and y must not occur free in s.

We can then provide the semantics of the closed wff of L as follows:

$$[p(e,d)] = 1 \quad \text{iff} \quad p(e,d) = 1;$$
$$[A\&B] = 1 \quad \text{iff} \quad [A] = 1 \text{ and } [B] = 1;$$
$$[\sim A] = 1 \quad \text{iff} \quad [A] = 0;$$
$$[\forall x A(x)] = 1 \quad \text{iff} \quad \text{for each } d \in D, [A(d)] = 1.$$

Let S be the theory defined by such models i.e. S is the class of sentences true in all models of L. Clearly, S includes all the universally valid sentences of first-order logic in one binary predicate letter.

So far, however, we have placed no constraints upon the interpretation of λ-abstractions. According to the above model-theory, they denote arbitary elements of D. Ideally, we require the following to be true in all our models:

(1) $p(\lambda x \cdot A(x,y_1, \ldots, y_n), d) \leftrightarrow A(d,y_1, \ldots, y_n).$

But this is impossible; from such a principle, Russell's paradox can be derived, using only minimal logic. One has only to compute $p(\lambda x \cdot A(x), \lambda x \cdot A(x))$ where $A(x) = \sim p(x,x)$, to reach a familiar conclusion.

We must certainly rule out the harmful instances of (1), but in a principled manner. The rest of this paper is devoted to the construction of theories, which seek to meet such desiderata.

3. A THEORY OF FEFERMAN AND GILMORE

One rather intriguing type-free theory is due to Gilmore (1974) and Feferman (1984). The latter develops the theory, from considerations arising from an approach to the paradoxes based on three-valued logic. The result of the analysis is the consistency, within classical logic, of the following schema:

(C1) ... $p(\lambda u \cdot A(u,y), x) \leftrightarrow A^+(x,y)$
(C2) ... $p(\lambda u \cdot \sim A(u,y), x) \leftrightarrow A^-(x,y),$

where A^+ and A^- are, in a sense yet to be made precise, "approximations" to A and $\sim A$, respectively. Although the theory is grounded in classical logic, there is a certain residue of the three-valued approach: in order even to state the theory we require two predication operators — a 'positive' one and a 'negative' one. Consequently, we are forced to extend the language, L, by the addition of a new binary relation constant ($\bar{p}$). Let $\bar{L}$ be the resulting language. We shall assume, as before, that all abstractions are represented as terms, and all terms denote themselves, as elements of the model. This facilitates the definition of A^+ and A^- as follows:

Definition   We define, for each wff of L,
3.1. A^+ and A^- by induction on A:

      (i)   If $A = p(t,s)$ then $A^+ = p(t,s)$ and $A^- = \bar{p}(t,s)$;
           If $A = \bar{p}(t,s)$ then $A^+ = \bar{p}(t,s)$ and $A^- = p(t,s)$;
      (ii) If $A = {\sim}B$ then $A^+ = B^-$ and $A^- = B^+$;
      (iii) If $A = B\&C$ then $A^+ = B^+\&C^+$ and $A^- = B^- vC^-$;
      (iv) If $A = BvC$ then $A^+ = B^+ vC^+$ and $A^- = B^-\&C^-$;
      (v)   If $A = \forall xB$ then $A^+ = \forall xB^+$ and $A^- = \exists xB^-$;
      (vi) If $A = \exists xB$ then $A^+ = \exists xB^+$ and $A^- = \forall xB^-$.

In order to interpret this new language we must extend our notion of model.

Definition   Let $P = \langle D,p \rangle$ be any predication frame.
3.2.   *The Negative Extension* of P, $\bar{P} = \langle D,p,\bar{p} \rangle$, where

$$\bar{p}(e,d) = \begin{cases} p(\lambda x \cdot {\sim} A(x,\bar{c}), d) & - \text{ if } e = \lambda x \cdot A(x,\bar{c}) \\ & \quad \text{for some A} \\ {\sim} p(e,d) & - \text{ otherwise} \end{cases}$$

The relations p and $\bar{p}$ are to be related by the following axiom:

   (Dis) $\ {\sim}[p(x,y)\&\bar{p}(x,y)]$

The importance of this property stems from the following result:

Lemma   Dis implies $A^+ \rightarrow A$ and $A^- \rightarrow {\sim} A$.
3.3
Proof. Trivial, by induction. $\square$

This justifies the use of the term "approximations" for A^+ and A^- .
    We shall, in fact assume, that (Dis) is true in all our models and forms part of the underlying theory S.
    Let $\bar{S}_0$ be the extension of S defined by (Dis) plus each instance of (C1) and (C2).
    Although $\bar{S}_0$ does not sanction the full axiom of comprehension it does permit us to conclude that properties which are "reducible" to each other are extensionally equivalent.

Definition   A *Reduces to* A' — written $A \triangleright A'$. This is defined by recur-
3.4   sion on the complexity of A as follows:

> (i)   If A is atomic of the form $p(\lambda z \cdot B, t)$, then $A \triangleright B(t)$.
> (ii) If $A = B \lor C$ then, if $B \triangleright B'$ and $C \triangleright C'$, then
> $A \triangleright B' \lor C'$.
> (iii) If $A = B \& C$ then, if $B \triangleright B'$ and $C \triangleright C'$, then
> $A \triangleright B' \& C'$.
> (iv) If $A = \,\sim B$ and $B \triangleright B'$ then, $A \triangleright \,\sim B'$.
> (v)   If $A(x) \triangleright A'(x)$ then $\forall x A(x) \triangleright \forall x A'(x)$ and
> $\exists x A(x) \triangleright \exists x A'(x)$.

Theorem   If $A \triangleright A'$, then, in $\bar{S}_0$, in each model for each c, $p(\lambda z \cdot A, c) \leftrightarrow$
3.5. $p(\lambda z \cdot A', c)$.

Proof
By induction on A.
It is straightforward given C1 and C2. □

This seems like an interesting constraint on any such property theory: $A \triangleright A'$ is certainly sufficient to ensure that A and A' induce the same property. It should therefore follow that they are extensionally equivalent. The converse, of course, would lead to some form of extensionality.

One of the unattractive features of $\bar{S}_0$ concerns its explicit dependence upon positive and negative approximations. From a classical perspective, such a dependence represents an unacceptable residue of the three-valued approach. In the next section we pave the way to its removal.

4. A REFORMULATION OF $\bar{S}_0$

Our main objective is to reformulate $\bar{S}_0$ so that it makes no explicit reference to such positive and negative approximations. We first state the revised version and then prove its equivalence to $\bar{S}_0$.

Axioms of Application and Abstraction

For each wff A, B of $\bar{L}$:

(S1) $A(x, \bar{y}) \rightarrow p(\lambda u \cdot A(u, \bar{y}), x)$ for atomic A
(S2) $p(\lambda u \cdot A(u, \bar{y}), x) \rightarrow A(x, \bar{y})$
(S3) $p(\lambda u \cdot (A \& B)(u, \bar{y}), x) \leftrightarrow p(\lambda u \cdot A(u, \bar{y}), x) \& p(\lambda u \cdot B(u, \bar{y}), x)$
(S4) $p(\lambda u \cdot (A \lor B)(u, \bar{y}), x) \leftrightarrow p(\lambda u \cdot A(u, \bar{y}), x) \lor p(\lambda u \cdot B(u, \bar{y}), x)$
(S5) $p(\lambda u \cdot \forall z A(u, \bar{y}), x) \leftrightarrow \forall z p(\lambda u \cdot A(u, \bar{y}), x)$

(S6) $p(\lambda u \cdot \exists z A(u, \overline{y}), x) \leftrightarrow \exists z p(\lambda u \cdot A(u, \overline{y}), x)$

(S7) $p(\lambda u \cdot \sim \sim A(u, \overline{y}), x) \leftrightarrow p(\lambda u \cdot A(u, \overline{y}), x)$

(S8) $p(\lambda u \cdot \sim p(\lambda v \cdot A(v), t), s) \leftrightarrow p(\lambda u \cdot p(\lambda v \cdot \sim A(v), t), s)$

These axioms have a rather different flavour to those of {Dis,C1,C2}. The above schema provide an axiomatic theory of abstraction and predication (or application). Essentially, this new formulation informs us how the operations of abstraction and predication interact with the logical connectives and quantifiers. Axiom schemes (S3), (S4), (S5) and (S6) are the axioms which govern conjunction, disjunction, universal quantification and existential quantification, respectively. Axiom schemes (S1) and (S2) tell us that, for atomic wff, the required equivalence $A(x, \overline{y}) \leftrightarrow p(\lambda u \cdot A(u, \overline{y}), x)$ holds. (S2), itself, guarantees that half of the equivalence always holds. Axioms (S7) and (S8) deal with negation. Observe we do not have the schema

$$p(\lambda u \cdot \sim A(u, \overline{y}), x) \leftrightarrow \sim A(x, \overline{y}).$$

If we did, (S7) and (S8) would follow, but the theory would be inconsistent.

Theorem $\overline{S}_0$ is equivalent to S1$-$S8.
4.1.

Proof
It is easy to verify that each of the axioms, S1$-$S8, follows from C1 + C2 + Dis. Conversely, we prove that C1, C2 follow from S1$-$S8, by induction on the wff of $\overline{L}$. The base step is just lemma 4.2, which follows. The induction steps follow directly from axioms (S3), (S4), (S5), (S6) and (S7). $\square$

Lemma   For each atomic wff, A, of $\overline{L}$, the following are consequences of
4.2.   S1$-$S8.

(i) $p(\lambda x \cdot A(x), s) \leftrightarrow A^+ (s)$

(ii) $\overline{p}(\lambda x \cdot A(x), s) \leftrightarrow A^- (s)$.

Proof
Part (i) is just a restatement of (S1) and (S2) since for atomic wff $A^+ = A$. Part (ii) is somewhat more involved. Consider the two possible cases of A(s) namely $P(t_1, t_2)(^x_s)$ and $\overline{P}(t_1, t_2)(^x_s)$. We can safely assume x is the only free variable of A(s). We illustrate the analysis by reference to the first case. The term t_1 can have three possible forms: $t_1 = x$ or $t_1 = c_i$ for some i or $t_1 = \lambda y \cdot B$ for some wff B. In all three cases $\overline{p}(\lambda x \cdot p(t_1, t_2), s) \leftrightarrow p(\lambda x \cdot \sim p(t_1, t_2), s)$ (by definition of $\overline{p}$). If $t_1 = \lambda y \cdot B$ then the latter is equivalent (by S8) to $p(\lambda x \cdot \overline{p}(t_1, t_2), s)$ which by part (i) is just $\overline{p}(t_1, t_2)(^x_s)$ as required. If $t_1 = c_i$

then by definition of $\bar{p}$, $p(\lambda x \cdot \sim p(t_1, t_2), s) \leftrightarrow p(\lambda x \cdot \bar{p}(t_1, t_2), s)$ and part (i) again yields the result. If $t_1 = x$ then by (Ab2) and (Ab1), $p(\lambda x \cdot \sim p(t_1, t_2), s)$ is equivalent to $p(\lambda y \cdot \sim p(s, y), t_2(^x_s))$. Since s is closed (since A(s) is closed) this reduces to the first two cases. $\square$

All this seems to be somewhat of a step-forward: we have a formulation of S_0 which makes no explicit mention of $\bar{p}$, A^+, A^- etc. Indeed, it is now quite easy to restrict the theory to L itself: let S_0 be the theory $S1-S8$, restricted to the language L. The theorem establishes that the original theory, based upon C1 and C2, is a conservative extension of S_0. In the next section we examine these theories in more detail, point out a certain curiosity, and suggest an amendment.

5. A REVISED THEORY

One curiosity of $\bar{S}_0$ relates to the properties defined by logical truths i.e. those of first-order logic. Certain intuitions demand that properties definable by logical truths or indeed by theorems of the underlying theory S, should be universally true:

$$(L) \quad p(\lambda x \cdot A(x, \bar{y}), u) \leftrightarrow A(u, \bar{y})$$

where $A(u, \bar{y})$ is wff of first-order logic, valid in all models of S. Unfortunately, (L) does not follow from $\bar{S}_0$. Indeed, adding such a principle renders the theory inconsistent. To see why, let $A(x) = p(x, x)$. By (L) we obtain

$$p(\lambda x \cdot [A(x) \vee \sim A(x)], u) \leftrightarrow A(u) \vee \sim A(u).$$

The right-hand-side, is always true, and so the left-hand-side must be. If we substitute $\lambda x \cdot \sim A(x)$ for u in the left-hand-side, take $p(x, x)$ for A and employ (S4), we are forced to choose between two alternatives: $p(\lambda x \cdot p(x, x), \lambda x \cdot \sim p(x, x))$ and $p(\lambda x \cdot \sim p(x, x), \lambda x \cdot \sim p(x, x))$. Presumably, one of these must be true. But, by (S2), the first alternative implies the second and the second implies $\sim p(\lambda x \cdot \sim p(x, x), \lambda x \cdot \sim p(x, x))$. But then we have a contradiction in both cases.

Given that we might wish to maintain the truth of (L), where are we to place the blame for this inconsistency? We certainly do not wish to abandon axiom (S2). This means we must relinquish (S4), in the direction left-to-right. Similar considerations will force us to abandon (S6), from left-to-right. We therefore amend S_0 and $\bar{S}_0$ accordingly. Let T be S_0, plus all instances of (L), minus (S4) from left-to-right and minus (S6) from left to right. Let $\overline{T}$ be T extended to all wff of $\overline{L}$. What are the consequences of this move?

Firstly, we can reformulate the theory more succinctly as follows:

The Theory $\overline{S}_1$

(1) $A(x') \rightarrow p(\lambda x \cdot A(x), x')$ for A atomic
(2) $p(\lambda x \cdot A(x), x') \rightarrow A(x')$ for any A
(3) $p(\lambda x \cdot (A \rightarrow B), x') \rightarrow (p(\lambda x \cdot A, x') \rightarrow p(\lambda x \cdot B, x'))$
(4) $\forall u(p(\lambda x \cdot A(x,u), x') \rightarrow p(\lambda x \cdot \forall u A(x,u), x')$
(5) $p(\lambda u \cdot \sim p(\lambda v \cdot A(v), t), s) \leftrightarrow p(\lambda u \cdot p(\lambda v \cdot \sim A(v), t), s)$
(6) $p(\lambda x \cdot A(x), u) \leftrightarrow A(u)$ for A any theorem of S

Leaving aside the problem of consistency for the moment, we are now under some obligation to say when we can maintain equivalence of the form

$$p(\lambda x \cdot A(x, \overline{y}), u) \leftrightarrow A(u, \overline{y}).$$

Obviously, (L) gives us a whole stock of such equivalences, but we can say more.

Theorem   In the theory $\overline{S}_1$,
5.1.   (i) If $A \leftrightarrow A^+$ then $p(\lambda x \cdot A(x, \overline{y}), u) \leftrightarrow A(u, \overline{y})$
            (ii) If $\sim A \leftrightarrow A^-$ then $p(\lambda x \cdot \sim A(x, \overline{y}), u) \leftrightarrow \sim A(u, \overline{y})$.
Proof
We prove (i), (ii) by induction on A. For the atomic cases, we argue as in 4.2, that

$$p(\lambda x \cdot A(x, \overline{y}), u) \leftrightarrow A^+(u, \overline{y})$$
$$p(\lambda x \cdot \sim A(x, \overline{y}), u) \leftrightarrow A^-(u, y).$$

The result now follows from the assumptions. We illustrate the induction step by reference to disjunction. By axiom (2), we have only to establish: $A(u, \overline{y}) \rightarrow p(\lambda x \cdot A(x, \overline{y}), u)$ and $\sim A(u, \overline{y}) \rightarrow p(\lambda x \cdot \sim A(x, \overline{y}), u)$. Let $A = B \vee C$ and assume A. By assumption, $A \leftrightarrow A^+$. Hence, A^+ i.e. $B^+ \vee C^+$. From Dis, $B^+ \rightarrow B$ and so B. Hence, $B \leftrightarrow B^+$. By induction, $p(\lambda x \cdot B(x, \overline{y}), u) \leftrightarrow B^+(u, \overline{y})$. By axiom S4 (right-to-left) we have $p(\lambda x \cdot A(x, \overline{y}), u)$ as required. Similar considerations yield the second part of the required equivalence. $\square$

This provides us with a condition sufficient to locate the appropriate equivalences. We immediately show it is not necessary.

Theorem   There exists an A such that
5.2. $\bar{S}_1 \vdash p(\lambda x \cdot A(x), u) \leftrightarrow A(u)$
       but
       $\bar{S}_1 \nvdash A \leftrightarrow A^+$, and not even $\bar{S}_1 \vdash A \rightarrow A^+$

Proof
Put $A(x) = p(x,x) \lor \sim p(x,x)$.
By (L), $\bar{S}_1 \vdash p(\lambda x \cdot A(x), u) \leftrightarrow A(u)$.
Assume $\bar{S}_1 \vdash A \leftrightarrow A^+$. Since $\bar{S}_1 \vdash A$ we have $\bar{S}_1 \vdash A^+$.
Hence, $\bar{S}_1 \vdash p(x,x) \lor \bar{p}(x,x)$. Let $t = \lambda x \cdot \sim p(x,x)$. Substitution, leads to
$\bar{S}_1 \vdash p(t,t) \lor \bar{p}(t,t)$. By (S2), the first disjunct implies $\sim p(t,t)$ and therefore
leads to the second disjunct $\bar{p}(t,t)$. This reduces, by definition of $\bar{p}$, to
$p(\lambda x \cdot p(x,x), t)$. This in turn, implies, by (S2), $p(t,t)$ — which is the already
rejected first disjunct. Hence, our assumption that $\bar{S}_1 \vdash A \leftrightarrow A^+$ must be
given up. □

The theories $\bar{S}_0$ and $\bar{S}_1$, although differing only slightly in form, are of considerable difference in content. The crucial difference relates to properties
definable via logical truths — $\bar{S}_1$ admits them as universal properties but $\bar{S}_0$
does not. Both theories are stated as axiomatic theories of predication and
abstraction, and relate the conditions under which

$$p(\lambda x \cdot A(x, \bar{y}), u) \leftrightarrow A(u, \bar{y})$$

holds.

6. CONSISTENCY PROOFS

This section of the paper is devoted to proving the consistency of the
theories $\bar{S}_0$ and $\bar{S}_1$. The consistency of S_0 and the consistency of S_1 are immediate corollaries. The actual constructions involved, offer some in-
teresting insights into the differences between the two theories. We do not,
however, have space to draw a complete comparison. We rather concentrate
on conveying the main ideas behind the proofs.

(i) *Consistency of* $\bar{S}_0$

Let $P = \langle D,p \rangle$ be any model of S which satisfies Dis with respect to its extension $\bar{P} = \langle D,p,\bar{p} \rangle$. There is no problem regarding the existence of such
a model. We then construct a new model $J(P) = \langle D,J(p) \rangle$ by

$$J(p)(e,d) = \begin{cases} [A^+(d,\bar{c})]_P - \text{if } e = \lambda x \cdot A(x,\bar{c}) \in \textbf{Form} \\ \\ p(e,d) \qquad - \text{ otherwise} \end{cases}$$

Clearly, $\bar{J}(P)$, the negative extension of $J(P)$, satisfies Dis since $\bar{P}$ does, and if P is a model of S so is $\bar{J}(P)$.

We now impose an ordering relation on the class of such models. Let $P = \langle D,p \rangle$ and $Q = \langle D,q \rangle$ be any two models. Define $p \le q$ iff for each $\langle e,d \rangle \in D \times D$, if $e \in \textbf{Form}$, then $p(e,d) = 1$ implies $q(e,d) = 1$; and if $e \notin \textbf{Form}$, then $p(e,d) = q(e,d)$.

Lemma   (i) $p \le q$ implies $\bar{p} \le \bar{q}$
6.1.   (ii) $p \le q$ implies $J(p) \le J(q)$.

Proof
(i) is obvious from the definitions. To prove (ii), we use induction on L, to prove:

$$[A^+(d,\bar{c})]_p \le [A^+(d,\bar{c})]_q$$
and $$[A^-(d,\bar{c})]_p \le [A^-(d,\bar{c})]_q.$$

Put another way, we prove by induction, that wff of the form A^+, A^- are monotonic in p. The details are straightforward.☐

Part (ii) informs us that J is a monotonic operator on models. As a consequence we obtain:

Theorem   The operator J has a minimal fixed point, i.e. there
6.2.   exists a minimal model P*, in the sense of $\le$, such that
              $J(P^*) = P^*$.

The proof is a standard one in the theory of inductive definability, and proceeds by defining an ordinal sequence of models, $P_\alpha = \langle D,p_\alpha \rangle$, and their extensions, $\bar{P}_\alpha$, where

(i) $p_0(e,d) = 0$, for all d where $e \in \textbf{Form}$.
(ii) $p_{\alpha+1} = J(p_\alpha)$
(iii) $p_\lambda(e,d) = \bigcup_{\alpha < \lambda} p_\alpha$, for λ limit ordinal.

Note that (iii) is well-defined because J is monotonic and, consequently, $\alpha < \beta \rightarrow P_\alpha \le P_\beta$. Also, it is clear that, if for each $\alpha < \lambda$, P_α is a model of S, then so is P_λ.

This result provides us with a model P* ($\bar{P}$*) such that:

$$p^*(\lambda x \cdot A(x,\bar{c}),d) = [A^+(d,\bar{c})]_{p^*}.$$
$$p^*(\lambda x \cdot \sim A(x,\bar{c}),d) = [A^-(d,\bar{c})]_{p^*}.$$

Moreover, $\bar{P}^*$ satisfies Dis. Hence we have a model of Dis, C1 and C2, and hence of $\bar{S}_0$. The details of the construction can be found in Feferman (1984) and Gilmore (1974). □

(ii) *The Consistency of* $\bar{S}_1$

For $\bar{S}_1$ we must be somewhat bolder in the process of model building; we must not, in the definition of the jump operation, restrict ourselves to monotonic wff. We require, among other things, the truth of

$$p(\lambda x \cdot A(x,\bar{y}),u) \leftrightarrow A(u,\bar{y})$$

for all logically valid A. Unfortunately, not all logical truths are monotonic, as Theorem 5.2 showed.

Let $P = \langle D,p \rangle$ be any model for L and $\bar{P}$ its extension to $\bar{L}$.

Define $K(P) = \langle D,K(p) \rangle$ where

$$K(p)(e,d) = \begin{cases} [A(d,\bar{c})]_p & - \text{ if } e = \lambda x \cdot A(x,\bar{c}) \in \textbf{Form} \\ \\ p(e,d) & - \text{ otherwise} \end{cases}$$

Let $\bar{K}(P)$ be the negative extension of $K(P)$. In this way we can define an ordinal sequence of models (and, implicitly, their negative extensions)

(i) $\quad P_0 = P$
(ii) $\quad P_{\alpha+1} = K(P_\alpha)$.

Of course, we must say what happens at limit ordinals. Here, we must proceed with care. The operator K, unlike J, is not monotonic. We cannot, therefore, define P_λ, at limit ordinals, as the union of its predecessors. In this case the union is not well-defined. To overcome this difficulty we follow the lead of Hertzberger (1982). We select those pairs, $\langle e,d \rangle \in D \times D$, which are locally stable in the following sense:

(iii) $\quad$ For limit ordinal λ, define
$\quad\quad\quad p_\lambda(e,d) = 1 \quad$ iff $(\exists\alpha<\lambda)(\forall\beta)(\alpha\le\beta<\lambda)(p_\beta(e,d) = 1)$.

Although we do not have monotonic behaviour, there exists a certain subset of values which are individually well-behaved.

Definition Let $\langle e,d \rangle \in D \times D$. Then $\langle e,d \rangle$ is *Positively Stable*
6.3. $\quad\quad$ iff $(\exists\alpha)(\forall\beta\ge\alpha)(p_\beta(e,d) = 1)$; it is *Negatively Stable* iff
$\quad\quad\quad (\exists\alpha)(\forall\beta\ge\alpha)(p_\beta(e,d) = 0)$.

For example, properties definable by logical truths are stable for all their arguments. Corresponding to fixed-point models we have the following concept:

Definition An ordinal α is a *Stabilization Ordinal* iff for each
6.4. $\langle e,d \rangle \in DxD$, $\langle e,d \rangle$ is positively stable iff
               $p_\alpha(e,d) = 1$.

The following theorem (6.6) is a direct application of a result of Hertzberger (1982).

Theorem There exists a least stabilization ordinal. Moreover, such
6.5.   ordinals occur with a regular periodicity.

Theorem Every stabilization ordinal α, $\overline{P}_\alpha$ is a model of $\overline{S}_1$.
6.6.

Proof
This is just a tedious but straightforward tour through the axioms of $\overline{S}_1$. $\square$

7. IN CONCLUSION

The majority of this paper has been devoted to the development of various type-free theories of properties. As such, its purpose has been very largely foundational. The actual application of these theories to a fragment of English, containing nominalized predicates, remains to be done. A detailed analysis might, for example, throw some light on the choice between such theories. Here, we have only indicated the need for some form of type-free theory. Another neglected topic is that of intensionality. We have employed a non-extensional framework but have neither defended it nor indicated its implications. Even the choice between a first or second-order theory requires further thought and discussion. Chierchia (1982), (1984) and Turner (1984) investigate second-order theories. Chierchia (1984), for example, argues strongly for a second-order theory on the basis of certain empirical facts about English. The theories developed here could be recast as second-order theories of properties, and so the present paper can be seen as very largely silent upon this issue. The choice of a first-order framework was dictated largely by pedagogical considerations. These topics will be further explored on another occasion. The full details of the theory S_1 can be located in Turner (1986).

REFERENCES

Bealer, G.: (1982), *Quality and Concept*, Clarendon Press, Oxford.
Chierchia, G.: (1982), 'Nominalization and Montague Grammar: a Semantics Without Types. For Natural Language', *Linguistics and Philosophy*, 5: pp. 303–354.
Chierchia, G.: (1984), 'Topics in the Syntax and Semantics of Infinitives and Gerunds'. Ph.D. Thesis, UMASS, Amherst.
Cocchiarella, N.: (1974), 'Fregean Semantics for a Realist Ontology', *Notre Dame Journal of Formal Logic*, 15: pp. 552–564.
Cocchiarella, N.: (1979), 'The Theory of Homogeneous Simple Types as a Second Order Logic', Notre Dame Journal of Formal Logic, 20: 505–524.
Feferman, S.: (1984), 'Towards useful Type-Free Theories I', *Journal of Symbolic Logic*, Vol. 49, pp. 75–111.
Gilmore, P.C.: (1974), 'The Consistency of Partial Set theory without Extensionality', *Axiomatic Set Theory*, Proceedings of Symposium in Pure Maths, Vol. 13, Part II, American Mathematical Society, Providence, R.I., pp. 147–153.
Gupta, A.: (1982), 'Truth and Paradox', *Journal of Philosophical Logic* 11: pp. 1–60.
Herzberger, H.: (1982), 'Notes on Naive Semantics', *Journal of Philosophical Logic* 11: pp. 61–102.
Kamp, H. (1983), 'A Scenic Tour Through the Land of Naked Infinitives' ms.
Landman, F.: (1985), 'Representation of Information and Information Growth' (this volume).
Turner, R.: (1984), 'Nominalization and Scott's Domains II', *Notre Dame Journal of Formal Logic* (forthcoming).
Turner, R.: (1986) 'A Theory of Properties', *Journal of Symbolic Logic* (forthcoming).

Chapter 7

VP Ellipsis in DR Theory*

Ewan Klein

1. INTRODUCTION

The title of this paper represents a somewhat arbitrary choice. Certainly a central portion of the subsequent text is concerned with an analysis of verb phrase ellipsis within Kamp's (1981) Discourse Representation (DR) Theory. Nevertheless, the starting point for the whole enterprise was an attempt to answer the following question: Can the rules for translating expressions of English into discourse representations be stated in parallel with the syntactic rules which assign a structural description to those expressions? As many readers will recognize, such a translation regime is embodied in Montague's (1974) fragments for English, and has been widely adopted in subsequent linguistic work. Assuming a context free phrase structure syntax, we get the following schematic pairing of syntactic with semantic rules:

$$\alpha_0 \rightarrow \alpha_1, \ldots, \alpha_n$$
$$\alpha_0' = f(\alpha_1', \ldots, \alpha_n')$$

where α_i' is the meaning of the constituent α_i, and where α_0' is defined as some function f of the meanings $\alpha_1', \ldots, \alpha_n'$. Semantic rules stated in this format are compositional: all the information relevant to constructing a meaning for a complex expression α_0 is locally present in the subconstituents of α_0. The reason why this enterprise seems challenging is that DR construction rules have typically been formulated as requiring reference to non-local information; for example, the rule which assigns a representation to an NP-VP sentence varies according to the identity of the determiner of the NP.

What is the justification for trying a different formulation? At least two

* The inception of this paper took place while I was a visitor at the Center for the Study of Language and Information (CSLI), Stanford, during summer 1984, and I am grateful to CSLI for their financial support and for providing such a stimulating and enjoyable environment. The credit for prompting me to look at VP Ellipsis within DR theory belongs to Ivan Sag. I am indebted to a large number of people for helpful comments and conversations at various stages in the development of this paper, in particular Gennaro Chierchia, Johan van Benthem, Keith Brown, Kit Fine, Hans Kamp, Barbara Partee, Barry Richards, Craige Roberts, Becky Root, Peter Sells, Stuart Shieber, Lesley Stirling, Mary Tait, Ray Turner, and Henk Zeevat. Finally, I wish to thank the SERC for longterm financial support in the form of an Advanced Research Fellowship.

reasons might be given. The first involves compositionality. As indicated above, DR theory appears to be less strictly compositional than, say, Montague grammar.[1] It is not obvious that strict compositionality is an indispensable feature of any adequate theory of natural language semantics; it might be the case that the proper treatment of anaphora is one in which compositionality is relaxed. On the other hand, to the extent that compositionality is a constraint on possible grammars, it would be interesting to determine exactly where it should be relaxed. Kamp himself claims:

... the conception of a perfect rule-by-rule parallelism between syntax and semantics is one that must be proved rather than taken for granted. [footnote omitted] In fact the data here presented point towards the conclusion that this conception is ultimately untenable. (1981, p. 298)

From a methodological point of view, it might be countered that it is the lack of parallelism which must be proved. One way of doing this is to cast DR construction rules in a compositional mould, and then to see at what point the mould becomes a Procrustean bed.

A second argument involves processing considerations. One of the appeals of DR theory is that it appears to provide an account of semantic representation in which the claims of model-theoretic semantics can be reconciled with those of automatic natural language parsing systems. It is far from clear, given the present state of our knowledge, what the optimal relation is between syntax and semantics in such systems. Nevertheless, the more flexibility there is between syntax and semantics, the better the chances of successfully incorporating DRSs in natural language parsers. The requirement that DR construction proceed top-down on syntactic parse trees would severely limit the design possibilities of any parser that incorporated DRSs as a semantic representation, and this again suggests that it is worthwhile exploring a rule-by-rule approach.

Despite these intentions, I shall not attempt to give a detailed reformulation of the required kind here (for some proposals in this direction, see Johnson and Klein (1985) and Reyle (1985)). Instead, I shall present the results of asking a subsidiary question: Assuming that each constituent in a phrase structure analysis of a sentence is to be assigned a DR translation, what is an appropriate representation and interpretation for a VP? It turns out that the evidence of VP ellipsis provides some useful clues about the answer to this. These issues form the subject matter of sections 3 and 4. They in turn raise further questions about the treatment of quantification and bound anaphora in DR theory, and this topic is briefly discussed in section 5. However, I start off in section 2 by giving a brief overview of some salient aspects of DR theory; the reader who is already familiar with Kamp (1981) may safely omit this section.

2. DR THEORY

Discourse representation theory[2] is a relatively new approach to the semantics of natural language. As the name suggests, a central tenet of the theory is that the basic unit of semantic analysis should be a discourse, rather than a sentence. Although this idea is not in itself very novel, DR theory is unusual in the way that it attempts to integrate techniques from model-theoretic semantics in a framework that also takes serious account of pragmatic aspects of language.

A key component of DR theory is the set of construction rules that convert natural language discourse into a formal representation of content, namely a Discourse Representation Structure. Existing proposals employ an algorithm that works top-down on syntactic parse trees. Starting off with a complex input, the procedure decomposes the parse tree into smaller and smaller units, while also indexing coreferential argument positions by means of reference markers. The procedure terminates when no further decompositions are possible.

In order to illustrate this, and other points, let us study some examples. We start by considering a two sentence discourse.

(1)   Lee owns a cat. It loves him.

We assume these sentences are assigned syntactic phrase markers of the usual kind. Application of the construction algorithm to the first sentence of (1) leads successively to the structures K_0 and K_1.

K_0:

x_0
Lee(x_0) x_0 owns a cat

K_1:

x_0 $\quad$ x_1
Lee(x_0)   cat(x_1)   own(x_0, x_1)

In the first step, K_0, the NP *Lee* licences the introduction of a discourse marker x_0 into the universe of the DRS. We also add two conditions: $Lee(x_0)$ – representing the information that x_0 stands for the bearer of the name *Lee* – and x_0 *owns a cat*, which is derived by replacing the subject of the S by the marker x_0. In the next step, the VP in this second condition is reduced further. The NP *a cat* licenses the introduction of discourse marker x_1 into the universe, and we add the conditions $cat(x_1)$, and *owns* (x_0, x_1). K_1

Processing of the second sentence now has to proceed relative to K_1. The natural interpretation of the pronouns *it* and *him* of this sentence is that they are anaphorically connected with the "antecedents" *a cat* and *Lee*. In terms of the construction algorithm, this means that the discourse markers which are introduced when the anaphoric pronouns are processed must be linked with the discourse markers x_1 and x_0 of K_1 that were earlier introduced for *a cat* and *Lee*. Thus the next two steps yield the following structure.

U. K_2

K_2:

x_0 x_1 x_2 x_3	*markers*
$Lee(x_0)$ $cat(x_1)$ $own(x_0, x_1)$ $x_2 = x_1$ $x_3 = x_0$ $love(x_2, x_3)$	*conditions*

Conk

This illustrates how a given DRS can serve as context for the processing of the next sentence, and how its discourse markers are essential to this function. Note that, according to this approach, the indefinite *a cat* is not treated as a quantifier, but simply as an expression that introduces a discourse marker together with some conditions.

context Kamp

The semantic content of K_2 is determined along lines which are familiar from model-theoretic semantics. An *embedding* function determines a correspondence between the formal representation and some situation. That is, K_2 is true in a given model M if there is an embedding function f which maps the discourse markers in the universe of K_2 into the universe of M, and if the objects in the range of f satisfy the conditions listed in K_2. More

Definition of embedding function

specifically, it is true if there is a function f which maps x_0, x_1 and x_2 and x_3 into objects a, b, c and d such that the following hold in M: a is Lee, b is a cat, a owns b, $c = b$, $d = a$, and c loves d. It transpires, therefore, that the existential force associated with an indefinite NP is determined by the embedding conditions for the DRS in which the NP is contained.

The following definition gives a more formal account of the way in which a truth conditional interpretation is assigned to a DRS.

Definition 1:

Let $K = \langle U.K, Con.K \rangle$ be a DRS where U.K is a set of discourse markers drawn from a nonempty set V, and Con.K is a set of atomic conditions. Let $M = \langle A, F \rangle$ be a model with universe A and interpretation function F. Let $f: V \mapsto A$ be a partial function. Then f *verifies* K, $f \models K$, iff U.K $\subseteq$ dom(f) and $f \models$ Con.K. And $f \models$ Con.K iff for each $S \in$ Con.K, $f \models S$.

Assume for the time being that a basic condition S is always of the form $R(x_1, \ldots, x_n)$, where R is an n-ary relation symbol, and $x_1, \ldots, x_n$ are reference markers. Then we have the following:

Definition 2:

$f \models R(x_1, \ldots, x_n)$ iff $\langle f(x_1), \ldots, f(x_n) \rangle \in F(R)$

Finally, we have:

Definition 3:

A DRS K is *true* iff there is some embedding function f such that $f \models K$.

Universally quantified NPs receive a somewhat different analysis to indefinites in DR theory. This point can be briefly illustrated with the help of a 'donkey' sentence such as (2).

(2)   Every farmer who owns a donkey beats it.

The problem in interpreting (2) is to provide a univocal treatment of *a donkey* which nevertheless accounts for the fact that it is perceived to have universal rather than existential force in this syntactic context.

166   *Ewan Klein*

K₃:

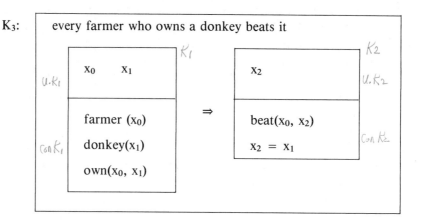

Universal sentences (and conditionals) licence the introduction of two subDRSs, the first of which represents the antecedent (e.g. *man who owns a donkey*), and the second the consequent (e.g. *beats it*). Informally, the embedding conditions associated with a DRS like K_3 go as follows: the DRS is true just in case every embedding function that verifies the antecedent box can be extended to an embedding function that verifies the consequent. By virtue of this analysis, every discourse marker in the universe of the antecedent box, including the marker x_1 which was introduced by *a donkey*, is universally quantified, and thus the correct truth conditions for (2) are obtained.

We can think of the split boxes in K_3 as being a new kind of condition, one in which ⇒ is a two-place relation whose arguments are DRSs. We write such a condition as ⇒ (K_1, K_2). Before giving it an interpretation, however, it is helpful to have some new notation (cf. Chierchia and Rooth (1984) and Zeevat (1984)).

Definition 4:

  Let $X \subseteq V$ be a set of discourse markers, and let f and g be partial functions on V. Then g is an *X-extension of f*, written $f \subseteq_X g$, iff dom(g) = dom(f) $\cup X$ and $f \subseteq g$.

That is, g is an *X*-extension of f iff g assigns the same values as f does to all the discourse markers in the domain of f, and moreover g also assigns values to all the markers in X. The next definition gives Kamp's interpretation of the universal/conditional arrow.

Definition 5:

  $f \models \Rightarrow (K_1, K_2)$ iff
  $\forall g[f \subseteq_{U.K_1} g \ \& \ g \models \text{Con.}K_1 \rightarrow \exists h[g \subseteq_{U.K_2} h \ \& \ h \models \text{Con.}K_2]]$

Suppose, for example, that we evaluated K_3 relative to an f whose domain is $\emptyset$, the empty set. Then for every g which is a $\{x_0, x_1\}$-extension of f and which verifies the antecedent subDRS of K_3, there must be a $\{x_2\}$-extension of g which verifies the consequent subDRS.

3. VP ELLIPSIS

As we saw in the preceeding section, Kamp's approach presupposes that when the DRS for a given sentence is constructed, a complete syntactic parse for that sentence has already been built. An alternative strategy would be to construct the DRS in a bottom-up fashion, so as to resemble the compositional construction of logical formulae in Montague semantics. What would the construction rules look like in this case?

Let us take as our model the Montagovian approach which is typically adopted in generalized phrase structure grammar (cf. Gazdar (1982), Gazdar *et al.* (1985), Klein and Sag (1985)). The grammar rules listed in (3) are pairs of phrase structure rules and translation rules:

(3)   a. $\langle S \rightarrow NP\ VP;\ NP'(VP') \rangle$
         b. $\langle NP \rightarrow Det\ Nom;\ Det'(Nom') \rangle$
         c. $\langle Nom \rightarrow N;\ N' \rangle$
         d. $\langle VP \rightarrow V;\ V' \rangle$

The translation rules dictate how the translation of the node on the lefthand side of the PS rule is built up from the translations of the nodes on the righthand side of the PS rule. So, for example, the translation rule in (3a) says that whenever a node S in a tree expands as an NP followed by a VP, the translation of that S constituent is obtained by combining the translation of the NP constituent (indicated as NP') as functor with the translation of the VP constituent (indicated as VP') as argument. The translations of NP and VP are derived in turn from the translations of their subconstituents by an inductive definition which takes as a basis the translations of lexical items into expressions of intensional logic. (4) gives a simple illustration, in which lambda expressions have been simplified where possible.

(4)

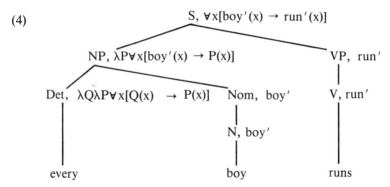

Taking (4) as our model, we could try to formulate analogues of (3) which would associate a subDRS with each constituent admitted by a PS rule. The tree in (5) gives a rough illustration of the way this might work.

(5)

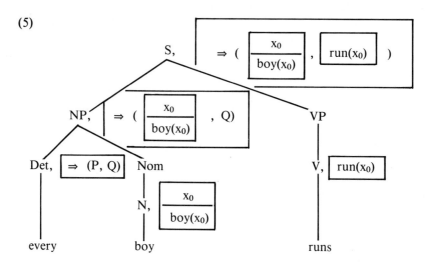

Notice that a structure has been associated with the determiner *every* in which P and Q are place-holders for subDRS arguments of $\Rightarrow$. Without going into details, I shall assume that there are operations which replace these place-holders with the appropriate subDRSs.

Even at this level of abstraction, a technical difficulty seems to arise. In order for the topmost DRS to receive the right truth conditions, it is essential that the same discourse marker (in this case x_0) occur as argument of both *boy* and *run*. However, it is not easy to see how to guarantee this result on a bottom-up translation process. That is, when some marker x_i is chosen to occupy the subject argument slot in the VP translation, this choice is independent of the discourse marker that is to occupy the argument slot in the Nom translation. It appears, then, that the DRSs associated with the Nom and VP in (5) do not represent the meanings of those constituents in a manner which is compatible with a compositional semantic analysis. The basis of a solution to this problem will be explored by examining the interpretation of VPs in greater detail.

The phenomenon of VP ellipsis in English has been subjected to close scrutiny in the literature, the central studies being Sag (1976) and Williams (1977). In the rest of this section, I shall investigate how DR theory might be extended to deal with some of the basic facts involving VP ellipsis. Despite the fact that many important and interesting issues will be ignored, the attempt to widen the coverage of DR theory in this way is interesting for its own sake, and will also give us some valuable clues as to the kind of representation that will have to be associated with VPs.[3]

Consider a discourse like the following:

(6)   Lee loves his cat. Gerry does too.

Without going into great detail about possessives, we might suppose that the DRS for the first sentence of (6) is something like this:

K$_4$:

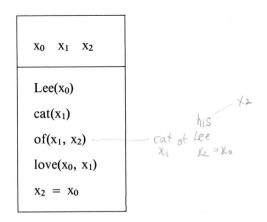

x_0 x_1 x_2
Lee(x_0)
cat(x_1)
of(x_1, x_2)
love(x_0, x_1)
$x_2 = x_0$

The NP *his cat* has been analysed as equivalent to *a cat of him*. Consequently, it licenses the addition of two reference markers x_1 and x_2 to the universe. We add the conditions *cat*(x_1) and *of*(x_1, x_2) and, assuming that *his* is anaphoric to *Lee*, we also add the link $x_2 = x_0$.

When we come to process the second sentence, we need to say something about the structure of the ellipsed VP *does*. Consider first a VP like (7) in which *do* takes a complement:

(7)   does like the cat

Following Gazdar, Pullum and Sag (1982), I shall assign it the following structure:

(8)

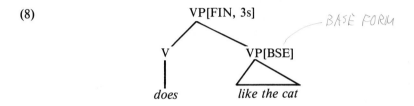

That is, it is analysed as a finite, third person singular VP consisting of a head V *does* and a base-form VP complement.

The ellipsed VP will be assigned exactly the same structure. The only difference is that we add the feature specification [+NULL] to the complement VP, and let such VPs expand as the empty string:

(9)

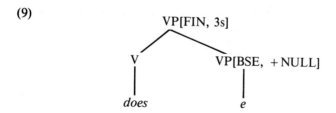

Let's assume that this complement is to be interpreted as a VP anaphor, and will itself license the introduction of discourse marker, say P. Ignoring the word *too*, we might therefore extend K_4 as follows:

marks verbs, predicates
? ?

K_5:

x_0 x_1 x_2 x_3 P
Lee(x_0)
cat(x_1)
of(x_1, x_2)
love(x_0, x_1)
$x_2 = x_0$
Gerry(x_3)
do(x_3, P)

This is a kind of verbal anaphora?

Now we are faced with the question: what can P be linked to? If we pursue the analogy with nominal anaphora, we are led to the conclusion that there should be an additional marker, say Q, which has already been introduced into the universe of the DRS, and whose value is constrained by the conditions associated with the VP of the preceding sentence. However, there is a problem in implementing this idea which is brought out in the attempted construction K_6. Here, we have grouped the conditions associated with *loves his cat* into a subDRS Q:

? ?

K$_6$:

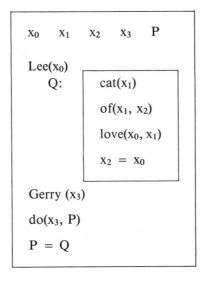

Let us suppose that all the reference markers in Q are assigned values by whatever embedding function is used to verify the superordinate DRS K$_6$. Then, in particular, x_0 will be assigned the value Lee. But this conflicts with the intention that Q should group together conditions that apply equally to Lee and Gerry. One way of dealing with this difficulty would be to invoke some kind of relettering operation which would make P equivalent to the result of replacing the relevant occurrences of x_0 in Q by x_3. An alternative would be to modify the subDRS Q so that it was interpreted as expressing a property that could be predicated of different subjects. There are two reasons why the second option is preferable. First, the deployment and analysis of properties has been much studied in formal semantics (see Chierchia (1984) for an interesting recent investigation), and other things being equal, it is sensible to build on established foundations. Second, Kamp (1983) introduces just the mechanism we require in the context of providing an account of definite noun phrases, so we already have independent motivation for such an extension to the theory.

Kamp suggests that, when a DRS is to be construed as a predicate, we add to its universe a distinguished reference marker "which plays the role of the individual to which the predicate is applied" (1983: 52). I will indicate the distinguished marker by enclosing it in square brackets. Thus, Q above would be modified to as follows:

Put [x₄] instead of x₀

Q:

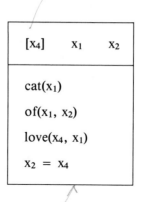

$$[x_4] \quad x_1 \quad x_2$$

$$cat(x_1)$$

$$of(x_1, x_2)$$

$$love(x_4, x_1)$$

$$x_2 = x_4$$

Let us call a structure like this a *predicate-DRS*, and call *P, Q, . . . discourse markers of the predicate type*, or predicate markers, for short. Moreover, we use the notation [x]K to represent a DRS which has a distinguished marker *x*. According to Kamp,

an object *a satisfies* [a predicate-DRS [x]K] if it is possible to extend the correspondence ⟨x, a⟩, between the object and the distinguished marker, to a proper embedding of the entire DRS. (1983: 53)

Thus, an object *a* satisfies *Q* if there are objects *b* and *c* such that *a* loves *b, b* is a cat, *b* is 'of' *c* and *c* is identical to *a*. Reverting temporarily to the notation of lambda-calculus, *Q* is equivalent under its intended interpretation to the following:

(10) $\lambda x_4 \, \exists x_1 \exists x_2 [love(x_4, x_1) \ \& \ cat(x_1) \ \& \ of(x_1, x_2) \ \& \ x_2 = x_4]$

This seems to be what we need. If *P* is linked to *Q*, then $do(x_3, P)$ will be true under an embedding *f* if $f(x_3)$ satisfies *Q*.

Given this new apparatus, the DRS K_6 can be revised along the lines shown in K_7 below.

The conditions (i) and (ii) in the subDRS *Q* in K_7 represent alternative, mutually exclusive ways in which we could link x_3 to a previous discourse marker. If we take option (i), then *Q* expresses the property of being a x_4 such that x_4 loves x_4's cat. Consequently, the discourse receives the so-called 'sloppy identity' reading, according to which Lee loves Lee's cat and Gerry loves Gerry's cat. Adopting condition (ii) instead gives rise to the 'strict identity' reading, where *Q* expresses the property of being a x_4 such that x_4 loves x_0's (i.e. Lee's) cat.

Before concluding this section, I wish to briefly consider an alternative analysis of VP ellipsis in DR theory. According to this alternative, there

K7:

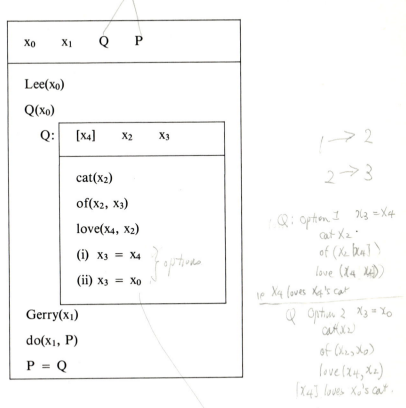

is no postulation of an anaphoric link between predicate markers. Instead, the conditions for a null VP are obtained by 'copying' the conditions associated with some previous VP in the discourse, accompanied by an appropriate relettering of the subject-position discourse marker.[4] To make things clearer, let us look at an example like (11).

(11)   Sam found a cat. Kit did too.

Suppose that K8 represents the first sentence.

K8:

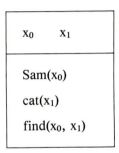

According to the alternative proposal, we can extend this DR to the second sentence of (11) in the following manner. First we add a condition (and discourse marker) for *Kit*, say $Kit(x_2)$. Next, we copy over both the VP conditions of the first sentence, replacing all occurrences of x_0 by x_2:

K_9:

x_0 $\quad$ x_1 $\quad$ x_2
$Sam(x_0)$ $cat(x_1)$ $find(x_0, x_1)$ $Kit(x_2)$ $cat(x_1)$ $find(x_2, x_1)$

But we now encounter a severe difficulty. By copying the VP conditions of the first sentence over to the second one, we have to use the same discourse marker to represent *a cat* in the ellipsed VP as we used in the full VP. According to the definition of truth, this means that Sam and Kit found the same cat. In other words, we are rendering (11) equivalent to (12):

(12)   Sam found a cat. Kit found it too.

And this of course is not at all what we want. Moreover, once we have adopted a copying analysis of VP ellipsis, it is difficult to see how this problem could be circumvented without radically changing the analysis of indefinites in DR theory.

Superficially, it might seem that the anaphoric approach that I have proposed would founder in the same manner. But first impressions are deceptive. The semantics that we independently require for predicate-DRSs says, in effect, that a structure of the form

K_{10}:

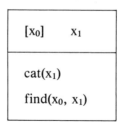

$[x_0]$ $\quad$ x_1
$cat(x_1)$ $find(x_0, x_1)$

denotes a function φ from individuals to sets of embedding functions such that for any individual a, a function f belongs to $\varphi(a)$ only if it verifies K_{10} when it assigns a as the value of x_0. (This will be elaborated more formally in the next section.) Since the values assigned to x_1 depend on the set of embedding functions associated with a given a, we can find a different cat for each a that satisfies K_{10}.

4. THE SEMANTICS OF PREDICATE-DRSs

I have not yet made clear how predicate markers are to be assigned values under an embedding function. The first step in rectifying this is to give a new definition of DRSs.

Definition 6:
(i)   The set V of discourse markers $= Ind \cup Pred$, where *Ind, Pred* are disjoint, nonempty sets. *Ind* is the set of individual markers and *Pred* is the set of predicate markers.

(ii)   A DRS K is a pair $\langle$U.K, Con.K$\rangle$, where each element of U.K belongs to V, and each condition in Con.K is either an atomic sentence or else an expression of the form $P:$ $[x]K'$, where P is a predicate marker and $[x]K'$ is a predicate-DRS with distinguished marker x.

This new kind of condition we have allowed, $P:$ $[x]K'$, says that P is a predicate marker whose value is constrained to be the interpretation of $[x]K'$. In order to spell this out in more detail, we have to be more specific about the semantic value which is to be assigned to predicate-DRSs.

As the name suggests, a predicate-DRS provides us with a means of representing a complex one-place predicate in DR theory. In standard first order logic, a one-place predicate denotes a function from individuals to sentence-denotations, i.e. truth values. The syntactic counterpart to a (non-atomic) sentence in DR theory is a DRS, and so the task of finding an appropriate denotation for a predicate-DRS involves finding an appropriate denotation for an ordinary DRS. The simplest solution would be to identify it with the set of embedding functions which make the DRS true. But this fails to take into account the particular role of discourse markers in the theory. Instead, I shall say that the denotation of a DRS K is a function which, relative to a partial embedding function f, yields the set of partial functions which extend f to U.K and which verify K.[5]

sounds good

re to the discourse markers

Definition 7:

Let f be an embedding function, and K a DRS. Then $\|K\|^f =$ $\{g: f \subseteq_{U.K} g \ \& \ g \models \text{Con}_{[x]K}\}$. Moreover, K is *true relative to f* iff $\exists g \in \|K\|^f$.

If we pursue this line of analysis, then the denotation of a predicate-DRS can be construed roughly as a function from individuals to DRS denotations, i.e. sets of embedding functions.

Since predicate markers will be assigned the same kind of values as predicate-DRSs, the notion of an embedding function has to be extended to take this into account. Since, in addition, an arbitrary DRS containing a predicate marker can always be made into a predicate-DRS which is contained within a larger DRS, the definition must be inductive.

Definition 8:

Let $M = \langle A, F \rangle$ be a model with universe A and valuation F. The set G of embedding functions into M is defined as follows:
(i) $G^0 = \{f: f \text{ is a partial function from } Ind \text{ into } A\}$
(ii) $G^n = \{f: f \text{ is a partial function which maps } Ind \text{ into } A \text{ and}$ $Pred \text{ into } \{\varphi:A \mapsto \text{pow}(G^{n-1})\}\}$
(iii) $G = \cup G^n$

Suppose that we determine the denotation of $[x]K$ relative to some function f. Then every g in the value space of $\|[x]K\|^f$ must be a suitable extension of f. By way of example, consider a DRS like K_{11}.

K_{11}:

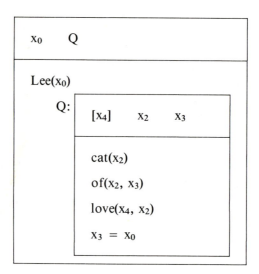

Let f be a function that verifies K_{11}, and let it assign to the predicate-DRS the value φ. For any $a \in A$, $\varphi(a)$ must be a set of embedding functions which extend f to the universe $\{x_2, x_3\}$ and which verify the conditions in the predicate-DRS when a is the value of x_4. But it is not adequate to require that every $g \in \varphi(a)$ be a $\{x_2, x_3\}$-extension of f. For f has to assign a value to Q, and the value of Q is set identical to the predicate-DRS. If $f(Q) = \varphi$ and every $g \in \varphi$ includes f, then f will be contained in its own function space and will not be well-founded. Notice, however, that this problem can be avoided if we impose the syntactic condition that a predicate marker such as Q cannot occur anywhere within the predicate-DRS that determines its value. We can then say that the embedding functions in $f(Q)(a)$ only have to extend f with respect to individual reference markers.

We use $f \mid X$ to denote the restriction of f to the set X.

Definition 9:

> If f is a partial function, then $f \mid X$ is that partial function $g \subseteq f$ such that $\text{dom}(g) = \text{dom}(f) \cap X$.

ie $f \mid X \equiv g$

$\text{dom}(f \mid X) = \text{dom} f \mid \cap X$

We now modify our definition of X-extension to take this restriction into account.

See definition 4

Definition 10:

> Let $X \subseteq V$ be a set of discourse markers, and let f and g be partial functions on V. Then $f \subseteq_{X \mid Ind} g$ iff $\text{dom}(g) = \text{dom}(f \mid Ind) \cup X$ and $f \mid Ind \subseteq g \mid Ind$.

f is restricted to Ind but extended to X

The interpretation of a predicate-DRS is defined as follows:

Definition 11:

> Let f be an embedding function, let $[x]K$ be a predicate-DRS with distinguished variable x, and let G be the set of embedding functions. Then $\|[x]K\|^f$ is that function $\varphi: A \mapsto \text{pow}(G)$ such that for any $a \in A$, $\varphi(a) = \{g: f \subseteq_{U.[x]K \mid Ind} g \ \& \ g[a/x] \models \text{Con.}[x]K\}$

Expressed in English, the extension of predicate DRS $[x]K$, relative to f, is a function φ with domain A that assigns to each argument a the set of embedding functions g which are $U.[x]K \mid Ind$-extensions of f and which verify all the conditions in $[x]K$ when they assign a as the value of x.

Finally, we spell out the way in which conditions of the form '$P: [x]K$' and '$P(x_i)$' are interpreted.

Definition 12:

> If P is a predicate marker and $[x]K$ is predicate-DRS, then $f \models P: [x]K$ iff $f(P) = \|[x]K\|^f$.

Definition 13:
     If P is a predicate marker and x_i is a reference marker, then
     $f \vDash P(x_i)$ iff $\exists g \in f(P)(f(x_i))$.

5. QUANTIFICATION

At this point, it is pertinent to see how our proposal meshes in with another important use of subDRSs, namely in the representation of universal quantification. Consider, for example, the standard DR analysis of (13).

(13)   Every boy who owns a cat loves it.

K$_{12}$:

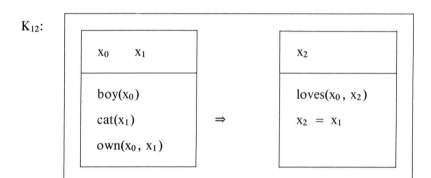

     Suppose that we wished to give a compositional interpretation to K$_{12}$. This would require assigning an interpretation to each subDRS, and interpreting $\Rightarrow$ as a binary relation on DRSs. If the subDRSs are to be taken as expressing properties, we arrive at an analysis which is strikingly reminiscent of the work on generalized quantifiers which treats determiners as binary relations on sets.[6] On such an approach, *every* denotes the relation D such that for any sets A, B, $D(A, B)$ is true if $A \subseteq B$. This analogy can be made more explicit if we modify K$_{12}$ to incorporate predicate-DRSs as follows.

K$_{13}$:

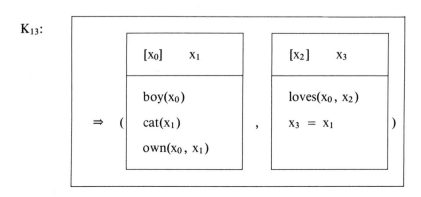

In the light of the preceding section, we might define the interpretation of ⇒ along the following lines:

(14)   Let $[x_0]K$, $[x_1]K'$ be predicate-DRSs. Then
       $f \vDash \Rightarrow ([x_0]K, [x_1]K')$ iff for all $a \in A$, for all g, if
       $g \in \|[x_0]K\|^f(a)$ then there is an h such that $h \in \|[x_1]K'\|^g(a)$.

Suppose that for a given individual a, there is some function g in $\|[x_0]K\|^f(a)$. Then by (14) and Definition 11, there must be a corresponding function h such that h is an extension of g to the universe of $[x_1]K'$ and such that $h[a/x_1]$ verifies $[x_1]K'$. To see that this gives the same results in the case of K_{13} as Kamp's definition, consider the following model:

(15) $F(boy)$ = { Lee }
       $F(cat)$ = { Tom, Felix }
       $F(own)$ = { ⟨ Lee, Tom ⟩, ⟨ Lee, Felix ⟩ }
       $F(love)$ = { ⟨ Lee, Tom ⟩, ⟨ Tom, Felix ⟩ }

The relevant reading of (13) is one on which every boy loves every cat that he owns. Thus we would expect it to be false in this model, since there is one cat owned by Lee which he fails to love, namely Felix. To see how things work out, let '$[x_0]$Nom' represent the first DRS argument of ⇒ in K_{14}, and let '$[x_2]$VP' represent the second argument. Then their extensions are given in (16a) and (16b), respectively.

(16)   a. $\|[x_0]\text{Nom}\|^f$ = { ⟨ Lee, { g, g' } ⟩,
                                        ⟨ Tom, Ø ⟩,
                                        ⟨ Felix, Ø ⟩ }

       b. $\|[x_2]\text{VP}\|^g$ = { ⟨ Lee, { h } ⟩,
                                        ⟨ Tom, Ø ⟩,
                                        ⟨ Felix, Ø ⟩ }

            $\|[x_2]\text{VP}\|^{g'}$ = { ⟨ Lee, Ø ⟩,
                                           ⟨ Tom, { h' } ⟩
                                           ⟨ Felix, Ø ⟩ }

       where

       $f = \emptyset$
       $g = \{ ⟨ x_0, \text{Lee} ⟩,$ $g' = \{ ⟨ x_0, \text{Lee} ⟩,$
              $⟨ x_1, \text{Tom} ⟩ \}$ $⟨ x_1, \text{Felix} ⟩ \}$
       $h = \{ ⟨ x_0, \text{Lee} ⟩,$ $h' = \{ ⟨ x_0, \text{Lee} ⟩,$
              $⟨ x_1, \text{Tom} ⟩,$ $⟨ x_1, \text{Felix} ⟩,$
              $⟨ x_2, \text{Lee} ⟩,$ $⟨ x_2, \text{Tom} ⟩,$
              $⟨ x_3, \text{Tom} ⟩ \}$ $⟨ x_3, \text{Felix} ⟩ \}$

According to the interpretation of $\Rightarrow$ given in (14) above, K_{13} is true under f just in case whenever a function $g \in \|[x_0]\text{Nom}\|^f(a)$, for any $a \in A$, there is also a function $h \in \|[x_2]\text{VP}\|^g$. But this fails. For although the function g in $\|[x_0]\text{Nom}\|^f(\text{Lee})$ has a corresponding function h in $\|[x_2]\text{VP}\|^g(\text{Lee})$, there is no function in $\|[x_2]\text{VP}\|^{g'}(\text{Lee})$ which corresponds to g' in $\|[x_0]\text{Nom}\|^f(\text{Lee})$. In fact, $\|[x_2]\text{VP}\|^{g'}(\text{Lee}) = \emptyset$

Our general strategy in constructing a DRS will be to associate a subDRS with each constituent in a sentence. Each subDRS will be labelled by a predicate marker, and it is convenient for expository reasons to let category labels such as 'Nom' and 'VP' be aliases for P_1, P_2, etc. In this way, we can make explicit what the syntactic origin of each subDRS is. K_{14} illustrates a DRS for (17).

(17)   Every boy loves his cat.

K_{14}:

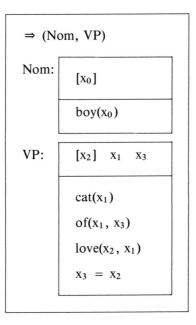

Since $\Rightarrow$ takes predicate markers as its arguments on this approach, we need to slightly modify its interpretation rule. This ensures that the embedding conditions for (17) are exactly the same as if we had directly used the subDRSs as arguments of the determiner.[7]

Definition 14:

$f \models \; \Rightarrow (P_1, P_2)$ iff for every $a \in A$, for every g, if $g \in f(P_1)(a)$
then there is an h such that $h \in g(P_2)(a)$.

On Kamp's approach, there are two differences between the treatment of *every* and *a*. The former triggers the introduction of two subDRSs, while the latter does not. And the latter triggers the introduction of a discourse marker, while the former does not. However, if subDRSs are associated with subconstituents in a sentence in the manner I have suggested, the first difference disappears. That is, suppose we are dealing with a syntactic structure of the following form.

(18)

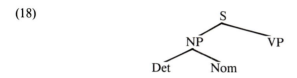

In order to obtain some generality in the DRS construction rules, I shall suppose that the subDRS associated with the Det constituent always involves a condition which contains a connective and two predicate-markers which are subsequently linked to the predicate-DRSs for Nom and VP. As we saw, this condition is '$\Rightarrow (P_1, P_2)$' in the case of the determiner *every*. The corresponding condition for *a* will be of the form '$\wedge(P_1(x_i), P_2(x_i))$', where $\wedge$ is a connective corresponding to conjunction, and x_i is a new reference marker whose introduction into the appropriate universe is licensed by the indefinite. The DRS K_{15} illustrates the resulting structure:

(19)   A boy loves his cat.

K_{15}:

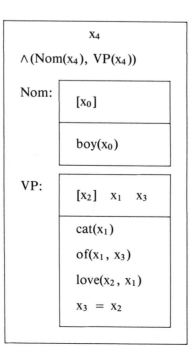

The connective $\wedge$ has an interpretation which is analogous to the one proposed for the conditional connective $\Rightarrow$. The main difference is we wish to admit conditions like '$P(x_i)$' as arguments of the relation. In the circumstances, it seems reasonable to first extend our notion of denotation so as to encompass arbitrary conditions within a DRS as well as a DRS itself.

Definition 15:

Let S be a condition. Then $\|S\|^f = \{\, g\colon \mathrm{dom}(g) = \mathrm{dom}(f)$ and $g \vDash S\}$

Definition 16:

Let S and T be conditions. Then

$f \vDash \wedge(S, T)$ iff there is a $g \in \|S\|^f$ and there is an $h \in \|T\|^g$.

It should be fairly easy to formulate an inference rule of $\wedge$-elimination which would render K_{15} equivalent to a more familiar DRS of the following sort:

K_{16}:

$x_1 \quad x_3 \quad x_4$
boy(x_4)
cat(x_1)
of(x_1, x_3)
love(x_4, x_1)
$x_3 = x_4$

One distinction that has frequently been drawn in the literature on anaphora is between pronouns that corefer with their antecedents and pronouns which are interpreted as variables bound by quantifiers.[8] It has recently been argued by Reinhart (1983) that all pronouns are interpretable as bound, regardless of whether the antecedent is a referring term or not, as long as the antecedent and pronoun meet her 'bound anaphora condition'. Ignoring problems of disjoint reference, this condition essentially reduces to the requirement that the antecedent c-command the pronoun. The main differences between referring NP and quantified NP anaphora follow, according to Reinhart, from the fact that pronouns can not only be bound by the former but also corefer with them. Within DR theory, as formulated by Kamp, the idea that some pronouns are interpreted as bound variables rather than coreferring terms seems to disappear.[9] Consider, for example, a 'standard' DRS for (17), namely K_{17}:

K_{17}:

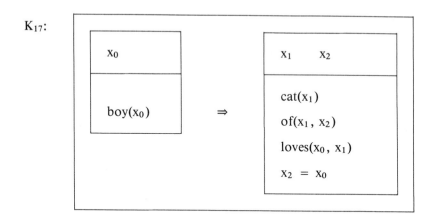

The pronominal *his*, which we might expect to be interpreted as a bound variable, receives a representation which is uniform with that accorded to other pronouns. That is, it licenses the introduction of a new discourse marker x_2, together with a condition that links x_2 to an accessible marker that was introduced at a prior stage in the construction. In this particular case, the relevant marker, x_0, occurs in the subDRS that represents the nominal sister of the determiner *every*, but it is difficult to relate this fact to the presence of a c-command binding relation between quantifier and pronoun.

By contrast, on the approach we are adopting, an analogue of the binding interpretation emerges rather naturally. Consider again the DRS K_{15}, which is our version of K_{16}. What seems to be relevant is that the reference marker x_3 that corresponds to *his* is linked to the distinguished marker $[x_2]$ which co-occurs in the universe of VP. This suggests the following idea:

(20)   A reference marker x_i occurring in the universe of a predicate-DRS $[x_j]K$ is *bound* just in case $[x_j]K$ contains the condition $x_i = x_j$.

Such a definition may be easier to motivate if we recall the standard account of quantifier binding in Montague grammar. In order for a variable x_i occurring in an expression β to be bound by a term α, we must employ a quantification rule with index i. The accompanying semantic rule yields $\alpha'(\lambda x_i \beta')$, i.e. it applies the translation of α to the result of abstracting over x_i in the translation of β. In effect, the pronouns bound by α are all those which translate as x_i and which are semantically bound by λx_i. Thus example (19), *A boy loves his cat*, would have a Montague translation roughly along the lines of (21), where the variable x_0 corresponds to a pronoun bound by *a boy*.

(21) $(a'(boy'))(\lambda x_0 [love' [x_0\text{'s-cat}'])(x_0)]$

A further point of interest is that although K_{15} assigns the pronominal *his* a bound reading, there is also a coreference reading which is truth-conditionally equivalent. To get this, we simply replace the condition $x_3 = x_2$ in VP by $x_3 = x_4$. A consequence of this fact is that indefinite NPs should be like definites in giving rise to the strict identity reading in VP ellipsis. That this prediction is indeed correct can be seen more clearly in an example like (22).[10]

(22)   A boy stroked his cat and my friend did too.

By contrast, where an anaphoric pronoun can only receive a bound interpretation, only the sloppy interpretation is available:

(23)   Every boy stroked his cat and my friend did too.

The correlation between the presence of both a bound reading and a co-reference reading for a pronoun with the presence of both a sloppy and strict identity interpretation in an associated VP ellipsis has long been established in the semantics literature.[11] It is striking that once predicate-DRSs are introduced, this correlation falls out in such a simple way.

At first sight, the generalized quantifier approach to NP interpretations seemed disturbingly remote from the approach adopted in DR theory. What I have tried to show is that we can have our cake and eat it too: assigning NPs to essentially the same semantic type is not incompatible with drawing a distinction between those NPs which trigger the introduction of a discourse marker, and hence give rise to discourse anaphora, and those NPs which do not.

6. SUMMARY

The main goal of this paper has been to lay the groundwork for an approach to DRS construction which would be compatible with existing approaches to semantic translation in extended Montague grammar. As a subgoal of this enterprise, I sketched a possible analysis of VP ellipsis in DR theory, on the assumption that this would give us some insight into an appropriate notion of VP interpretation. Starting from the assumption that the relation between the ellipsed VP and its antecedent should be treated as special case of anaphora within DR theory, I introduced the construct 'predicate DRS' to serve as the representation of a VP and defined a model theoretic semantics for it. I then showed that this allowed us to give an account of the sloppy/strict ambiguity analogous to one using lambda abstracts.

I suggested that predicate DRSs could also be deployed in the analysis of quantification, that is, by treating them as arguments in the representation of the determiners *every* and *a*. Such a relational representation brought the DR account of determiners into line with the large body of work on generalized quantifiers, while retaining the advantages of Kamp's analysis of donkey sentences. A further advantage was that we could establish a link between the sloppy/strict distinction and the bound anaphora/discourse anaphora distinction, as proposed by Reinhart. Indefinite NPs were assimilated to the pattern of generalized quantifiers, yet also triggered the introduction of a discourse marker in the usual fashion. This captured the fact that, like proper names, but unlike universal NPs, indefinites also give rise to the strict/sloppy distinction in VP ellipsis.

NOTES

1. For some discussion of the issues, see Janssen (1983), Landman and Moerdijk (1983), Partee (1984) and Zeevat (1984).
2. Apart from Kamp (1981, 1983), see also Heim's (1982) file card theory.
3. After completing the main substance of this paper, I became aware that a study of VP ellipsis within DR theory has also been carried out by van Eijck (1985). The points of agreement between the two treatments probably outweigh the differences.
4. Roberts (1984) briefly proposes such an analysis, which she attributes to Hans Kamp.

Sells (1985) presents some interesting data involving contrasts between anaphora with *which* and anaphora with VP ellipsis; he points out that only the former exhibits the sensitivity to scope restrictions which is typical of pronominal anaphora. He argues from this to the conclusion that VP ellipsis should involve some kind of copying operation. Unfortunately, I do not have an explanation for the facts pointed out by Sells; it remains to be shown that an appeal to copying will substantially improve matters.
5. This is very similar to the proposal in Zeevat (1984), according to which the denotation $\|K\|$ of a DRS K with universe U.K. is a pair $\langle$ U.K, G$\rangle$, where G is the set of (total) embedding functions which verify K. Given the denotation I have suggested, Zeevat's structure is definable as $\langle \{ x: \forall f \in \|K\|^{\emptyset} [x \in dom(f)] \}, \{ g: \exists f \in \|K\|^{\emptyset} [f \subseteq_v g] \} \rangle$ (where $\emptyset$ is the totally undefined embedding function).
6. See, for example, Barwise and Cooper (1981), and van Benthem (1983).

It is interesting to note that in more recent work, Barwise (1984) proposes a treatment of 'donkey' sentences which is rather similar to the approach adopted here.
7. It should be briefly mentioned at this point that although we have treated $\Rightarrow$ as a relation on predicate-DRSs, minor modifications suffice to also interpret it as a relation on ordinary DRSs.
8. Partee has consistently emphasized the importance of this issue, and one of the earliest discussions is Partee (1970).
9. This point has also been made by van Eijck (1985) in the same connection as the present

one; viz. accounting for the sloppy/strict ambiguity in a DRS approach to VP ellipsis.

10.   The difficulty with a present tense example like *A boy strokes his cat* is that it invites a generic interpretation, something which I do not wish to consider at present.

11.   See, for example, Keenan (1971), Partee (1978), Reinhart (1983), Sag (1976) and Williams (1977).

REFERENCES

Barwise, J.: (1984), 'A model of the treatment of anaphora in situation semantics', unpublished paper, CSLI, Stanford University.
Barwise, J., & Cooper, R.: (1981), 'Generalized quantifiers and natural languages', *Linguistics and Philosophy* 4, pp. 159–220.
Van Benthem, J.: (1983), 'Determiners and logic', *Linguistics and Philosophy* 6, pp. 447–478.
Chierchia, G.: (1984), *Topics in the syntax and semantics of infinitives and gerunds*, unpublished PhD thesis, distributed by Graduate Linguistic Student Association, University of Massachusetts, Amherst.
Chierchia, G., Rooth, M.: (1984), 'Configurational notions in discourse representation theory', NELS 14, Graduate Linguistic Student Association, University of Massachusetts, Amherst, pp. 49–63.
Van Eijck, J.: (1985), *Aspects of quantification in natural language*, unpublished PhD thesis, University of Groningen.
Gazdar, G.: (1982), 'Phrase structure grammar', in Pauline Jacobson and Geoffrey K. Pullum (eds.) *The Nature of Syntactic Representation*. D. Reidel, Dordrecht, pp. 131–186.
Gazdar, G., Klein, E., Pullum, G., & Sag, I.: (1985), *Generalized phrase structure grammar*, Blackwell, Oxford.
Gazdar, G., Pullum, G., & Sag, I.: (1982), 'Auxiliaries and related phenomena in a restrictive theory of grammar' *Language* 58, pp. 591–638.
Heim, I.: (1982), *The semantics of definite and indefinite NPs*, unpublished PhD thesis, distributed by Graduate Linguistic Student Association, University of Massachusetts, Amherst.
Janssen, T.M.V.: (1983), *Foundation and applications of Montague grammar*, unpublished PhD thesis, Mathematisch Centrum, University of Amsterdam.
Johnson, M., Klein, E.: (1985), 'A declarative formulation of Discourse Representation Theory', Paper presented at the summer meeting of the Association for Symbolic Logic, July 15–20 1985, Stanford University.
Kamp, H.: (1981), 'A theory of truth and semantic representation', in Groenendijk J., Janssen, T., Stokhof M. (eds) *Formal Methods in the Study of Language, Part 1*, Mathematical Centre Tracts 135, Mathematisch Centrum, Amsterdam.
Kamp, H.: (1983), 'SID without time or questions', unpublished chapter of *Situations in Discourse*.
Keenan, E.: (1971), 'Names, quantifiers and a solution to the sloppy identity problem', *Papers in Linguistics* 4.
Klein, E., Sag, I.A.: (1985), 'Type-driven translation', *Linguistics and Philosophy* 8, pp. 163–201.
Landman, F., & Moerdijk, I.: (1983), 'Compositionality and the analysis of anaphora', *Linguistics and Philosophy* 6, pp. 89–114.
Montague, R.: (1974), *Formal Philosophy: Selected Papers of Richard Montague*, R. Thomason (ed), Yale University Press.
Partee, B.: (1970), 'Opacity, coreference and pronouns', *Synthese* 21, pp. 359–385.
Partee, B.: (1978), 'Bound variables and other anaphors', in Donald Waltz (ed.), TINLAP-2, Association for Computing Machinery, pp. 79–85.

Partee, B.: (1984), 'Compositionality', in Veltman, F. & Landman, F. (eds.) *Varieties of Formal Semantics*, Foris Press, Dordrecht.

Partee, B., & Bach, E.: (1981), 'Quantification, pronouns and VP anaphora', in Groenendijk, J., Janssen, T., Stokhof, M. (eds), 445–481. *Formal Methods in the Study of Language, Part 2*, Mathematical Centre Tracts, 136 Amsterdam: Mathematisch Centrum.

Reinhart, T.: (1983), 'Coreference and bound anaphora: A restatement of the anaphora questions', *Linguistics and Philosophy* 6, pp. 47–88.

Reyle, U.: (1985), 'Grammatical functions, quantification and discourse referents', to appear in Proceedings of IJCAI 1985.

Roberts, C.: (1984), 'Anaphora, coreference and the binding theory', unpublished paper, University of Massachusetts, Amherst.

Sag, I.A.: (1976), *Deletion and Logical Form*, Garland Press, New York.

Sells, P.: (1985), 'Anaphora and Semantic Constituency', paper presented to the 4th West Coast Conference on Formal Linguistics, Los Angeles, March 1985.

Williams, E.S.: (1977), 'Discourse and logical form', *Linguistic Inquiry* 8, pp. 101–140.

Zeevat, H.: (1984), 'A compositional approach to discourse representations', unpublished paper, Erasmus Universiteit, Rotterdam.

Chapter 8

A Treatment of Belief Sentences in Discourse Representation Theory*

Henk Zeevat

0. INTRODUCTION

Discourse representation theory (DRT) has been applied with considerable success to a group of problems involving anaphoric relations. Here it has succeeded in explaining a group of notorious open problems, the most famous of which is the problem of donkey sentences. There have been several attempts at applying the theory to indirect contexts, but the results here are not spectacular: it is not very clear what the theory says about the philosophical problem of the nature of thoughts, and it is not clear what it is about discourse representation structures (DRS) that makes some of the suggestions made here seem so promising. It is mainly towards the last two questions that this paper hopes to make a contribution. The formal account of belief is, in a broad sense, a variant of the approach sketched by Hans Kamp in several talks.

I set out working on DRT because I was interested in a realist theory of thought. On a realist theory of meaning the meaning of any expression is either a constituent of reality such as an object or a property, or is a logical construction out of such constituents. An unsatisfying aspect of such a theory is that it must choose a form for thoughts in the absence of any criterion or evidence by which one could decide between the different kinds of logical syntax that one could use here. Now DRT provides a logical syntax, that is non-standard and claims that by its use various semantical puzzles can be solved. Thereby it becomes plausible to assume that natural language and thought are more similar to DRS-like systems than to, say, predicate logic. So what I wanted to do was to define a realist theory of thought that would use a notion of logical form derived from DRT. This would doubtless also have led to a more satisfactory treatment of coreference.

Unfortunately, it turned out that it is not possible to do so. But two conclusions could be drawn. First of these is that there seems to be no interpretation of DRT as a realist theory[1] of propositions in the sense sketched

* I wish to thank Barry Richards, Ewan Klein, Hans Kamp, Jeroen Groenendijk and Martin Stokhof for commenting on and suggesting improvements to earlier versions of this paper.

above. Secondly there are problems that cannot be handled by a realist theory (or at least lead to a considerable uneasiness) but can be handled in DRT.

These problems are treated in section (1). An alternative, more phenomenological, account of thoughts is discussed in section (2), and related to DRT in sections (3), (4) and (5). Section (6) contains some ideas on how thought, reality and language are related. In section (7) a more formal account is given, which is applied in section (8) to several classical problems with belief sentences.

1. REALISM AND DE DICTO TERMS

Though it seems that other versions of realism towards thoughts fall prey to the complex of problems around de dicto terms discussed here, my version of realism appears to be a good starting point. My realist would be defending the thesis that meanings are always ultimately constituted by real objects, properties and relations, and that thoughts correspond with the meaning of sentences. The simplest candidate for the meaning of singular definite terms is here the object to which it refers. So the meaning of a proper name would be the bearer of the name, and the meaning of a definite description the unique object satisfying the description.

It is well known however that this approach leads to problems in intensional contexts: there substitution of identicals is not always possible, and names (or other singular terms) may fail to have a referent. The standard solution (that can be carried out within the realist's assumptions) is to construct a meaning for de dicto occurrences of terms, that treats them as a quantifier, in exactly the same way as this is done for general terms.

In conjunction with the doctrine that proper names are hidden descriptions, most of the problems can be treated, though some uneasiness remains. Nevertheless, this approach is bound to fail in the end, as can be seen from Geach's famous example:

Hob believes that a witch poisoned his cow and Nob believes that she killed his pig

where de dicto terms are considered together with coreference. Though it is impossible by the non existence of witches to construct 'a witch' as a de re term the coreference between 'a witch' and 'she' requires some sort of identity between the witches Hob and Nob have their beliefs about. This is not rendered by the requirement that both terms have the same de dicto meaning: this would just guarantee that both beliefs are about a witch.

The phenomenon is quite common. The fact that it only has a de dicto interpretation does not seem to limit the pronoun binding abilities of a term, provided that the pronoun is not in an extensional context. It does not seem that there is a way to solve this problem, that on the one hand complies with semantical methodology[2] and on the other hand remains realist.

2. A PHENOMENOLOGICAL ACCOUNT

What the situation seems to call for is a different kind of object: an object that is not 'given in the world', but exists in the way we enter into contact with the world and try to grasp it. Such an idea is hardly new, since it is implicit in the analysis of representation ("Vorstellung") given by philosophers such as Brentano or Meinong. Where the realist looks at a potential belief subject and studies his relation with the objects, properties and relations in reality and finds out whether he is in sufficient contact with them so that he is able to intend them and form complex ideas about them, the phenomenologist remains on the side of the subject.

Since the subject cannot distinguish between successful and unsuccessful intentions of objects, one can make no distinction between the one kind of intention and the other: to the subject they both appear as objects. Moreover, there seems to be no reason to stop here, once we have the notion of an internal object of a belief subject: when a general thought is considered intentions of objects are again involved. These, however, can be distinguished internally: they are not intended as intentions of objects in reality, but play a role in the constitution of a general thought. By the internal role they play in the thinking of a subject, we can distinguish possible, impossible, arbitrary, hypothetical, fictional, determinate, indeterminate and other objects.

Most of these objects play a role in natural language coreference. Compare the following three examples:

A square circle does not exist. It would have to have four angles and be smooth at the same time.

Every farmer owns a donkey. He always treats it kindly.

Hamlet is the protagonist of one of Shakespeare's plays. He is a prince of Denmark.

All these cases appear to involve something like 'coreference'. But if by 'coreference' we mean what the term suggests viz. reference to the same thing, then what we have here would be reference to the same non-existent object. In the first case it could be called an impossible object. In cases like these the second clause must be similar to the first for coreference to be possible. Without the irrealis coreference appears to be impossible. In the second example we meet an arbitrary as well as a hypothetical object. In this case it is required that the second clause is general ("always"). In the third example the first clause introduces a fictional object. It seems that the pronoun in the second clause meets a contextual restriction.

In belief sentences and other propositional attitude sentences we are concerned with a particular kind of object: the objects that are the intentions of thoughts expressing the beliefs of a subject. The other kinds of objects noted above are not immediately treated in the framework developed below.

The phenomenological approach has two considerable disadvantages when one compares it with a realist approach: both the relation between thought and reality and the relation between thought and language become obscure. On a realist account the relation with reality can be understood from the ultimate constituents of the thoughts and logic. The relation with language is just as simple since in language we have names for the ultimate constituents and syntactical functions to describe complex thought using these names.

On the phenomenological account this simplicity is lost: whether a correspondence of an internal object with an external one can be assumed involves the nature and history of the private object. There is a similar problem with the relation to language. The mere fact that a subject connects a particular expression with a particular internal object is not sufficient. His use of the expression must also fit the syntactical and semantical conventions[3] governing the use of that expression.

3. DISCOURSE REPRESENTATIONS

One of the claims of this paper is that DRT can be used (in its role as a theory of logical form) as an interpretation of the phenomenological theory of thoughts. In order to make this more precise it is necessary to take a closer look at DRS's. The version I will give of them differs in three respects from the treatment given in Kamp [1981]: total assignments are used, a linear format is employed, and the treatment of variables introduced by proper names is different. DRS's are here given as formulae with the following recursive definition.

There are five kinds of atomic formulae:

1. proper names with a superior index (a natural number), e.g. $john^4$
2. common nouns with superior indices, e.g. $donkey^2$
3. intransitive verbs with an inferior index, e.g. run_5
4. transitive verbs with two inferior indices, e.g. $love_{4,2}$
5. $\perp$, the absurdum.

From these atomic formulae complex formulae can be formed[5] by the following rule:

If S_1 and S_2 are formulae that share no superior indices, both $S_1 S_2$ and $(S_1 \rightarrow S_2)$ are formulae.

Some examples, with a natural language equivalent:

(1)   a. *John owns every donkey.*
        b. $\text{john}^1 \, (\text{donkey}^2 \rightarrow \text{own}_{1,2})$

(2)   a. *If a farmer owns a donkey, he beats it.*
        b. $(\text{farmer}^1 \, \text{own}_{1,2} \, \text{donkey}^2 \rightarrow \text{beat}_{1,2})$

(3)   a. *John likes no girl who likes him.*
        b. $\text{john}^1 \, (\text{like}_{1,2} \, \text{girl}^2 \, \text{like}_{2,1} \rightarrow \perp)$

(4)   a. *John owns one donkey who likes him.*
        b. $\text{john}^1 \, \text{own}_{1,2} \, \text{donkey}^2 \, \text{like}_{2,1} \, (\text{donkey}^3 \, \text{own}_{1,3} \, \text{like}_{3,1} \rightarrow =_{3,2})$

In order to give the semantics it is necessary to introduce four syntactical notions.

Definition 1.
CN-indices. *(common noun index)*
    i is a CN-index of S if S is of the form x^i where x is a common noun or S is of the form $S_1 S_2$ and i is a CN-index of S_1 or S_2.

Definition 2.
PN-indices. *(proper noun index)*
    i is a PN index of S iff S is of the form x^i where x is a proper name or S has a subformula of that form.

Definition 3.
Primary Index. *A primary index is either a common noun index or a*
    i is primary in S iff i is a CN-index of S or i is a PN-index of S. *proper noun index*

Definition 4.
Sentence.
    A formula is a sentence iff every inferior index occurrence of an index i occurs in a subformula S′ of S where i is a primary index of S′.

The four examples cited above are all sentences in the sense of the definition. Parts of them e.g.

$(\text{like}_{1,2} \, \text{girl}^2 \, \text{like}_{2,1} \rightarrow \perp)$

or

own$_{1, 2}$

are not since in these cases the inferior index 1 (and in the second case the inferior indices 1 and 2) is not primary in any subformula.

The semantics is very similar to the normal semantics for predicate logic. Models $M = \langle A,F \rangle$ are used where A is the domain of the model, and F an interpretation function that assigns to the proper names objects in A, to CN's and IV's sets over A and to TV's two place-relations over A. As normal, assignments to indices are functions $g: IN \rightarrow A$. We define simultaneously:

   g is correct for S with respect to M   *index*

and

   g satisfies S with respect to M ($M \vDash S [g]$)

Definition 5.
   g is correct for S with respect to M iff for every primary index i of S and atom A^i that introduces i to S g satisfies A^i with respect to M.

Definition 6.
1. $M \vDash PN^i [g]$ iff $g(i) = F(PN)$.
2. $M \vDash CN^i [g]$ iff $g(i)$ in $F(CN)$.
3. $M \vDash IV^i [g]$ iff $g(i)$ in $F(IV)$.
4. $M \vDash TV_{i, j} [g]$ iff $\langle g(i), g(j) \rangle$ in $F(IV)$.
5. $M \vDash \bot [g]$ never holds.
6. $M \vDash S_1 S_2 [g]$ iff $M \vDash S_1 [g]$ and $M \vDash S_2 [g]$.
7. $M \vDash (S_1 \rightarrow S_2) [g]$ iff g is correct for $(S_1 \rightarrow S_2)$ and for every f such that f is equal to g except maybe for the CN-indices of S_1 and $M \vDash S_1 [f]$, there is an h that is equal to f except maybe for the CN-indices of S_2 such that $M \vDash S_2 [h]$.

Definition 7.
Truth.
   A sentence S is true on a model M iff there is a g such that $M \vDash S [g]$

The above definitions give a version of the syntax and semantics of DRS's that is orthodox except for the treatment of proper names. In Kamp's approach proper names introduce discourse referents on the highest level of the DRS under construction. In the bottom up approach used here it is impossible to follow Kamp in this respect. Therefore a distinction is made between CN-indices and PN-indices. Only the second are primary indices in an implication in which they occur. Correctness, and the fact that their interpretation does not vary in the interpretation of the arrow makes that any assignment that fulfills a phrase in which the proper name occurs assigns the referent of the name to the index introduced by it no matter how deeply embedded the name occurs. So e.g.

If John finds a unicorn, he rejoices.

that gives rise to the formula:

$$(\text{john}^1 \ \text{find}_{1,\,2} \ \text{unicorn}^2 \ \rightarrow \ \text{rejoice}_1)$$

can only be satisfied by an assignment g such that $g(1) = F(\text{john})$, even if the implication is trivially true because its antecedent can never be fulfilled. This makes it possible to continue the discourse with new facts about John, like e.g.

He has never yet found one.

4. MEINONGIAN OBJECTS

One of the claims of this paper is that the syntax of DRS's makes it possible to interpret Meinongian objects. The claim is that we may speak of certain primary indices in DRS's, conceived of both as logical formulae, or as concretely given representations, as if they were objects out of one of Meinong's types. Properties like "inexistent", "arbitrary", "possible" or "fictional" can than be predicated of them either by their position in the DRS, by the logical properties of the DRS in which they occur, or by the way in which the DRS is given. Such speech admittedly takes a psychological realism for granted: a DRS must be taken as characterising aspects of the form of thought.

This section is not intended as a reconstruction of Meinong's views, especially not if one takes him as implying that the objects subsist independently of thinking[6]. It might however be worthwhile to pursue the idea that our way of structuring logical languages, that derives from the work of Frege, is to a certain extent responsible for the misunderstanding of Meinong's work. It would be interesting to see how far one could come in the interpretation of Meinong against the background of DRT.

Roughly one can say that meinongian objects are primary indices in DRS's of a special form, or in DRS's with a special logical property, or in DRS's that play a special role. Let us start with the first kind. Within a DRS

CN- and PN-indices may occur at various depths. The prototypical kinds can be distinguished as follows:

a. primary indices.

These are the objects that from the point of view of the DRS itself are *existent*: they are judged to exist by anyone who judges the DRS to be true.

b. CN-indices of S' in a DRS S of the form (S' → ⊥).

These are the objects that from the point of view of the DRS itself are *nonexistent:* anyone who holds S must judge them to be absent.

c. the CN-indices in S' in a DRS S of the form (S' → S''). These may be termed *arbitrary*. Anybody who holds S to be true is committed to defend S'' for any choice of (real) objects that satisfies S'.

d. the CN-indices in S'' in a DRS S of the form (S' → S'').

These may be called *hypothetical*. A person who holds S, must also hold that they correspond to real objects, under the hypothesis that S' is satisfied.

The second distinction among kinds of objects is given by the logical properties a given DRS S may have. S can be true, false, logically true, logically false or contingent. Accordingly we can distinguish five kinds of objects among the primary CN-indices of S:

a. *existent*
b. *nonexistent*
c. *necessary*
d. *impossible*
e. *possible*

A second group of the same kind may also be distinguished. Let i be a primary index of a DRS that is satisfied. We can call i a *determinate* object if on every way in which S can be satisfied i stands for the same object. Similarly i is *indeterminate*, if i stands for different objects in different assignments that satisfy S.

These notions can be connected with necessity as well. i can be necessarily indeterminate or determinate, or possibly indeterminate or determinate.

The third type of objects comes into being at the point where we take DRS's seriously as representing mental states, or as representations of the meaning of a given piece of discourse or text. Accordingly we can call the primary indices of a DRS that represents somebody's beliefs an *object of belief*. In a similar way one might characterize *objects of desire, fictional objects, hypothetical objects* (this time from an explicitly given hypothesis) and *theoretical objects*.

In the rest of the article we will concentrate on one kind of object: the objects of belief.

5. A HYPOTHESIS

In the light of the preceding sections it is useful to introduce a simple hypothesis: the belief state of a person is structurally similar to a large DRS. There are two reasons to be interested in this hypothesis. The first is the success of DRT as a theory of logical form (a success that must to a large extent still be established by extending the approach to more problems in semantics). The second argument can be distilled from the last two sections: the hypothesis allows objects that are not real as constituents of thoughts. One might think there is a third argument that could be invoked: the role DRS's play in DRT as a theory of meaning, where they function as an intermediate level of analysis between the syntactic structures and the truth conditions. I do not think that one can argue in a decisive way for such a role for DRS's; it is possible to eliminate DRS's completely from DRT by employing a compositional translation mechanism as in Montague grammar.[7]

There are variants of the hypothesis that are just as plausible. It could e.g. be argued that the beliefs of a subject do not constitute a whole but are typically divided into unrelated parts. It does not seem proper to make a choice here. The hypothesis is to be taken in a very empirical manner, so that a decision on these matters is relegated to further inquiry.

An obvious problem with taking a belief state as a kind of DRS is the role natural language played in supplying the ultimate constituents. This is a difficulty, since we want to ascribe beliefs not just to creatures endowed with the gift of speaking English, but also to speakers of different languages, to people who lack the power of speech and to animals.

Moreover it is clear that natural languages contain only names for a rather small selection of the objects, properties and relations we and other creatures with perceptual powers can distinguish. It seems therefore best to start in the following way. Instead of employing constants taken from a natural language to build our atoms from, we assume a large collection of signs, for every possible subject of belief, from which the belief state is made up. It is easiest to think of those signs as constituting a finite segment of the natural numbers. It is not assumed that when two subjects employ the same number in their beliefs there is any relation between what they represent with those numbers: the numbers are private signs that a subject uses for his own purposes, and can be thought of as the equivalents of the common nouns, verbs and other non logical constants one finds in natural language. There are minor differences with the account of DRS's given a few pages back. There we took any proper name or common noun to introduce a superior index of its own. It seems normal to assume that an object falls under more than one proper name or common noun[8]. One can account for this fact by allowing common noun equivalents to carry inferior indices. Secondly there seems no need for having proper name equivalents as well since their superior indices are already available.

So I assume that a belief state can be represented by a large DRS in an abstract language that is particular to the subject. Each of us employs a different one. To fix ideas one may describe it in the following way: There are some numbers k, l, m such that

a. $\langle x, 1 \rangle$ is a common noun equivalent if $x < k$.
b. $\langle x, 2 \rangle$ is a intransitive verb equivalent if $x < l$.
c. $\langle x, 3 \rangle$ is a transitive verb equivalent if $x < m$.

And there are atoms of the following forms:

a. ^{i}
b. $\langle x, 1 \rangle^i$
c. $\langle x, 1 \rangle_i$
d. $\langle x, 2 \rangle_i$
e. $\langle x, 3 \rangle_{i, j}$

And from these DRS's can be constructed in the normal way. A belief state should correspond with a DRS that is a sentence.

In themselves the constants used in these DRS's do not mean anything. It is their connection with the perceptual and other powers of their subject that makes them relate to anything at all. The next sections are devoted to the problem of assigning meaning to these utterly private constants.

6. THOUGHTS, REALITY AND LANGUAGE

The more phenomenological approach towards thoughts leads to two related problems. On a realist theory a thought is related to elements of reality by the ultimate constituents that it is built up from. A name in a natural language like English for one of the elements of reality is thereby automatically a name for the corresponding constituent of a thought. A thought conceived along the lines of the preceding section is constituted by a mental primitive created by a subject as a reaction to information reaching him through the senses or by communication. Therefore, there does not exist an intrinsic relation between the constituents of thoughts and what the thoughts are about. Nor is a name in a public language automatically a name for one of those constituents. In this section I try to settle the question under which circumstances a private object (a primary object in the belief state or an index standing for a predicate) is a counterpart[9] (corresponds) to an object or relation and the question under what circumstances a name in some public language is a name for a private object.

The answers will sound familiar. There is clear convergence with David Kaplan's notion[10] of a name that represents its denotation for the subject such as defined in his *Quantifying In*. Moreover the notion of a counterpart by communication has a lot in common with a solution[11] of Hans Kamp for the Hob Nob sentences, and the general conception of DRT. The context of this approach is different however.

Counterparts by experience

I argued that the indices occurring in a belief state can be taken as meinongian objects. Though one might call every such index an object of belief, the only indices the subject assumes to correspond with something in reality are the primary indices of the belief state and the indices that stand for predicates. The other variables play a role in coding general information, and so one does not need to take the subject to believe that there is something corresponding to them in reality. Consequently I will use "object of belief" only for those indices that one might call "existent objects of belief". Under certain circumstances one can assume that the primary and predicate indices are related to real objects and relations: namely when the indices in question derive from experience of those objects and relations.

One may describe the genesis of such an index in the following way. The subject is affected through one or more of his senses. Moreover, he understands this as being affected by one object and accordingly forms a new index to store the information he obtains by his experience. In a similar way a property may be experienced and understood as a property, so that again an index is created as a result of the experience. It is also possible that the experience leads to a recognition. The subject in that case assumes that his experience is of an object that corresponds already with a private object in his belief state. Again, the same thing can happen in the case of properties and relations.

I will say that in these cases the private object (that may be identified outside the DRS of which it is a part with the ordered pair of the subject and his primary index) is a counterpart by experience of the experienced object, property or relation.

The process does not lead to a 1-1 relation. Many private objects come into being by other processes than experience. Many objects are never experienced. A real object may have two distinct private objects as counterparts by failure of recognition. Again two different real objects may have the same counterpart for a subject, by his failure to distinguish them. Private objects come into being by hypothesis and by communication as well. The first does not seem to lead to a comparable relation of the private objects with other things. One can use as a criterion that if a subject has a private object that is a counterpart of something else, the subject should intend to use his private object only as a means to store information that is about its counterpart. But a subject can not have such an intention in case the object is not related to him independently of its existence as one of his private objects.

Counterparts by communication

The criterion just mentioned does apply in case the private object is derived by communication. Suppose somebody says to you:

> *There is a car outside*

If he is sincere, one must attribute to him a thought of the form:

$$\langle k, 1 \rangle^j \langle i, 2 \rangle_j$$

A private object $\langle a, j \rangle$ standing for the car must be assumed. Suppose now that you believe the speaker but have no idea what car he is referring to. You can then add a belief of the form:

$$\langle l, 1 \rangle^r \langle m, 2 \rangle_r$$

to your belief state, where r must be a new index in the belief state. (I am assuming here that you already possess counterparts of being outside and carhood.) Now you intend r to stand for the same car the speaker intended the term to stand for and thereby your object $\langle b, r \rangle$ has become a counterpart of the speaker's $\langle a, j \rangle$ that may in turn be a counterpart of the car that stands in front of your house. Of course you may immediately think that it is the taxi you ordered 15 minutes ago. In that case there is already a private object $\langle b, 1 \rangle$ present and you just add

$$\langle m, 2 \rangle_1$$

to record the fact that it is now outside. But by the communication your object $\langle b, 1 \rangle$ has now become a counterpart of the speaker's $\langle a, j \rangle$.
    Let us try a definition:

> $\langle a, i \rangle$ is a counterpart by communication of $\langle b, j \rangle$ iff
> $\langle a, i \rangle$ is a's referent for the term T in an utterance by b to a in which T refers to $\langle b, j \rangle$ for b.

Again the process need not result in a tidy relation. As before two private objects of somebody can share a counterpart and two private objects of the same person can be counterparts of the same private object of somebody else.
    The notion of counterpart by communication can lead to a notion of a chain of private objects that are linked by the counterpart relation. The idea that the name 'John' (or any other name) is used correctly by a language

user only if such a chain connects his idea of John with the original dubbing can be treated in this way.

Names of private objects

Many belief subjects are language users. At first sight this may seem to alleviate our task. It is plausible to assume that many private objects have a name, in virtue of the connection of the private name with the subject's use of language. But a speaker may have a deviant use of certain names. One does not want to say that John has the belief that clouds talk, if he associates with 'cloud' and 'talk' counterparts of doghood and walking respectively.

A word in English, that is a name of an object, a property or a relation, stands for something that is publicly given by a convention among the users of English. Even if a name lacks a referent there are conventional limits on its use. E.g. it is not appropriate to use 'unicorn' for a thing that is not an animal or lacks horns.

Since private objects are not public it follows that an English word cannot be a name of a private object in the normal sense, but only in a derived sense. We must therefore state the conditions under which a word in English or another language can be called a name for a private object. The following two criteria seem to work:

1. Let S be a sign in a language L. An S-chain is a chain of counterparts by communication, each of which has become a counterpart by an act of communication in which it served as a referent for S. An S-chain is founded if it originates in the private object associated with S by the originator of the present use of the sign S. S is a name for any of the private objects in a founded S-chain.

One can explain a sentence like:

Charles is in love with Madame Bovary.

by attributing to Charles a private object that is a counterpart by communication of Flaubert's idea of Madame Bovary, and that has become a counterpart by Flaubert's use of the sign 'Madame Bovary'. Or in the same way:

John believes that Vulcan is covered with craters.

by assuming that John takes part in a Vulcan-chain that goes back to the astronomers that hypothesized Vulcan.

The second criterion is the following:

2. S is a name for ⟨ a, i ⟩ iff
   a. S is a name of x
   b. ⟨ a, i ⟩ is a counterpart by experience of x
   c. there is nothing in a's beliefs that prevents a from entering into the convention that governs the use of S, using ⟨ a, i ⟩ as his private meaning for S.

Admittedly, clause (c) is vague. It is designed to deal with problems like the following two.

Let us assume that there is a Babylonian who by regular observation of the heavens has acquired two counterparts by experience of the planet Venus: one associated with its morning appearance, the other with its evening appearance. Among other things he believes of one of them that it is visible in the evening sky. By (a) and (b) alone we must say that he has the following three beliefs:

that Venus is visible in the evening sky
that Hesperus is visible in the evening sky
that Phosphorus is visible in the evening sky

But (as we all know) he does not have the third of these. Clause (c) provides two possible explanations. The convention governing the use of 'Phosphorus' originates in a dubbing connected with the morning appearance of Venus. Our Babylonian, unaware of the fact that he could have morning experience of the object the counterpart of which is the private object that was caused by the evening appearance of Venus, cannot participate in this aspect of the convention.

There is another way to explain why attributing the third belief is strange. There is a simple rule in our convention concerning the use of 'Phosphorus', namely to call it 'Phosphorus'. Now the Babylonian already has a different private object that he calls 'Phosphorus', so he cannot participate in our convention.

The second example needs the second explanation:

John believes that woodchucks are bigger than groundhogs.

Both his private object for woodchuckhood and his private object for groundhoghood can be counterparts by experience of woodchuckhood.

Still he does not believe that groundhogs are bigger[12] than woodchucks. The only explanation here seems the linguistic one: John cannot participate in the 'woodchuck' convention by his private object for groundhogs since he already has a different private meaning for 'woodchuck'.

There is a seeming absurdity here. Suppose that John has had experience of woodchucks on two occasions, but has failed on the second occasion to recognise them as the same animals he had experience of on the first occasion. Suppose moreover that he has no idea of what the animals were called. Then both counterparts can be called 'woodchucks'. But if John now acquires the name 'woodchuck' one of the counterparts loses this name. So a word can cease to be a name for a counterpart of its referent, by the subject's entering into a convention to use it for a different private object.

Translation

The theory of belief that I am working out has many characteristics in common with a syntactical theory of belief. Therefore it may seem to do badly on one score: the explanation of the closure of belief under translation. On the treatment above one can say the following. A word in one language may be governed by the same or a very similar convention as a word in another language. So the French 'Londres' and the English 'London' are governed by almost the same convention: they share referents, connotation, origin and, but for a minor variation, the form of the sign. The correspondence can be less perfect, but the minimum one requires of a good translation is the matching of reference and connotation. Matching of connotation is of course not always completely achievable.

Now if the conventions in one language match the conventions in another to a sufficient degree, one might count John's use of 'London' and 'big' as equivalent with the use of 'Londres' and 'grand' in French. Under such an equivalence, the configuration in John's belief state that stands for John's belief that London is big, contains indices that have the French names of 'Londres' and 'grand'. But it is not clear that belief sentences can always be translated. E.g. John's belief that groundhogs are smaller than woodchucks cannot be rendered in another language, e.g. French even if it contains two different names for woodchucks, since we do not have a criterion for deciding which French name corresponds to which English one. It is not very different with translation in general: though quite often a good translation is possible, quite often also one must remain content with an approximation.

Though it is not possible to assume complete closure of belief under translation, a large part of it can be handled by relativising the clauses in the definitions on the previous pages where necessary by adding "or a conventionally equivalent word in another language".

The identity of thoughts

If a thought is identified with a piece of inscription in the belief state of a subject, it follows that the subject of that state is the only one that can have the thought. Nobody else can have the same thought; another can have at best a different but analogous one.

The counterpart relation provides a different account of what a thought is. Consider any way to assign to every constant of a DRS a real or private object, property or relation that is named by it, and to every primary index of it an object that satisfies the atom that introduces it or that satisfies it privately. (I.e. the assignment to the constant in the atom must be a private object of the same subject as that of the assignment to the superior index and the application of the first to the second must belong to the belief state of that subject.) Now under such an assignment the DRS determines a possible thought, that is independent of any particular subject, since it is a determinate question for any belief state whether it contains a counterpart to it. So in this sense, we do have a notion of independent thoughts, though they need not be composed exclusively by real objects, relations and properties, as the realist would have it.

7. A FORMAL TREATMENT

The most direct way to treat the ideas from the previous sections is to have an operator that turns DRS's into names of thoughts. There would be a syntactic clause:

if S is a DRS then so is $[S]^i$.

and a corresponding semantical clause that says:

g satisfies $[S]^i$ iff g(i) is the thought named by S under g.

Belief would then be a relation between people and thoughts.

There are however two reasons to prefer another approach here. In the first place syntactic clauses like the one above lead to self reference. From the point of view of natural language one need not worry about this. Natural languages contain various devices that lead to self reference and it is only fitting that a theory that attempts to do natural language semantics should bring this out. But our way of interpreting DRS's does not naturally lead to a way of dealing with self reference. In the second place we would have to develop thoughts as objects that can be the value of a variable and this is not straightforward.

Belief states are therefore now modelled as normal DRS's instead of as the abstract ones introduced in section (5). The relation between those and the normal ones can be taken as given by the discussion in section (6) of the circumstances under which a public constant is a name of a private index: the predicate indices are replaced by the English words that name them, and N^i is added whenever N is a name for the private object i.

Instead of saying that g assigns a thought to an index i bound by [S]^i we now say that g is correct for [S] iff g assigns objects to the primary indices of S that satisfy, or satisfy privately the atoms that introduce them. In this way we capture a part of the more elaborate conditions under which g would assign a thought named by S to i.

Belief is now treated as an operator and not as a relation.

Adaptations and additions

In order to give a formal treatment of belief sentences in the light of the discussion above, it is first of all necessary to give a definition of the logical form of belief sentences.

1. New formulae.
   If S is a DRS and i is an index then believe$_i$ [S] is a DRS with the same primary indices as S.

For the interpretation it is necessary to add two new elements to the models we considered earlier: the counterpart relation (CP) and an assignment of belief states (DRS's) to possible belief subjects. So we arrive at the following notion:

2. New models.
   $\langle$ M,B,CP $\rangle$ where
   a. M is an old style model.
   b. B: A $\rightarrow$ DRS
   c. CP $\subseteq$ (A $\times$ IN) $\times$ (A $\cup$ (A $\times$ IN))

Since private objects (here pairs in A $\times$ IN) can be assigned to terms in belief complements, the definition of assignments must be adapted.

3. New assignments.
   G = { g: IN $\rightarrow$ (A $\cup$ (A $\times$ IN)) }

The notion of correctness of an assignment, that was discussed in the preceding section as an alternative to the idea that an assignment assigns a thought of the appropriate form to a propositional term leads to the following definition.

4. Correctness.
   g is correct for S iff g assigns to every primary index of S an object that satisfies the atom that introduces it to S or a private object $\langle$ x, n $\rangle$ such that if A^k is the atom introducing the primary index k then A^n is a part of B(x).

There seems to be no immediate way of making this definition into a compositional one. As it stands we define with correctness (and the embeddability conditions) a set of new one place predicates. In order to make out whether a belief state contains a counterpart of a given thought, it must be defined what counts as a counterpart of a given thought. This will again be a syntactical object that is obtained by replacing indices (external indices) that stand for particular objects or private objects for indices that are their private counterparts for the belief subject.

5. CP-preserving relabeling.
   S' is a CP-preserving relabeling of S under g for x iff
   a. S' comes from S by uniform substitution of indices.
   b. Whenever i is free or primary in S and is replaced by j in S'
   $CP(\langle x, j\rangle, g(i))$ holds.

The next definition is a syntactical definition of what it means that one can embed a given DRS into another one.

6. Part of.
   Part of ($<$) is the smallest relation among DRS's satisfying (a), (b) and (c).
   a. $S < S; S < SS'; S < S'S$.
   b. If $S < S'$ and $S'' < S'$ then $SS'' < S'$.
   c. If $S < S'$ then $(S'' \rightarrow S) < (S'' \rightarrow S')$.

After these preparations it is possible to give the full definition of satisfaction for belief sentences.

7. believe$_i$[S] is satisfied by g under $\langle M,B,CP\rangle$ iff
   a. g is correct for S.
   b. there is a CP-preserving relabeling S' of S under g for g(i) such that S' is a part of B(g(i)).

Intuitively definition (7) can be read as: g satisfies a belief sentence S iff its complement denotes a thought under g that has a counterpart that constitutes a part of the beliefs of the subject of S under g.

8. APPLICATIONS

The following section contains a discussion of some of the problems connected with belief sentences. Though the limitations[13] adopted in the previous section lead to certain difficulties, it seems that the resulting picture agrees reasonably well with our intuitions on belief sentences.

De re and de dicto

The classical account of the de re/de dicto distinction among terms in a belief complement uses scope ambiguity. De re terms have a scope that includes the verb "believe", where de dicto terms have a scope that is limited to a part of the complement. In principle an account of this kind could be adopted here as well. There are however both linguistic and philosophical arguments against such a treatment. If one were to have a mechanism that can transport a term from the complement to a higher position (such as quantifying rules in Montague Grammar, elimination rules for the iota-operator, or various forms of quantifier raising) it would be possible to have general terms in the belief complement that could bind pronouns outside the complement. But this is not possible, witness the following examples:

That no man owns a donkey is believed by him.
That every man owns a donkey is believed by him.

A more philosophical argument could be distilled from Heidelberger's problem. A version of this problem is given by the following story. A person is introduced in a room where there are two porcelain vases. He is now allowed to choose one of them. He is therefore anxious to pick out the most valuable of the two. In order to make his choice he may look at them and touch them after being blindfolded. Thereby two de re attitudes come into being. The first one is his preference for the blue vase on the basis of seeing. The second one is his preference for the smooth vase on the basis of feeling it. The puzzle now comes into being if we ask ourselves how we can predict on the basis of his beliefs which one he will choose. It is the case that he has a de re preference for both vases and if one of the attitudes is the cause of his choice why is it not the other?

The problem shows the need, when one wants to use a de re attitude in explaining action (and it appears that this is the typical use of de re attitudes), for a specification of how the res is given to the subject, since otherwise the explanation is incomplete. The analysis of de re belief given here is in fact a theory that meets this demand. A de re attitude is analysed as involving at the same time an (existing) object and a specification of that object. Even if a specification is omitted, like in sentences with explicit quantifying in, where it is outside the belief complement, the existence of a private object requires a way in which that object is given to the belief subject.

The analysis of explicit quantifying in such as in:

John believes of no man that he owns a donkey.

involves the wide scope reading: it can be rendered as:

john^1 (man^2 believe $_1$[own$_{2, 3}$ donkey^3] → ⊥)

The de re/de dicto distinction, however, is not conceived here as a semantical ambiguity but rather as a difference in the way in which a belief sentence may be satisfied. Consider:

Harry believes that a witch killed his cow

and suppose that the sentence is true. There can be three ways in which this sentence is satisfied with regard to the term 'a witch'. An assignment that fulfills the sentence can assign to the term either a private or a public witch and if it is a private witch either a private witch of Harry or a private witch of somebody else. The following scheme can be given;

Type	Interpretation	Relabeled
de re	a real witch x	Harry's witch ⟨ harry, m⟩ that is a counterpart of x to itself
de dicto	Harry's witch ⟨ harry, m⟩	
in between	a person z's witch ⟨ z, k⟩	Harry's witch ⟨ harry, m⟩ that is a counterpart of ⟨ z, k⟩

A similar distinction can be applied to definite terms: a proper name or description can be used in the same three senses. So the problem of names without reference can be treated by both the de dicto and the inbetween reading. Also de dicto and in between readings for proper names can be assumed. Compare:

1. *John believes that Vulcan is round*
2. *John believes that Hesperus is larger than Venus*
3. *John believes that the widow he wants to marry is rich*

De dicto or in between readings are needed in the first case since Vulcan does not exist. Such readings can be used in the second case to explain the absence of a contradiction in John's beliefs (when he has no de re beliefs about Venus). In the third case, they can explain cases where John's widow does not exist, or has not yet assumed a definite identity.

Though the availability of a de dicto reading is all that is required for the truth of a belief sentence considered in isolation, there are many contexts in which other readings must be assumed. Compare:

John believes that his cow is ill but in fact it is only in a bad mood.

In this sentence a de re reading for 'his cow' is needed since the second conjunct contains a coreferential 'it' in an extensional position.

Hob Nob sentences

The following sentence:

Hob believes that a witch killed his cow and Nob believes that she poisoned his pig.

rendered in the system above by:

$$\text{Hob}^1 \quad \text{believe}_1 \, [\text{witch}^2 \quad \text{kill}_{2,3} \quad \text{cow}^3] \quad \text{Nob}^4 \quad \text{believe}_4 \, [\text{poison}_{2,5} \quad \text{pig}^5]$$

has caused many difficulties for systems trying to deal with coreference. The simplest reading is a de re one: one assumes there is a real witch of whom Hob believes that she killed his cow. This real witch then is the witch of whom Nob believes that she killed his pig.

But witches do not exist, so this reading is not available. Let us then assume that Hob has told Nob that a witch killed his cow and that Nob has, partly thereby, acquired the belief that his pig was poisoned by the same person. But we need not even assume that. If Hob and Nob never talk we can still give a coreferential reading: viz. an in between reading. Here Hob and Nob acquired their private witches from the same source, e.g. a rumour going around in the village.

These three interpretations correspond precisely with the different ways of satisfaction that were distinguished above.

Exportation

Under which circumstances can one infer from sentences like:

John believes that Harry comes at ten.
John believes that the proprietor comes at ten.
John believes that a plumber comes at ten.

to the following conclusion:

There is something such that John believes that it comes at ten.

In order to treat this problem one must first of all agree about the analysis of 'something'. Let us assume that it means the same as 'a P' where P is a trivial property. We can then render it as

T^i

where

g satisfies T^i iff g(i) is an element of A.

Moreover it seems reasonable to assume that:

g is correct with respect to T^i iff g(i) is an element of A or g(i) is an element of A × IN.

So the conclusion would be rendered as:

T^i John^j believe$_j$ [come-at-ten$_i$]

It now follows that in all three cases the existence of a de re reading is a sufficient condition for exportation. Assume that

John believes that a plumber comes at ten.

rendered as:

john^j believes$_j$ [plumber^i come-at-ten$_i$]

is true in a de re sense. There is then a real plumber a such that John has a counterpart k of a and believes of k that it is a plumber and that it comes at ten. So that means that the same assignment g that fulfills the premiss also fulfills the conclusion.

In fact we have here what seems a variant of the conditions for exportation given by David Kaplan. A difference is that the conditions under which a name is a name for a private object are weaker; it is here also allowed that the speaker is not aware of a name for the object or of the name that is used in the belief sentence.

Downwards Closure

It does not do to identify the logical operations under which the set of beliefs of a person are closed with the deduction rules that would give a complete theory of first order logic. Though the operations under which one can assume that belief is closed must all be valid in a logical sense a complete logic would lead to automatic belief in any tautology, and, on the assumption that at least one contradiction has, unnoticed by the subject, slipped into his set of beliefs, to the conclusion that the subject believes everything.

The ones one can allow and that seem natural are all bound to the particular way in which the beliefs are stored. In fact our semantics restricts closure to such operations. By the notion of 'part of' it gives us only rule-schemes like the following:

a. conjunction to conjuncts:
  $believe_i[SS'] \rightarrow believe_i[S]$
  $believe_i[SS'] \rightarrow believe_i[S']$
b. conjuncts to conjunction[14]:
  $believe_i[S]believe_i[S'] \rightarrow believe_i[SS']$
c. internal exportation:
  if a^i is a conjunct of S, or a is a proper name and a^i occurs in S
  $believe_j[S] \rightarrow believe_j[T^i/a^i S]$

Others may be formulated to capture 'part of' with respect to implication. So one can infer that a complement is a belief from the fact that another one is iff it is both logically entailed by it and forms a syntactical part of it.

Substitution and identity problems

The existence of a de re reading is not sufficient for substitution of identicals in a belief complement in the way it is for exportation. The reason can perhaps be given as follows: in exportation one passes to a belief complement with less information: that the name in the complement is a name of the counterpart of the res is no longer required for the truth of the conclusion. In a substitution however one first removes this information and then adds a different name so that the counterpart must now also have a different name. This may be false even if the reading was a bona fide de re one.

The inference below can be blocked for this reason.

John believes that Cicero was a famous orator.
Tully is Cicero.

_____

John believes that Tully was a famous orator.

'Tully' is a name for John's Cicero on either of two conditions: John participates in a convention to call Cicero 'Tully' that involves his counterpart of Cicero or John's Cicero is a counterpart by experience of Cicero and nothing about John's beliefs prevents him from joining a convention to call it 'Tully'.

Now the first case seems mainly interesting if we are dealing with de dicto or in between belief: in this case the history of the word is completely determined by the history of a chain of private counterparts. In the second case the word no longer distinguishes: any name of the object can be a name for the private object, if there is no reason to assume that the name can not be used for it by the subject. Now suppose John is unaware of the name 'Tully'. Then it is hard to imagine how the name 'Tully' can be blocked, since John is in no way predisposed towards that name. So on our account the inference holds in this case.

Still it is possible to explain why John in this case would not consent to the complement of the belief in the conclusion. The word 'Tully' would be a new name for him, and on hearing it he would create a private object that would be different from his counterpart by experience for Cicero. So one may assume that there is at best a pragmatic reason here for not allowing the inference. My guess on this score is that the example convinces since most people on hearing it for the first time do not know the name 'Tully' and thereby find themselves in precisely the situation John would be in if he were asked the question.

But suppose that John knows that 'Tully' is a name. Then there are two possibilities. Either he associates the name with the same private object he associates with Cicero, or with a different private object. In the first case the inference is valid, in the second case he associates the name with a different private object. Now the name 'Tully' is not a name of the private object John associates with 'Cicero', since John cannot enter into a convention to use 'Tully' for Cicero if he uses 'Tully' already for something else.

There is a series of closely related problems involving the substitution of identicals in belief complements. The oldest one, derived from Frege's work, is the explanation of the following paradox.

Assurbanipal believed that Hesperus rises in the morning.
Hesperus is Phosphorus.
Assurbanipal believed that Phosphorus does not rise in the morning.

The interesting problem here is to explain how both terms can have a de re reading while all three sentences are cosatisfiable. A version of the first and third sentence in the formal system is the following:

assurbanipal^1 believes$_1$ [hesperus^2 rise$_2$]
assurbanipal^1 believes$_1$ [(phosphorus^3 rise$_3$ $\rightarrow$ $\perp$)]

The explanation is simple in this case: there are two de re counterparts for Assurbanipal of the planet Venus; one named by 'Hesperus' and one named by 'Phosphorus'. The first has the property of rising in Assurbanipal's beliefset, but the other has the negation of that property.

A harder version of the same problem is Kripke's puzzle. Here we find a case where on the story Kripke gives the following sentence holds:

Pierre believes that London is a nice city and that London is not a nice city.

Here there can be no difference between the first and the second case because of the names. But it is possible and plausible on the terms of the example to assume that Pierre here has two private objects that are counterparts of London, and that 'London' is a name of both. The formula can here be given by:

pierre^1 believe$_1$ [london^2 nice$_2$ (london^3 nice$_3$ $\rightarrow$ $\perp$)]

Notice that on the same story one cannot say

Pierre believes that London is nice and that it is not nice.

by the account given here since 'it' can only be relabeled to the same private object that is already chosen for 'London'. This seems in accord with our intuitions.

The case of the man who suffers from amnesia so that:

John Smith believes that he is not John Smith.

can be treated along the same lines. There are two counterparts of John Smith, one that is linked to John Smith's experience of himself, and the other to his private object linked to the name 'John Smith'. Both can be counterparts by experience for John Smith of John Smith. The seemingly equivalent:

John Smith believes that he is not himself.

again comes out as false.

Conclusion

I have tried to give a philosophical interpretation of DRT as a theory about the form of thoughts. Though the spirit of the approach is phenomenological, it does not seem to be idealist. The theory just involves a realism towards mental representations. On this basis I have given a relatively simple account of the semantics of 'belief' that seems to be in accord with most of our intuitions on belief sentences.

It seems worthwhile to pursue this approach in three directions. In the first place the abstract approach that seemed to give the most natural and acceptable philosophical explanation of the use of DRS's in a treatment of 'belief' should be worked out. This must involve looking for a different and hopefully more intuitive semantics for DRS's than the present model theoretic one. The second direction is the application of the ideas sketched here for coreference with objects of belief to the different objects distinguished in section (4). It seems that the ideas used here can be generalised without any problem to the other psychological attitudes and to e.g. fiction. It is however difficult to see how something similar could be made to work for general and nonexistent objects. The third direction would be to give a more dynamic theory of belief states. In such a theory one would be able to account for the fact that a belief state is but a phase in an ongoing process that allows for the influx of new information by the senses or by communication and the use of inference to organise, extend and revise belief states.

NOTES

1. It would be necessary in order to find a realist theory that follows DRT to give a version of DRS's that does not use variables any more. I doubt whether there exists such a version. For realist theories of the proposition see e.g. Bealer [1982] or my own [1983]. The position of Barwise and Perry is not a realist theory in this sense, since they rely heavily on socalled indeterminates that are not understood as constituents of the world in the way objects and properties are.
2. Semantical methodology is here invoked to rebuke pragmatical treatments of the problem or approaches that would get hold of hidden descriptions involved in the reference, that cannot be found from the meaning of the expressions occurring in the term in the belief complement.
3. A lot more on this matter will be said in the later section on "Names of Private Objects."
4. This section can be skipped without harm on a first reading. It is not intended as a first introduction to discourse representations. See Kamp [1981] for such an introduction.
5. Superior indices are similar to discourse referents in Kamp's formulation. The presence of a formula with superior indices, e.g. $horse^3$ can be taken as indicating the presence of the discourse referent x_3 and the atom "$horse(x_3)$". The requirement in the rule that S_1 and S_2 share no superior indices can be seen as an analogue of requiring new variables in the construction of a DRS.
6. Meinong is best understood as a philosopher who complies with methodological solipsism in the theory of knowledge. When one understands him in this way there cannot be a distinction between objects that are existing in the thought of a thinker and objects that are really there. Since our enterprise is to understand communication, it is not possible to follow Meinong in this respect: we must clearly distinguish between what exists for an individual and what exists for a group of participants in communication.

7.   This is possible, but involves some complications, such as the introduction of variables into the semantics, and a complex indexing mechanism in the syntax.

8.   I assume here that the belief set contains no positive identities. I.e. someone's belief in the identity of two of his private objects is treated as constituting their identity.

9.   My notion of counterpart is not the same as David Lewis's one. Both notions however share the idea of a non essential correspondence between unrelated objects.

10.   Kaplan's notion has three parts:
   the name must be a name of its referent for the subject
   it must be sufficiently vivid
   it must be a name of the referent.

There are three differences. Vividness is ignored. Even complete ignorance of the name by the subject is allowed. Secondly a private object may fail to have any denotation at all. Thirdly, it is not assumed that the private object is some kind of meaning for the name.

11.   Kamp considers 'anchorings' of discourse referents to discourse referents that are given in the representation of the preceding conversation. The coming into existence of discourse referents in the interpretation of a sentence is a basic idea of DRT. What is added here is that the term that prompts the introduction of a discourse referent makes it a counterpart of the object that caused the term to be uttered.

12.   Using an asymmetric relation here shows that is does not suffice to require (for pragmatic reasons) that the names used in the complement are different.

13.   E.g., the woodchuck/groundhog examples cannot be treated any more.

14.   The validity of this inference scheme depends crucially on the assumption that the beliefs form one large DRS. If one does not think this is true, and allows for the beliefs of a subject to be organised in unrelated parts, the scheme becomes invalid for conjuncts taken from two different parts.

REFERENCES

Bealer, G.: (1983), '*Quality and Concept*. Oxford.

Kamp, H.: (1981), 'A Theory of Truth and Semantic Interpretation'. In: Groenendijk, Janssen & Stokhof (eds). '*Formal Methods in the Study of Language*'. Vol. I. Amsterdam.

Kaplan, D.: (1971), 'Quantifying' In. In: Linsky (ed). *Reference and Modality*. Oxford.

Zeevat, H.: (1984), 'Belief' in Landman & Veltman (eds). '*Varieties of Formal Semantics*'. Dordrecht.

Zeevat, H.: 'A Compositional Approach to Discourse Representations'. (to appear).